ETO*
MEMORIES

By
LEON D. OSTRANDER, JR

PROCTOR PUBLICATIONS LLC

Copyright © 2001 Leon D. Ostrander, Jr.

All rights reserved. No part of this book may be reproduced in any form or by any electronic or mechanical means including information storage and retrieval systems without permission in writing from the publisher.

Proctor Publications, LLC
PO Box 2498
Ann Arbor, Michigan 48106
1-800-343-3034

Publisher's Cataloging-in-Publication
(Provided by Quality Books, Inc.)

Ostrander, Leon.
    ETO memories / by Leon D. Ostrander, Jr. -- 1st ed.

    p. cm.
    LCCN: 2001 132082
    ISBN: 1-928623-09-3

    1. Ostrander, Leon. 2. World War, 1939-1945--Personal narratives, American. 3. World War, 1939-1945--Reconnaissance operations, American. 4. Soldiers--United States--Biography. 5. World War, 1939-1945--Europe. I. Title.

D811.088A3 2001   940.54'8173'092
                            QBI01-700584

This book is dedicated
to my wife,
Louise,
and to our children
Leon III, Jane and John.

PREFACE

This is an account of one young American soldier's experiences in the European Theater of Operations (ETO) during the final months of World War II. The narrative is a series of anecdotes about people and events and the setting in which the tale unfolds. It is a story of civilians in uniform, young men struggling to perform their military duties while often frustrated, confused and frightened by the seeming chaos in which they operated. It is also a story of the entire range of human behavior from selfless devotion to duty and one's comrades to the other extreme of selfishness, greed and depravity.

One might wonder about the accuracy of this account written so long after the events, but I can assure the reader that the incidents in the narrative occurred as I describe them. The many letters I wrote from Europe were saved and became invaluable reminders of the chronology of events. The occurrences left such indelible memories that I shall never forget them.

I have substituted aliases for the real names of all the people in the story except Arthur Robarge and General Cota, for I have no desire to embarrass any of my old comrades by public disclosure of their less savory behavior or silly antics even after so many years.

A brief description of the personnel and equipment of a cavalry reconnaissance troop will help the reader to understand the story. A troop was roughly equivalent to an infantry company, an organization of about 150 men and officers under the command of a captain.

The executive officer, usually a first lieutenant, was second in command, directed the headquarters platoon, and worked with the first sergeant to convey the captain's orders to the entire troop.

Headquarters platoon included the kitchen, supply, communications and motor pool sections, each under the direction of a staff or technical sergeant and manned by appropriate enlisted ranks such as cooks, mechanics, drivers and radio operators. In addition to these sections there were two armorers, a clerk, a mailman, several messengers, and sometimes one or two misfits who could only be used for odd jobs at headquarters.

Half tracks, six by six trucks and jeeps transported the personnel, equipment and supplies of headquarters platoon. The half track was an eight ton armored vehicle with wheels on the front and tracks under the rear half of the body. One half track carried powerful radio transmitters and served as the principal communications vehicle, while others were designated to carry supplies to platoons in the field.

The six by six truck was the workhorse hauler of the army, a carrier pictured so often that it is probably familiar to most readers. The name came from the six wheel drive option which allowed the trucks to negotiate unbelievable depths of snow or mud. It came with either a closed or open cab, and the cargo area could be protected by a heavy canvas cover suspended on large wooden hoops like a modern day covered wagon. The passenger seats were wooden benches along either side of the cargo box which could be folded up when freight was hauled. The trucks were strictly utilitarian without a hint of comfort, but the soldiers always referred to the "six-bys" with real affection, for they were the tough, reliable transporters of nearly everything the army used.

The three field platoons conducted reconnaissance patrols and other combat missions as ordered by the troop commander. Each unit consisted of 33 enlisted men and one officer, usually a lieutenant, who was the platoon leader. The platoon was divided into three sections of eleven men each, the smallest field unit and equivalent to an infantry squad. Headquarters section was led by the platoon sergeant, who was also second in command of the entire platoon. He was usually a staff sergeant. The leaders of the other sections were "buck sergeants", the lowest ranking three stripers, and each section had a corporal as second in command. The other men in the section were technicians or privates according to their duties.

A section rode in two jeeps and an armored car. The first jeep was armed with a .30 caliber machine gun which was mounted on a pedestal just behind the front seats. It also carried a short range radio transmitter and receiver. The crew consisted of the driver, a machine gunner and his assistant, and the corporal. The M8 armored car was a nine ton vehicle which resembled a small tank except that it rode on six wheels instead of tracks. It was armored against small arms fire and had a rotating turret where a 37mm gun was mounted. A .50 caliber machine gun was mounted on a circular track around the top of the turret. The M8 carried large radios so that messages could be sent and received over distances of many miles. The driver and chief radio operator sat low inside the hull at the front of the car, and the assistant radio operator and sergeant rode in the turret and manned the guns.

The second jeep carried a 60mm mortar, a weapon designed to be fired from the ground. It consisted of a baseplate, barrel and bipod and was fired by dropping a shell down the muzzle of the tube. The projectile landed on a firing pin, was discharged, and shot out in a high trajectory arc from which it plummeted silently down and exploded hundreds of yards away. The mortar was operated by a gunner and his assistant, while the third crew member of this vehicle was the driver. The mortar folded down so that it could be stored any place that was convenient for the crew, and the shells were carried in a box built under the rear seat of the jeep so that this perch was elevated about a foot and a half above its usual height. The crew was literally riding on a load of TNT, a sobering thought when driving on mined roads.

These were the alignments of the official table of organization, the "TO", for mechanized cavalry reconnaissance troops, but in reality units were usually under strength, and officers and noncoms rode wherever they wished.

In addition to the weapons I have mentioned, each section had at least one rocket launcher ("bazooka"), the armored cars carried a supply of antitank mines, all vehicles were issued grenades, and many men carried pistols, submachine guns or an M1 rifle as well as their issued weapon, the .30 caliber carbine.

This was a cavalry reconnaissance troop, a completely mechanized, highly mobile, and heavily armed organization. If one had to be involved in ground warfare such a unit had advantages over infantry. Every man rode in a vehicle and could carry almost unlimited amounts of gear, the assignments were less dangerous than the assaults of the foot soldiers, and the conveyances were endlessly fascinating for car crazy young Americans. The movement of one such troop afforded me an opportunity to observe many aspects of the military and civilian scene in Europe during the final months of the war.

Table of Contents

Preface iv

1. Welcome to France 1
2. The Depot and The Train 18
3. The Troop 46
4. Combat 72
5. The Big Move 115
6. The Monschau Forest 144
7. The Pursuit 193
8. Civilians 217
9. An Uncertain Future 249
10. Beyond the Rhine 266
11. Odd Jobs 298
12. Occupation Duty 327

ETO*
MEMORIES

*European Theater of Operations - WWII

1

WELCOME TO FRANCE

I climbed out of the hold of the dingy old freighter and stood unsteadily on the heaving deck while my gaze drifted over the flotilla of ships and beyond to the blur of green and white that was France. Was I really part of this scene, or was it only an outlandish dream from which I would soon awake? The hazy morning sun gave the vessels and distant shore a shimmering, ethereal quality, the sort of image one recalls from a dream, but the unceasing chop of the gray-green sea was real enough to remind me of my chilled body and churning stomach. Yes, I was truly here, waiting to land at LeHavre, a replacement among thousands of others with whom I had made the journey from the States.

I thought less about what awaited me on shore than what a relief it would be to get off the ship and to be free of the queasiness which threatened to erupt again into seasickness, a near constant affliction during the entire voyage from New York to the Firth of Clyde. I had eaten little for a week and had no opportunity to catch up during the 18 hour journey by train from the Clyde to Southampton. Now, on the cross channel transport, my stomach was signaling its rebellion against too little food and a resumption of the pitch and roll of a ship at sea.

Conditions aboard the rusty, salt caked old tub did nothing but aggravate my nausea. Hundreds of men were crammed into filthy cargo holds where they tried to sleep in hammocks or on long tables in an atmosphere of stifling odors emanating from unwashed bodies and the ship's accumulated grime from years of service without a thorough cleaning. One look at the dirt encrusted galley, unkempt cooks, and nauseous food drove me and others below decks to nibble C rations. The only latrines were elongated outhouses suspended over the sides of the vessel, but waves and spray dashed up the gunwales to douse those using the crude facilities.

The wait seemed endless, indeed I had almost decided that we were destined to wallow in the rough channel for the day, when the engines began to throb and the transport slowly wended its way around other ships on a course toward the shore. By this time it was midday, and the mist had thinned so that the land was quite distinct as we approached a seawall outside the harbor. When we rounded this barrier the port of LeHavre lay before my view in bright sunshine. I could hardly comprehend the scene, an incredible panorama of destruction. As we moved closer to the shore I realized that not a building was left standing along the waterfront. Indeed, every wharf, quay, and warehouse had been smashed to rubble.

The complete lack of port facilities compelled ships to anchor off shore from where landing craft transported men and cargo to several gravel beaches. These small vessels were about 50 or 60 feet long and had a bow ramp which was lowered to disembark passengers and freight when the craft nudged onto the beach. A score of such boats crisscrossed the harbor in a tedious shuttle to unload the ships. As soon as our transport was anchored, cargo nets were lowered over the side, and the landing craft began ferrying men to the beach, but disembarking 2,500 men from the grimy old freighter was a slow procedure that consumed more than two hours.

When it was my turn to go over the side I realized how weak I had become. I clung to the cargo net above the bobbing landing craft and hoped that my 70 pound pack and duffle bag would not drag me off the rope strands. I clumsily started down the net, ever aware of the man above me, who might step on my fingers, and yet trying to avoid the same mishap to the fingers of the man below. I was shaking and sweating when I finally dropped onto the deck of the small vessel, and I immediately felt a wave of nausea from the bobbing motion of the boat. Fortunately the craft cast off before the queasiness could worsen, and the ride was quite smooth once we were under way.

While crossing the harbor I was stunned by the nearly total destruction of all installations. The Germans had built concrete bunkers to defend the port, but bombs had cracked them like walnuts. Huge hunks of concrete stood at odd angles, and the reinforcing steel bars and mesh were twisted into grotesque shapes. The barrels of artillery pieces poked out of the rubble like bent toys, the only equipment still recognizable in the fortifications. Other port facilities, piers, warehouses, cranes, railroads, streets and offices were either demolished or so damaged as to be unrecognizable.

A jolt redirected my attention to the landing craft which had beached on the stony strand. The men disembarked over the bow ramp, which fortunately reached dry land and saved us a wade in the cold water of the harbor. After we assembled on what was left of a waterfront street we answered a roll call, by now an old and familiar ritual that had been repeated at least twice daily since we had left New York. As usual, all men were present, so we marched away from the waterfront over a pockmarked road and then onto a cobblestone street that was in better condition. Even when we began to see recognizable buildings a good distance from the harbor the bomb damage was appalling.

At first I felt comfortably warm from the exertion of lugging my gear up the long grade leading away from the waterfront, and I even imagined that the bright sun radiated some heat from its position low in the southern sky. But then a clammy sweat told me that the warmth was only a sign of my weakness, which manifest itself by shaky knees and a surprising shortness of breath. Fortunately the officers were as deconditioned by their journey as the men, so we stopped for brief rests. Each halt made me more aware of a chill wind that mocked the sunshine and laced me with what felt like hundreds of icy needles. Because we were cavalrymen each trooper was outfitted with a finger tip length gabardine coat with a wool lining rather than the standard service overcoat made of heavy wool and extending below the knee. Our coats were designed for convenience in getting in and out of vehicles, but at that moment I longed for the regulation overcoat to protect my lower body from the frigid blasts. The little wool beanie that fit under my helmet was much too small to keep my ears and neck warm, so I covered them with my hands at each stop to ease the sting of the nippy breeze. Even my gloves, thin wool affairs with a leather palm, were better suited to spring or fall wear than protection from subfreezing weather.

I saw a few French civilians who were shabbily dressed and behaved as though they were chilled to the bone as they scurried from one building to another. Half a dozen boys, perhaps eight to twelve years of age, tagged along next to our irregular column begging for cigarettes, candy, and food. The occasional adults eyed us malevolently, and some of the men muttered angrily as they skirted our formation in crossing the street. It was hardly a cordial welcome, and I was shocked by the obvious animosity of the French.

Taken together, French hostility and deficiencies of my clothing were hardly a propitious start for my stay in the ETO. If the others felt as I did, it was hard to tell from any outward signs. None of the men said much during our march, and most seemed preoccupied with their own thoughts, or perhaps it just seemed that way to me because of my own peculiar feelings, a kind of inner numbness. It was almost as though I could not accept that this was really happening to me, a queer sensation that the heavy load of gear, cold wind, inadequate clothing, unfriendly civilians, hunger and fatigue were all part of a nightmare from which I would awake. With this, a wave of self pity began to build, but before I could wallow too deeply in such emotions I noticed that my queasiness was gone and replaced by a mounting hunger. I felt as though I had not eaten in weeks, and, as I thought about it, I realized that I had indeed eaten very little since leaving New York. Soon I was not only hungry, I was famished, and food became an obsession. I could think of nothing else. Yes, it would solve all of my problems; it would assuage my hunger, warm by body, and strengthen my muscles. Yes, that was it, all would be well when we reached the camp at the top of the hill where surely warm barracks and a bounteous mess hall awaited us.

In fact, we had made progress, and the column was now on the outskirts of the LeHavre, beyond the destruction and surely near the camp. I could almost smell the aroma of hot food wafting my way from that giant mess hall. It must be close now, it had to be, I told myself, because the sun was setting. Light was already fading when we turned off the main highway and followed a lesser road to where it led into a grove of fir trees. The limbs of the evergreens were bent by accumulations of snow, and the stuff was ankle deep on the ground now that we were off the heavily traveled thoroughfare. Then I saw army tents scattered among the trees, a disappointing sight for one anticipating barracks and a mess hall. The tents were as burdened by snow as the trees, the splotches of white indenting the tops of most, and several were partially collapsed by their icy load.

The column halted in a clearing where our lieutenant conferred with a sergeant from the camp. Another roll call followed, and then we were ordered to count off by fours. By this time dusk had settled, and the sergeant appeared like a dark blur as he told us that two groups of four were to occupy each tent of a cluster on the far side of the glade. The good part of his message was that we were to go through a mess line that was setting up on one side of the clearing as soon as we had deposited our gear in one of the tents.

I needed no second invitation as I hurried to a tent, dropped my pack and duffel bag on a canvas cot, and headed for the food as though drawn by a magnet. The others were pulled as irresistibly as I to the assorted cooks and helpers who were doling out chow on the far side of the glade. I was ecstatic when the servers slapped generous portions of greasy Spam, reconstituted dried potatoes, canned green beans, bread, and canned fruit on my upturned mess kit and poured a cup of scalding hot coffee into my cup. It was the answer to all my wild food fantasies of the late afternoon, a true delight, and I wolfed it down in short order and returned to the line for more. The hot food was gone, but I helped myself to a couple of bread crusts and another cup of coffee, which I savored while I munched slowly in the lee of the kitchen truck. Even washing the mess kit was a pleasure, as the hot water in the wash and rinse cans radiated a warmth that almost made me forget the chill night that had descended while I ate. My euphoria reached a peak when I contemplated sleeping without the pitching and fetid odors of the old transport.

Leon D. Ostrander, Jr.

When all the men had finished eating we were ordered to assemble in the clearing for instructions from a captain who stood in the illumination of a gasoline lantern. I could not discern his features clearly in the uncertain light, but his message was delivered rapidly and mechanically as though he had said the same thing so often that it had become an incredible bore. He told us that LeHavre was off limits for us because American troops had been attacked by French civilians there. This did not surprise me, but I wondered why anyone would want to go to that pile of rubble and misery. He then indicated that we must use straddle trenches in certain designated areas as latrines, and we were strictly forbidden to urinate near the tents, surely a temptation on a cold night. Then he told us of the dire penalty for desertion in a war zone and assured us that the army would catch and punish any man who tried it. I listened to this last with mixed wonder and irritation. I could not conceive of any man in his right mind deserting here. Where would he go? What would he do? Who would shelter him? It was all too fantastic for my youthful mind to comprehend. At the same time I resented the tone and implications of all that he said. It was almost as though we were convicts being transported from one prison to another rather than American soldiers in France to fight for our country. The captain ended his orientation and curtly dismissed us with the parting admonition to get some sleep because we would leave the camp early in the morning.

This last comment cheered me; I reasoned that no place could be worse than this camp, so the sooner we left the better. I groped my way to my tent, which was undulating slightly in a breeze that now whipped a few snow flakes against the canvas. When I entered I found that several men were pushing their cots together on the advice of a camp noncom. This would allow each pair to better utilize their blankets and shelter half. The latter was a large piece of canvas which could be attached to another like section to form the fabric portion of a "pup" or small two man tent. When not used for that purpose it was a water repellent cover for the two wool blankets in the bed roll part of each man's pack. A collapsed wooden pole and pegs were included in the roll, and when I opened mine an almost forgotten can of shoe impregnite rolled out. This was a waxy substance that was to be applied to boots for protection against certain types of poison gas. Each bed roll had been bent into a horseshoe shape and attached to the pack harness so that it rode above and to either side of a musette bag, a square rucksack containing small items of clothing, toilet articles, and other odds and ends. This was the first time most of us had opened our bed rolls since we had carefully packed them at Camp Kilmer, New Jersey.

With a mounting wind knifing through the porous tent I don't recall anyone taking off a single piece of clothing except boots as we gingerly prepared for sleep by the dim illumination of a single flashlight. I crawled between the blankets — coat and all and wished I had more when I realized that even the two blankets and a shelter half above and below were barely enough to keep me warm. My partner on the double cot was Charley Clark, like most of us an eighteen year old, who seemed as nonplused as I by our situation.

Charley put on a brave face with a weak attempt at humor. "Well, it's better than that lousy boat, it doesn't smell and it stands still. If you don't kick me with those big feet I guess we'll get along."

I replied in the same vein, "Just don't try to hog the bed, it isn't worth fighting over, but the blankets are different. Better hang on to your part because I might get pretty grabby before the night is over."

Hans Schmidt, a big boisterous kid from Kalamazoo, elicited a few snickers when he exclaimed, "We won't have to worry about some damn horny queer fuckin' around, he'd freeze his damned cock off."

In spite of fatigue and a full stomach, I did not fall to sleep. The cold was pervasive, not intense enough to make me shiver, but a constant presence that kept me awake. I heard none of the usual sounds of night in a barracks, no snoring, no heavy slow breathing, no garbled words from sleep talkers. I was sure the others were as wakeful as I.

Suddenly Hans reared up like an angry bear and growled, "It's too damned cold to sleep in this fuckin' tent. You guys got any ideas about warming this place up?"

George Lane replied sarcastically, "What do you think we can do, Hans, all light a match?"

There was a moment of silence and then Schmidt exclaimed, "Well, by God, that's at least the start of an idea. We all have those damned tent poles and pegs and that shit for our boots. Hell, we'll never use that stuff, so let's burn it and get warm."

There was a momentary stir of dissent, but then the chilled men crawled out of their cocoons and rummaged in their belongings for the makings of a fire. Poles, pegs, and shoe impregnite were piled together in the center of the tent and set afire. The wood ignited into a crackling, cheery blaze, but the fire only lasted a few minutes. The impregnite produced a candle-like flame that radiated no noticeable warmth and cast the interior of the tent into weird shadows after the wood burned out.

For a short time after building the fire I felt warmer, probably more from the activity than any increase in temperature of the tent, but in a few minutes the cold again engulfed me and mocked my puny efforts to stay warm. I slept fitfully in spite of fatigue, and I awoke frequently between bizarre dreams and seemingly endless turning on the cot in futile quest of a warmer and more comfortable position.

After what seemed an eternity I was roused to full wakefulness by a noncom shouting for us to get up for breakfast. I crawled out of the blankets and awkwardly groped for my boots in the dark. All was confusion as seven other men struggled to get up from their cold pallets, find their boots, and get them on. In spite of what seemed extreme clumsiness I managed to get myself together and out of the tent with surprising speed, spurred on by cold and hunger. Thoughts of dinner, my only pleasurable experience since landing in France, gave me hope of another satisfying meal, and I was not disappointed. I felt better after moving about and eating, but I fumbled maddeningly as I reassembled my bedroll and pack in the cold half light. My fingers were numb from working without gloves to secure the fastenings, and I barely completed the task before we were called to assemble in the clearing.

After the usual roll call we waited for trucks that would transport us to our next destination. After nearly an hour I heard the familiar growl of engines in the distance, and then a line of six by six trucks appeared on the narrow road leading to the clearing. Snow was falling steadily now, and the flakes danced in the headlights of the trucks. Someone ordered us to count off by fours, and other noncoms shepherded the foursomes into groups of sixteen, the quota for each six-by. It seemed like too many when I thought of the bulky packs and duffel bags, and my fears were justified when I clambered into the cave-like interior of my assigned vehicle. I could barely move my feet and legs once I was seated on the wooden bench along the side of the box, but at least the heavy canvas cover provided shelter from the wind and snow. I decided it would be tolerable if we were not going too far, and even if it were a long journey, almost anything seemed preferable to another night in the tent camp.

About 15 minutes after boarding the truck, shouts from a camp noncom told me that we were about to leave, and then the engines roared to life, gears shifted, and we slowly jounced out of the clearing. As the truck accelerated on reaching the highway, snow swirled into the open rear of the vehicle and coated men near the tailgate with a white crust. Trees lining the road were ghostly blurs through clouds of snow and exhaust smoke, and yet they were the only objects I could see besides the headlights of the following truck. There was little conversation over the roar of the engine and the whine of wind, and speech seemed somehow pointless anyway. I felt a sense of quiet resignation mixed with a slowly mounting discomfort induced by cold and crowding. My fate seemed completely out of my control, the future was as murky as the view over the tailgate, and I fell into a trance like state which dulled my appreciation of the harsh environment and my personal unease.

I was only roused from my torpor when the truck stopped and someone nearby shouted, "OK you guys, piss call, ten minutes break. Don't get lost." The latter was followed by a guffaw as the unknown noncom laughed at his own little joke.

I climbed stiffly out of the truck, stretched, urinated, and walked around trying to restore circulation to my numb feet. As I came opposite the truck ahead I saw a road sign that said Rouen 10 km. I recalled that Rouen was between LeHavre and Paris, so I concluded that our destination was probably near the French capital. While I was looking at the sign the truck driver turned from the ditch where he had been urinating and announced that he would be damned glad to get to the 9th Replacement Depot at Fontainebleau. This confirmed my impression from the sign, since I also recalled that Fontainebleau was near Paris. That our destination was a replacement depot scotched a recurrent rumor that had circulated since we left Ft. Riley on December 15. I had heard again and again that we were going somewhere for "advanced training" but the details were always vague and the site of the training constantly moved toward the battle front. The rumor probably grew from a large dose of wishful thinking seasoned by the unstated fear that we were not yet a match for the veteran Wehrmacht. Still, deep down I think most of the men knew they were going overseas to replace men who were casualties of the fighting, and our movement to a replacement depot assured us that our ultimate destination would be a frontline outfit.

When we climbed back into the truck each man tried to shift about enough so that he could find a less cramped position than on the first leg of the journey, but our efforts were futile. The six-by was just too crowded. During the next two hours of the trip I gradually added hunger to my vexations, and when we finally stopped we were introduced to K rations. Each box was slightly larger than a Cracker Jack and contained hard crackers, a can of meat or cheese, hard candy, powdered coffee, cigarettes, and olive drab toilet paper. I devoured it enthusiastically and was pleasantly surprised by how it satisfied my appetite, but the K would win no prizes for taste.

As we continued our journey it seemed that my comrades were a jumble of drab statues in a dark tunnel, immobile and mute, except for Clark, my cot mate of the previous night, who had become a snowman. After each stop he ended up sitting next to the tailgate, so that he was exposed to more wind blown snow than anyone else. He had gradually rotated so that his back bore the brunt of the weather and was covered by an icy crust, but his chest, arms and legs were also white and his helmet was completely glazed. Even his face looked like Jack Frost with spicules of icy snow bristling from his brows, eyelashes and two day growth of beard. And yet he insisted on sitting next to the tailgate, so I thought no more about his frosted appearance.

It seemed as though we had been in the truck for days, and in fact the early winter twilight was settling when I caught glimpses of buildings and pedestrians in what I hoped was Paris. If so, we must be near our destination, I reasoned. Suddenly we stopped, and then I heard the convoy leader's jeep chugging from one truck to another. After several minutes the truck turned around and retraced its route, a sure sign that we were lost. Soon we left the city, or at least I could see nothing but darkness outside the beams of the headlights of the following truck. I fervently hoped that we were near our destination because I was becoming ever more aware of my numb and painful feet, stinging fingers and ears, and sporadic shivering. I could feel the men on either side of me shaking intermittently, so I knew that I was not alone in my misery.

After an interval that could have been 15 minutes or an hour and a half the truck stopped once again and I could hear the jeep moving along the line of six-bys. A few minutes later the convoy turned around again, moved slowly along the country road and then made a sharp right turn and proceeded at an even slower pace. After crawling a few more minutes, during which I prayed that we were not lost again, we stopped next to what appeared to be a steel link fence, a sign of some sort of human establishment. After the engine was turned off I could hear snatches of conversation, which became more heated and louder and seemed to involve the convoy leader and another American.

The latter shouted, "I'm tellin' you for the last time, you can't bring your goddamned men in here. I don't care how many bunks we have, we can't have replacements from the states in this camp!"

Our leader retorted angrily, "Don't give me that chicken shit excuse, these men are damned near frozen and it'll be your ass if anything happens to them; we gotta have a place to eat and sleep, and I know you can take care of us. There's no way in hell we can find our way to the Ninth tonight, so don't give me any more of your shit!"

This last salvo with its threat of blame seemed to clinch the argument, and we were admitted to a camp that more nearly conformed to my expectations of an army facility than the cold tents at LeHavre. After the inevitable roll call we were directed to several one floor barracks that were dimly visible in the half light from two hooded street lamps. I noticed a few men lounging on cots when we entered the building, and I sensed their curiosity when I dropped my gear on a vacant bunk. One man asked if we were just over from the states and our affirmative replies elicited exchanges of glances among the denizens of the barracks. I thought no more about our new comrades as I hurried to the mess hall for a hot meal and contemplated the luxury of sleeping in the relative warmth and comfort of our temporary quarters.

Later, after eating and while preparing to go to sleep, Hans Schmidt asked one of the men why he was in the camp. The question set off such agitation in the soldier that he seemed almost too nervous to reply.

After a seemingly painful effort to compose himself the man exclaimed in a taut, almost shrill voice, "They think they're sending me back up on the line, but I'll be damned if I'll go. I'll shoot my damned foot off before I'll go back up there! It's just hell up there, you boys'll see what I mean, just you wait. Look at Manny over there," he continued, pointing to a thin, dark haired young man who peered out at us like a cornered rodent from his cot in the dimmest corner of the room. "The poor bastard wakes up screaming every night, thinks the fuckin' 88's are shooting at him. Hell, one night he even climbed up in the rafters before he calmed down. Tell 'em what it's like, Manny."

The young soldier seemed too unnerved to reply, visibly upset by even a reference to his terror. Finally, after a series of abortive starts, he spoke in a halting, husky, half whisper with a pronounced Southern accent.

"Oh, it's jest hell up there, ah never been so scairt in mah whole life. Them krauts jest drive a man crazy. You don't hear nothin', and then they's a God awful noise 'n' everythings blowed to hell and gone. Ah was like to go outa mah haid when ah got hit and took to the hospital. Ah jest wish ah coulda stayed there, but them potlickers is sending me back — oh, God!" and with this he began to sob.

After Manny subsided into muffled whimpers other men added personal anecdotes of a similar but less dramatic sort. All had been wounded and were recovered enough to return to their units. These men made me very uneasy, they were so different from my expectations of combat veterans. My feelings ran the gamut from awe to pity to embarrassment. Of course I had not expected all front line soldiers to share a heroic image, but neither had I anticipated an entire group as distraught as these men. I wondered if I too would soon suffer the same fate, to be killed or wounded or so traumatized mentally that I would become a craven emotional cripple like the hapless Manny.

Fortunately the effects of profound fatigue, a full stomach, and a warm room quickly overcame this morbid introspection, and I fell into a deep sleep marked by a series of vivid dreams of a unique sort to which I was becoming accustomed. These nocturnal visions had started when we left New York and were so real that awaking to reality seemed to be the bad dream. They were invariably images of joyful times with family or friends and seemed to occupy most of my sleep time. I cautiously asked several other men who would not be likely to laugh at me if they had similar dreams and was relieved to learn that they did, but none wanted to talk about this experience for fear of ridicule.

Night passed quickly, and I was surprised by how much better I felt after adequate food, shelter and rest. I recalled only one outburst by the unfortunate Manny during the night, but I had been so tired that I may have slept through other disturbances. We ate breakfast quickly, assembled our gear, and boarded the trucks for what we were told would be a short trip. The day was cloudy, but at least the snow had stopped falling so we could see the villages and occasional pedestrians as we rumbled along the road. The shepherding jeep moved confidently among the convoy vehicles, and after little more than an hour we entered a larger town with cobblestone streets. The convoy moved unerringly through the narrow, crooked byways until we stopped before a high stone wall pierced by a gateway that was guarded by an American sentry. We were ordered out of the trucks, and an officious sergeant herded the men through the portal into a courtyard about the size of a football field. The wall formed one side of this rectangular space, and four story stone buildings enclosed the other three sides. These structures resembled old college dormitories, dignified and architecturally attractive but in need of paint and repair. Another sergeant stood in the center of the yard yelling for us to fall in for roll call and further instructions.

After it was ascertained that nobody had deserted during the ride from the other camp, a brusque captain laid down the rules in no uncertain terms. He said we were at the 9th Replacement Depot and housed in part of the old palace of Fountainebleau. We were ordered to refrain from any sort of vandalism while quartered in this French national historic preserve. We would be billeted in the servants' section of the palace, but the entire complex had immense historical significance. He pointed in the general direction of one corner of the courtyard where he said we would find firewood. Under no circumstances were we to forage for wood in the nearby forest because it was a national park. The mess hall was on the first floor of one of the buildings where it intersected the wall, and lavatory facilities, including showers, were in the building opposite the wall. Then, after looking reprovingly at our ranks throughout his speech, the captain ordered us to wash and shave before dinner. With this he turned and slouched off toward the depot headquarters, and the sergeant assigned us to quarters, described our duties, and told us how to get passes to go to town.

Thus I began my stay at the 9th Replacement Depot with more enthusiasm than I had been able to muster for any other stop during my trip from the states. I told myself that at least the buildings were intact, there was a mess hall, lavatories, and firewood, and I might even see some of the sights because the sergeant had mentioned passes. It wasn't even snowing at the moment, so maybe the ETO was not so bad after all.

2

THE DEPOT AND THE TRAIN

Noncoms led groups of replacements into buildings on one side of the courtyard, where I plodded along in a straggling line of my fellows, each bent by his duffel bag and pack as he stumbled through a doorless entrance to the old structure. We climbed two flights of wooden stairs and turned down a barren hall, where we stopped at successive rooms while the sergeant distributed men to quarters.

I was assigned to a room with seven other men, including George Lane and Dave Morton, whom I had known throughout basic training. Another man, Caulkins, had been in the same compartment on the train from Scotland to Southampton, and I liked him from the moment we met. I knew who the others were, but only to associate a name with a face. Each move, each change of quarters, shuffled my friends and acquaintances so that I was forever losing track of those I knew and liked and meeting new men with whom I had to develop relationships. Except for Morton, all those who had been close friends at Fort Riley had been assigned to other units, and, while I had made new friends, now I was separated from many of them as well. I hoped that the constant shuffling would ultimately deposit me among some congenial comrades, for I knew that one could not make it by himself. It was an absolute necessity to have at least one or two confidants with whom a man could share his thoughts. I think most of the men recognized this need, for we made friends far more quickly than was usual in civilian life. Almost instinctively I knew which of my fellows I wanted to befriend, so relationships developed nearly instantly.

We dropped our duffel bags and packs next to the four double deck steel bunks in the room, a drab chamber about 12 feet square with only a fireplace on one wall to relieve its cell like character. The only decoration of the grimy, paintless walls had been supplied by a former occupant, a Nazi, who had neatly stenciled in old German script the words "Ein Reich, Ein Volk, Ein Führer". A later inhabitant had added a fourth item in similar script but slightly different color and character size, "Ein Fooey", a refreshing American touch.

Another feature of the room added to its austerity, a total lack of wood trim around the door and window casings and the fireplace. Lines of dirt marked the limits of the missing trim, but at the moment I thought no more about this unusual deficiency as we all concentrated our attention on the fireplace. A few ashes told us that it was functional, and I immediately visualized the cozy comfort of a crackling fire.

While we arranged our bedrolls on the bunks and dug toilet articles out of our musette bags, I asked if anyone recalled where the wood pile was located. Most thought it was in the farthest corner on the opposite side of the courtyard, and we agreed that each man would carry as much wood as he could manage when he returned from the latrine.

The washroom was a bitter disappointment. There was no hot water, and even the cold water flowed ever so slowly from ancient faucets into filthy, dilapidated wash bowls. A single dim bulb cast little light on the cracked, discolored mirrors above the basins, so that I shaved more by touch than sight. I had anticipated a hot shower, but the trickle of water on the floor next to the shower stall had frozen, an icy damper on my desire for cleanliness. I washed and shaved as fast as I could, eager to get out of the dismal lavatory and to look for firewood.

I joined several of the others in the far corner of the yard where we hoped to find logs, but after searching along the entire wall we found nothing but bits of bark and splinters where we had kicked the snow aside. Suddenly I recalled the missing wooden trim in our room and the mystery was solved. There had been no firewood for a long time, and previous residents had burned everything they could lay their hands on in an effort to keep warm. The others made the same depressing connection, and we looked at each other with a mixture of disbelief and anger.

Bob Wilson, a big husky kid from the state of Washington, broke the silence, "Those bastards! They were just kidding us all along. The guys before us used up all the wood and there's nothing for us. Hell, if one of those noncoms'll loan me an axe, I'll go into the damned forest and cut enough wood for the whole damned place."

"If you get an axe, I'll help you, Hunk," Bud Henry piped up. "You cut it, I'll carry it."

Henry was also from Washington and a friend of Wilson since basic training. The rest of us assured the two that we would help too, if by some miracle Bob, or Hunk as he was known to his friends, could lay his hands on an axe. It was beginning to snow again, so we returned to our cheerless room to wait for our would-be woodsmen. It was but a few minutes until we knew the outcome of our comrades' inquiry by the bellows echoing from an enraged Hunk as he stamped down the hall toward our room.

When the two burst into the room it was the usually quiet Henry, now a bristling little rooster, who sputtered out the story.

"Those pissants just laughed at us," he exclaimed. "They said the whole damned forest is some kind of national park, 'n' the frogs won't let us even take the dead wood outa there. Some shitass Frenchman is supposed to deliver wood, but they haven't seen the son of a bitch in about a month 'n' think he's making too much on the black market to bother with the wood job."

When Henry paused for breath Hunk continued, "Hell, I've taken dead stuff outa national parks back home and the rangers thanked me. I told the damned sergeant I'd take all the blame if I got caught if he'd just get me the axe, and do you know what that son of a bitch did? He laughed at me! Another thing, those bastards have plenty of wood for themselves over in the orderly room, yeah, it's so hot in there they sit around in their shirtsleeves!"

After everyone had his turn griping about the wood problem Hunk declared soberly, "Say, I almost forgot, we found out something else. You guys know Charley Clark?" Without waiting for a reply he continued, "The poor bastard froze his ass off, no shit, he really did! That damned sergeant thought it was funny, said we were luckier than our buddy 'cause he had to go to the hospital with a frost bitten ass and frozen piles or some such thing. I don't know anything about that stuff, but it sounds like old Charley's in trouble."

I teetered between laughing at the bizarre thought of a man actually freezing his rear and sadness at the thought of Clark's plight. The others must have shared my feelings, because the news provoked a few nervous titters and uneasy glances.

Williamson, a man from cooks and bakers school at Fort Riley, said, "I told him to find a place inside the truck, to sit somewhere besides the tailgate, but he said he liked it better there, and now the poor guy's in real trouble."

We murmured assent and sat morosely on the edges of the cots. I realized that I was very hungry as well as cold and wondered if they had failed to provide food for us too. It was already dark and the single light bulb in the room had flickered on and off several times adding darkness to our irritations. Before I could get more disconsolate in my self pity I heard someone shout "chow", and we came to life as though a switch had been turned. The promise of food had a magical effect on hungry eighteen year olds.

The room used as a mess hall was too small for the purpose, but the crowding and heat from the stoves was a welcome relief from the chill of our room. I stood against the wall eating out of my mess kit and thought how strange it was to revel in such a plain dinner, but the meal was so much better than anything else that had happened at Fountainbleau that I hated the thought of leaving. The others shared my reluctance to return to the dismal room, and we discussed the possibility of getting passes so we could explore the town and perhaps find a warmer place to spend some time. When he returned to the chow line for seconds Hunk asked one of the cooks if the town was worth a visit.

The server, a red faced, unkempt fellow in his late twenties, was patently contemptuous of a bunch of green kids and replied brusquely, "If you're not fussy you can get a piece of ass and some cognac." Then he added as an afterthought and with obvious disdain, "Or some of you boys might like the Red Cross Club, coffee, doughnuts and games."

As we plodded back to our room we discussed the pros and cons of a visit to town. We fit the Red Cross Club pattern but wondered if we could get into the place. Miserable as it was, the depot had an aura of security, while the town was unknown, foreign, and possibly unfriendly. We had only huddled in the bleak room a few minutes when the light went out again and the decision was made, we would try the town.

The corporal in the orderly room produced passes and with a smirk cautioned, "Now you boys stay outa trouble and come back by 2200, you hear? Don't get too drunk or go to fightin' over them French whores."

I asked, "Could you tell us how to get to the Red Cross Club?"

"Well now, I guess I can't help you on that one," he replied insolently. "I reckon it's there, but you'll have to ask someone else. Hell, I don't know any of the boys from here that's been there."

Once we walked out of the gate I was buoyed by curiosity about the town and elated to be free of the oppressive atmosphere of the depot. Most of the pedestrians were American soldiers, and the few French civilians on the streets appeared indifferent to our presence, but at least they were not hostile. The shops were closed and shuttered except for a few cafes, but the dim street lights cast enough illumination so that I was struck by the omnipresent pictures of De Gaulle in windows of both business places and residences. The shadows on the snow gave the town an even more picturesque appearance than I had appreciated from the truck. None of us had ever visited a foreign country other than Canada or a border town in Mexico, so we gawked and chattered about everything like any other group of tourists.

When we reached the main square I saw a long line of soldiers apparently supervised by a French policeman who strutted up and down the avenue like an officious doorman at a first run movie theater. He issued occasional commands in French, which were surely unintelligible to most of the soldiers. I asked him if the line was for the Red Cross Club, speaking loudly and with exaggerate slowness and clarity, as though somehow the Frenchman would understand English if only I tried hard enough. Of course he didn't understand a word I said, but with an accommodating smile, a nod of his head, and an unmistakable gesture to get in line he seemed to affirm my assumption that the men were waiting their turns for coffee, doughnuts, and ping pong. We followed his direction but began debating whether it was worth the wait.

A pair of soldiers ahead of us in the queue turned around and one exclaimed, "It all depends on how much you want to get fucked. The pimp who runs the place keeps the price low, but he only allows 20 minutes, so you better start playing with yourselves at the door to get your money's worth."

I stammered, "But I thought this line was for the Red Cross Club."

The two men burst into laughter and assured us that we were waiting to get into Fountainebleau's largest brothel. They had no idea where the Red Cross Club was.

We sheepishly mumbled our thanks and slunk away. I began to wonder if there was a Red Cross Club as we wandered aimlessly about the windswept streets of the town. Just when we were ready to give up and return to the depot two soldiers came around a corner from a different direction. Fortunately they were coming from the elusive club and directed us to a building only half a block away.

We were delighted to find it a roomy, light, warm and hospitable haven. We made for the ample supply of doughnuts and Coca Cola, which was standing up well to the onslaught of the twenty or so men milling around in the place. The building had probably been a large residence, and some of the couches and chairs had been left for those who wanted the luxury of a soft seat while they stuffed themselves. Two young American women circulated among the men answering questions and explaining the range of facilities. There were three ping pong tables and a pool table in the large rooms, and several alcoves housed small tables or desks where men could find stationery and pencils for writing letters. It was comfort that I had almost forgotten in the course of our pell mell journey, and I savored every minute of it, the edibles, a couple of games of ping pong, a few minutes on a soft couch, and a brief conversation with one of the hostesses.

The time passed all too rapidly, and by 10 o'clock we were again in our barren cell gazing at the lone light bulb and wondering when it would blink off again. By then I was ready to sleep and gladly crawled into my bedroll. Nobody called us until nearly eight the next morning when one of the depot noncoms yelled that breakfast was being served.

After eating we had our usual roll call, and then the sergeant dismissed us with a warning to stay near our quarters. We sat on the lower bunks in our coats, cold and uneasy with nothing to do and nowhere to go. The low mumbling of our griping was interrupted by a cracking sound from above, apparently on the top floor of the old building where there were no billets and supposedly no people. The strange noise was repeated, and then we heard the unmistakable clomp of GI boots.

"I wonder what's going on up there," Hunk mumbled idly after a big yawn.

After a long pause George responded half-heartedly, "Maybe we should go up there and have a look."

Even such faint interest in investigating the odd sounds was a measure of our complete boredom. Five of us got up slowly and sauntered down the hall to the stairway, where we hesitated as though we might be invading someone's privacy if we climbed to the fourth floor. We looked at one another, laughed nervously, and started up the steps.

I felt better when Caulkins said, "Well, nobody said we had to stay in our room, they just said to stick around."

When we got to the top we found nothing to explain the strange noises; the hall looked exactly like the one below. We decided to explore a little anyway since we were there, and anything seemed more interesting than sitting and staring at one another in our icy room. The only difference between the rooms on the top floor and those below was the slant of the ceiling to accommodate the sloping roof.

When we entered a large chamber roughly over our room we immediately recognized the cause of the mysterious sounds. Many floor boards had been torn from their supporting joists; some shivering GI's had found an answer to the wood problem. To see was to act, and we enthusiastically set to work ripping up more boards and carrying them down to our room. The strips were three quarter inch hardwood, so it was difficult to break off proper lengths for the fireplace without tools. Some yielded to a technique of laying one end on the edge of a bunk and the other on the floor and jumping on the board, but the sizes were still unpredictable and we bent one steel bed support as well. Finally we decided to lean the boards against the wall, and two men would coordinate blows from their booted feet against the middle of the piece until it broke or the men got tired, a method that was no more accurate in providing proper lengths, but one that at least left the beds intact.

When we had accumulated a sizeable pile of boards less than two feet in length we used the morning "Stars and Stripes", the army newspaper, as tinder to start a fire. The men broke into smiles of wordless satisfaction as the dry wood caught fire and radiated a glorious warmth.

Leon D. Ostrander, Jr.

We decided to burn the longer pieces that we could not break into lengths to fit the fireplace by putting one end in the fire and gradually advancing the board as the burned end was consumed. This practice was potentially hazardous, particularly when we left the fire unattended while we ate, but we wanted to use the wood efficiently to limit the number of forays to replenish the supply.

We spent the entire day loafing before the crackling fire, apparently forgotten by the command of the depot. It was necessary to fetch more wood several times, which was accomplished without incident. We heard the other foragers at the same task on a couple of occasions and were emboldened by the knowledge that others were as guilty as we in desecrating the old building. In spite of the fire the room was not really warm, but at least it was tolerable. Our conversation was a languid and relaxed succession of anecdotes about our homes and families, interests and hopes, a pleasant mix of nostalgia and anticipation. The day was so comfortable that we decided against another trip to the Red Cross Club and spent the evening chatting around the fireplace.

The fire was only dead ashes in the morning, and before we could rekindle it we were marched out of the courtyard to an unknown destination. The snow had stopped, but the leaden sky threatened more and the stuff was deep under foot. The cold air had a damp, penetrating quality, so I was glad when the column halted at a building no more than six blocks from the depot. The town looked shabbier by day, but the walk through the narrow streets was a welcome break from the monotony of the compound. The corporal in charge of our column had said nothing about where we were going, the usual army practice of keeping the troops ignorant of even the most inconsequential activities. It turned out that our goal was a theater, a dilapidated hall to be sure, but a real theater, where we found about a hundred other men already seated when we entered. The place was unheated, so the men started to grumble as they thought of the fireplace back at the depot and decided that we were to be subjected to either another propaganda film on "why we fight", or worse yet, a venereal disease movie.

When the screen lit up I didn't know whether to cheer or laugh, for the film was a Red Skelton comedy with a staple slap stick formula and many scantily clad girls. It was a better outcome of our mysterious morning excursion that I could have anticipated, but why the secrecy and early showing? Many of the men had seen it the previous summer and the old newsreel was ridiculous, so there were many hoots and jeers as well as belly laughs during the performance, but still it was diversion for the restless men and better than sitting around killing time.

As soon as we returned to our quarters we made another foray to the top floor for wood. Two men ripped up boards while the others carried them downstairs and broke them into pieces. Just as we were leaving the area of destruction we passed a little French carpenter coming up the stairs laden with tools and several new floor boards. He smiled amiably and greeted us with a friendly "bon jour" in spite of the telltale evidence of our depredation.

Hunk laughed and said, "He oughta just haul the boards to our room and let us use his saw to cut 'em up, it'd save us all a lot of trouble."

We chuckled at the thought of the carpenter diligently replacing the floor boards while the soldiers just as industriously pulled them up. We were in a mellow mood, toasting by our hearth and becoming better friends by the minute. In midafternoon we were ordered to assemble again and marched to a supply room where we were issued carbines and two more blankets. Both were welcome, the blankets for their immediate utility and the carbines because they were cavalry weapons. If we went to the front as infantry we would be issued M-1 rifles, so at least for the moment we were still cavalry. With the additional warmth of four blankets each, the cheery fire, and the seeming assurance that we were not headed for an infantry company we again chose to stay in our room rather than seek another pass to town. Williamson, the cook, had helped out in the kitchen because one of the regular cooks was sick and had managed to swipe enough chocolate bars to treat his roommates. We were contented indeed that evening, sitting before the fire, swapping tales and munching chocolate. The scene epitomized how men in the army could seize momentary pleasure without apparent thought about what had gone before or what the next day might bring. This live for the moment psychology was probably an important mechanism for the men to maintain their morale in the face of hardship and uncertainty.

The next morning was bright and sunny, although still cold, but the palace and town looked much more attractive in the sunlight than at any time since our arrival. We spent most of the morning loafing around in the courtyard, discussing the latest rumors, and speculating about the weather, the war, and our ultimate destination. In the afternoon we marched to the firing range to sight our new weapons, an outing which lifted my spirits even further. The range was in a forest clearing, and we marched for several miles through the woods to get there. The boys from the Pacific Northwest ridiculed the French forest, calling it a "toothpick farm", but in spite of their disdain I admired the carefully tended, parklike character of the preserve made even more attractive by the mantle of glistening snow that clung to the trees.

As soon as we returned to our quarters we made another raid on the wood suppy and found that the carpenter had repaired much of the floor and was nearly keeping pace with the destruction. The floorboard farce fed our exuberance until we were overcome by hilarity at the slightest mention of floorboards. We sat and made small bets about when the "frog" electric light would next fail in a mood that could only be described as giddy.

The next day the weather reverted to clouds and snow flurries and our tempers became as somber as the grey sky. We had nothing to do but write letters and fetch wood. We met and greeted the carpenter again but even that continuing comedy seemed to have lost its sparkle. By this time we knew everyone's life history and were thoroughly fed up with hearing each other's favorite stories. I hoped I would never hear another talk of the woods in Washington, or of the wreck of a train in Dave's home town or the rodeo in Caulkin's, and I am sure they had their fill of my stories about the Detroit Tigers and Michigan Wolverines. We were getting on each other's nerves and needed activity to relieve the tedium.

The boredom was shattered instantly when a sergeant strode in the door and shouted, "Attention!"

A lieutenant close behind quickly took in the scene and snapped, "Where did you men get that wood?"

At first there was no reply; we stood at rigid and terrified attention, too stunned to say a word. I know I was struck dumb under the officer's withering gaze.

Then someone mumbled, "In the courtyard, sir."

The lieutenant's face turned a bright red at this blatant lie made even more ridiculous by the telltale pieces of flooring protruding from the fire.

"Dammit, I want the truth," he exclaimed.

Finally we stammered out the story of the floorboards, which I'm sure he already knew.

"Do you men realize you can be court-martialed for what you have done?" He paused to let this sink in and then continued, "Now I don't want to get you men in a lot of trouble, so I'm not going to press this thing unless you step out of line again. If you do, you'll go to the front as prisoners. The sergeant will find something for you to do in the morning so you won't have time to destroy property."

With that he turned and left, and the sergeant took our names and told us to look at the duty roster that evening because starting tomorrow we would have no more time to rip up floors. Visions of an unheated room and constant kitchen police or latrine duty shifted my thoughts to the desirability of getting out of the depot and to a permanent assignment even if it were a combat unit. We had been in limbo for nearly a month and the combination of uncertainty and boredom made almost any change an improvement.

To my surprise none of our names appeared on the duty roster that evening, a sure sign that we were about to leave Fountainebleau. Because lavatory facilities were uncertain once we left the depot I decided to grit my teeth and take a shower. The patch of ice was still on the floor outside the shower stall, the water was still as cold as the ice, and worst of all the process was agonizingly slow. The trickle of water was simply too slow for one to lather and rinse quickly, so my shower became an interminably prolonged cold water torture. I vowed to take no more showers until I could wash in warm water, even if I had to wait until spring. Afterward I ran to the mess hall to warm myself by the stoves; I could not face even a short wait in the frigid room. The fat cook who had told us about the pleasures of the town asked why I was there before chow call, and when I told him that I was getting warm after a shower he looked at me with a mixture of incredulity and disdain. It was obvious that he was not a man to suffer any discomfort for cleanliness, but at least he did not object to me sitting in the warm room.

In the morning we were told to pack our gear and be ready to move out at any time. We were issued ammunition so that our load of gear had increased to nearly 90 pounds. It was not easy to make a bedroll from four blankets that would fit into a pack and around the musette bag, so most of us stuffed one of the new covers in the duffel bag. The carbines were an awkward addition to our load, and I just hoped that we would not have to ride far in a six-by or more of us might end up with some portion of our bodies frostbitten.

After the noon meal we were ordered to assemble in the courtyard with our gear, where we stood in a cold, blustery wind and watched the snow whip around into curious spiral clouds. Waiting is normal for the army, but after we had stood there for a half hour with no sign of action some of the men began to grumble and stamp their feet as much from frustration as the cold. Just when the waiting seemed to be approaching the intolerable stage all eyes turned to a scene that instantly quieted the grumbles and distracted the mens' attention from their discomfort.

Two mongrel dogs appeared from somewhere, a male and a female in heat. The male mounted the bitch to the cheers and whistles of the troops. After copulating the male had trouble extricating himself, he was "hung up" as some of the more knowledgeable dog fanciers put it. Speculation mounted as to how and when the two curs would separate and bets were made on all aspects of the elemental scene. At last the dogs separated, but in less than 5 minutes the male again mounted the bitch to the delight and cheers of the soldiers.

We missed the conclusion of this canine reproductive drama when we were ordered to fall in, count off, and board trucks parked outside the gate. My worst fears seemed to be realized when again sixteen men were assigned to each truck and the additional gear made the crowding worse than on the trip from LeHavre. As soon as we were loaded the trucks left, bumping through the streets of the town only to stop next to a line of boxcars in a railyard. The brief truck ride was a relief, but the wooden railcars were tiny by American standards and I could not help but wonder how many of us they would pack into each little wagon. While I studied the boxcars a high pitched toot sounded behind me, and I turned to see a small steam locomotive puffing along on another track. It was in scale with the boxcars, and we fell to joking about the miniature French trains until we were interrupted by an order to fall in and count off so that we could be assigned to a particular car.

A man next to me, interpreting the faded inscription on the side of a car, 40 Hommes, 8 Cheveaux, said, "I hope they carry the 8 horses on a different trip."

I turned to look at him, a man of medium height, about 30, with a New England accent and an air of slightly ironic good humor.

I smiled and replied, "I get it, 40 men, 8 horses. You must understand French."

His thin face broke into a smile and his bright blue eyes sparkled as he answered, "I know about enough to get by, but I'm used to Canadian French, not the kind they speak here."

The car was nearly full when we clambered in, so that I ended up near the door. It was not as crowded as the trucks, but movement was limited by equipment and the darkness of the interior of the car. I thought of Clark, and wondered whether my position near the door would expose me to too much cold and snow, but it seemed preferable to the dark recesses of the corners, and, favorable or not, I could do nothing about it.

A corporal poked his head in the door and yelled, "Shut up in there so I can tell you fuckers a few things about this damned train. Keep your fuckin' heads inside if you want to stay alive. When the train stops, stay on board until the whistle blows twice; these frog trains stop all the time, but the engineer will let you know when it's piss call. If you get off other times you may get left and then you're shit out of luck, they treat you like a deserter. Watch it getting off in the dark; the trains run under blackout and you may not see or hear the damned thing until it kills you. Any questions? If not, a couple of guys jump down here and load these ration boxes, if you want to eat while you're in there."

I hopped out with two others, and we tossed 4 boxes of K rations into the car. This crowded us even more, but it also told us that we would be on the train for a long time. Each man had a full canteen of water, so we seemed to be ready for the journey.

After at least an hour of sitting in the railyard we felt the jar of a locomotive coupling onto the line of cars. I had passed the time watching occasional trains chug by with their ridiculous little teakettle engines, high pitched whistles, and diminutive freight cars. I was struck by the high proportion of cars that had what looked like a large barrel or vat lying on its side on a flat car.

My French speaking acquaintance laughed when I mentioned this and said, "Jesus, these people must wash in wine, those barrels on the cars are full of the stuff."

This observation drew a few guffaws, and one man noted that a couple of bullets through a wine barrel would make a handy bunghole.

Suddenly the shrill whistle sounded, the train jerked, and we began to move slowly out of the yard. When we reached the main line it seemed as though we were flying with much rocking, rumble and roar, but I doubt if we ever went over 25 or 30 miles per hour as judged by the passing objects. Those of us near the door wanted it shut because of the cold draft, while men in the dark corners of the car complained that they had no light or ventilation. After several adjustments we settled on leaving the door on one side of the car open about 3 or 4 inches to provide a shaft of light and a more or less tolerable breeze.

The train stopped frequently as the corporal had predicted, usually to allow another shrieking little demon to pass, but sometimes the reason for a stop was not evident. After moving in this halting fashion for about an hour I could see that we were in a large city, which could only be Paris by my reckoning. Electric commuter trains glided by on adjacent tracks, and the passengers had an urban air about them in spite of their shabby clothes.

As dusk began to settle we stopped opposite a station on the outskirts of the city. Everyone was grumbling about the cold, cinders, hunger, crowding, the need to urinate, and whatever else came to mind. We opened the door wider to catch the fading light and a breath of fresh air. Although there were no signs of previous equine occupants, the car had a musty, unpleasant odor which was evident at my position near the door and must have been much worse in the farther recesses of the boxcar.

One man cried, "Hey, look, the frogs have a fire in that depot. Let's run over there for a minute and get warm."

Voices of caution sounded as some recalled the warnings about leaving the train, but eight of us dashed to the station anyway. A few French civilians were sitting quietly on benches near an old fashioned heating stove when we burst into the room. The heater was radiating a magnificent warmth as we crowded around to toast our chilled bodies.

Suddenly one man said, "This sucker would fit in the boxcar, someone give me a hand 'n' we can carry her right over to the train. The rest of you guys grab as much wood as you can and some stove pipe, and we'll keep that damned car warm."

Without a moments hesitation we fell to the task, and, before the startled occupants of the station could so much as move, the stove, wood, and a few pieces of stove pipe were seized, carried across the tracks on the run, and hoisted into the boxcar. The last man was just climbing aboard when the whistle sounded and the train started to move to the cheers of the men in the car. Departure was barely in time to escape the wrathful stationmaster, who had just emerged from his office screaming wildly in frustrated rage at our brazen theft. The cost of the heist had been scorched gloves for the principals and even less space for everyone. The stove rocked unsteadily as we picked up speed, and the car filled with smoke as the wind played havoc with our improvised flue, but we laughed madly at the success of our audacious coup. We convinced ourselves that the smoke would not be a problem once the stove pipe was adjusted properly, and those of us near the heater were sure it would provide plenty of warmth. Men who were not in almost direct contact with the stove were more dubious about the whole scheme but seemed willing to give it a trial. The boxcar was so uncomfortable that anything offering hope of even slight improvement would get a chance.

We munched K rations in the dark while the train rattled through the snow covered countryside. I was scrounging around like a dog getting ready to lie down when the wheels gave a louder than usual clack, the car swayed and swerved, and we slowed down on a siding. As we ground to a complete halt the whistle shrieked twice, and we threw open the door and tumbled out to stretch and relieve ourselves. No moon or stars brightened the dark of night, and even the blanket of white snow was barely perceptible as we bumped against one another and clumsily tried to find a place to urinate without wetting another man or losing track of our own boxcar. I moved away from the train a few paces with a few others and stumbled over another track. As I glanced to my right I saw a tiny white light and heard the sound of a locomotive.

I shouted, "Look out, there's a train coming," and lurched back toward the car, jostling several men in the process.

Before the impact could elicit the usual oaths others sounded the alarm, and a shrill whistle alerted all to the rapidly approaching train. It was on us in seconds, and we huddled against the boxcars until it passed before finishing our business. We groped around for more fuel for the stove, but it was too dark to distinguish coal or wood from anything else along the right of way. Soon the whistle sounded and we climbed back into our "GI pullmans" to continue the journey.

I have no clear recollection of much of the time in the boxcar, only blurred memories of trying to restore feeling to my cold, numb feet, subsisting on K rations, sleeping in snatches, getting out to urinate, and tending the stove.

On the second morning the train stopped in a railyard where the snow seemed even deeper than at the previous stops, and it was still falling steadily. I could see a little of what appeared to be a town, where a fire was burning fiercely in several buildings giving forth clouds of smoke which blended with the snow to obscure the landscape. I felt the urge to have a bowel movement, and at the same time a wave of nausea swept over me. The piece of canned cheese on crackers that I had eaten for breakfast felt leaden in my stomach, but I gritted my teeth, kicked the snow aside, dropped my pants and drawers, and squatted. As the icy wind laced my bare bottom with particles of snow that felt like a hundred tiny needles, all impulse to defecate left me and I hastily pulled up my clothes and started walking about to restore feeling to my feet. As I moved about I recalled a lieutenant in basic training who warned us always to heed the urge to have a bowel movement or else "all the crap just backs up on you and the first thing you know it gets into your appendix and you get appendicitis." While I didn't believe this bit of GI wisdom, I wondered to myself what would happen if one of us developed appendicitis or any other illness while on the train. We seemed to be in a world of our own and completely disconnected from the life where people had recourse to hospitals or other facilities of civilization.

I tried to change my wet socks to keep my feet in good condition, but snow invariably got into my boots at each stop and soon all my socks were wet, and my feet were just as numb and cold as ever. One man tried to dry his socks on the stove during a time when we had fuel, but the only result was half burned and half wet socks.

My French speaking acquaintance returned from a walk to the head of the train and reported that we were in Neufchateau, wherever that was. Apparently we had been scheduled to leave the train there, but the officer in charge of our group was in discussion with two other officers who had arrived in a jeep. The train crew had departed for whatever pleasures they might find in the town, so it looked as though we would sit in the snowy railyard for a while.

We scrounged more wood and coal for the stove, which functioned quite well while we were not moving. Most of the men took turns sitting next to it, where one could get some sensation of warmth, but the little heater had never been intended for use in the open. At least the smoke went up the stovepipe and the air was bearable in the car while we were stopped, but this minor improvement in our level of misery had little effect on my own melancholy mood. Try as I would, I could not get my mind off my cold, wet feet, fatigue and hunger for hot food. Now the apparent confusion about our destination disheartened me even more.

After nearly two hours the whistle sounded and the train backed out of the town and seemed to be retracing much of the route we had covered the night before.

One man probably spoke for all of us when he commented bitterly, "Hell, they can back me all the way to the states if they want to. I've had enough of this ETO shit already, and I guess I ain't even all the way there yet."

The grumbling increased when we divided up the remaining K rations. Only the least palatable rations were left, mostly a nauseous concoction of congealed fat labeled "corned pork loaf with carrots and apple flakes."

After several hours of backing interspersed with numerous stops that consumed much of the day, we halted on a siding in a railyard. A string of wine cars stood on another track and the next events were inevitable. Shots were fired, men crowded around the fountains of wine spurting from the bullet holes, and cups and canteens were filled with the dark liquid. An officer and two noncoms appeared at the sound of the shots and shouted for the men to get back into the cars. The officer threatened dire but unspecified punishment while he urged the men to board the train.

One man from our car called, "What will you do to us, lieutenant, send us to the front?"

This drew bitter chuckles from the sullen men, and the irony was not lost on the officer, who replied, "Just keep it under control men. Don't shoot any more holes in those barrels or go too heavy on that wine. We're all in this together, but it's my ass if you get way out of line. Hell, I might have some of that frog grape juice myself, since it's running out on the ground anyway."

The men murmured their grudging approval of this conciliatory reply, but the mood was still testy as they faced a third night on the train. Everyone seemed to be quarrelsome and ready to make an issue out of the slightest discontent, so that when the train pulled out of the siding, one faction in our car demanded that the stove be jettisoned because they got no benefit and objected to the choking clouds of smoke that filled the car. Even those of us close to the heater had to admit that it was not much use, but there were several men who seemed to hold out for sheer cussedness. The last to agree to pitch the stove was the man who had suggested that we filch it in the first place. At last even he acquiesced, and we shoved the little monster out the door as we rode atop an embankment. I watched in fascination as the stove bounced down the slope, scattering embers that culminated in a final explosion of sparks and coals when it struck the bottom. I must admit that we had more room and could close the door without risking asphyxiation, and I was no colder that night without the stove than I had been the two nights when we had it.

When we opened the door in the morning we were on a siding in a hilly area where fir trees dotted the hillsides and bent under heavy burdens of snow. All the rations had been eaten, and I was so hungry that I would have welcomed even the hated corned pork loaf with or without carrots and apple flakes. A train passed and then our locomotive gave a toot, jerked the cars, and slowly steamed out onto the main line. It started to snow heavily, and we could see nothing that would give us a clue to our location even when we peeked out the crack where the door was left slightly ajar. Some sat dumbly on the floor and others stamped their feet in a vain effort to keep warm in the frigid car, and all grumbled and cursed in their misery. I wondered if I would ever be warm or have a decent meal again as the ordeal of the train seemed to go on forever.

About eleven o'clock the train swung into another siding and ground to a stop. When we slid the doors open I spotted a convoy of trucks parked near the tracks, so at least the rail portion of our trip to the front was over. I never thought that I would actually welcome another ride in a six-by, but after three days and nights on the train I was ready for anything that might take me to food and shelter. We crawled out dragging our packs, duffel bags and weapons and assembled in a ragged formation for the first roll call since boarding the train. We were assigned to trucks, and I stiffly crawled into my six-by while I silently prayed that the trip would be short. Then transportation corps men heaved K rations into each truck, a welcome development to alleviate our hunger, but an ominous sign that we still had a long way to go.

The ride in the six-bys was a fitting climax to our ordeal since leaving Fountainebleau. The roads were snow covered and steep with many curves, and the terrain seemed to get more rugged the farther we went. The trucks were driven by Negro soldiers of a transportation battalion, a disquieting fact by itself. It was generally agreed among whites at that time that Negroes were irresponsible, stupid, lazy, dishonest and incompetent to perform difficult mechanical tasks, but here we were racing along treacherous mountain roads in the snow and at the mercy of what one man called "a bunch of crazy, jazzed-up niggers." Thus fear compounded our physical discomfort and made us more than a little edgy. I had known and liked a few Negroes at college, but when we stopped for a "piss call" it was clear that our drivers had nothing in common with my acquaintances at school except their race. They had a jaunty nonchalance that bordered on insolence and called everything and everybody a "mother fucker" while jiving among themselves.

It seemed as though we were in a race as the convoy gunned away into the swirling snow and entered ever more mountainous country. Suddenly we were braking and the truck slewed on the slippery road and came to a stop half off the road with the front bumper of the following truck nearly touching the rear of ours, proof enough to the tired and frightened troops that the drivers were a bunch of wild men who would probably get us all killed before we ever got to the front. To make matters worse, we had missed a turn, so the convoy had to turn around, a tricky operation on a narrow road clinging to the side of a snow covered mountain. Our truck pulled up and then started backing toward the edge of the road, which was separated from a sheer cliff by only a narrow shoulder.

As the driver edged closer and closer to the abyss, Joe Colleto, a native of Boston who was seated next to the tailgate, screamed, "Stop the truck, you black mothah fuckah! You're backin' us off the cliff!" The truck stopped momentarily and then crept back farther while a chorus of screams rose from the terrified occupants. We then inched forward, followed by another chilling backward move, and at last we moved forward and away from the yawning chasm. I hoped that we were indeed on the right road as the convoy then sped recklessly along the mountain highway, but I somehow felt totally drained of all emotion. I think the others shared my numbness of body and emotion, for we sat hunched on our seats like a row of olive drab dummies, and I don't recall how long it was before I heard Colleto yelling again.

"Damn, I gotta take a piss, that niggah scared it right outa me."

Others probably felt the same urge, but Joe seemed to be in real agony as he futilely shouted at the driver, "Stop, you black son of a bitch. I gotta take a piss. If I wet my pants, I'll shoot yoah black ass!"

Of course the driver could not stop until the rest of the convoy stopped, and Joe became ever more frantic. We urged him to go over the tailgate and assured him that we would hang onto his belt so he would not fall out as we lurched along the road. He tried but could not accomplish his objective and finally sat down muttering to himself.

This commotion roused me to pay more attention to our surroundings, and I noticed several trucks going in the opposite direction. In the first it looked as though a lot of men were lying on top of one another, which didn't arouse my curiosity as it should have in my introspective mood. When the next six-by passed I realized that we had witnessed the return trip from the front for some American soldiers, for the trucks were loaded with dead bodies.

A shiver ran over me just as one of the others gasped, "God, did you guys see that?"

Only those near the tailgate could have observed the grisly cargoes, but word spread to the others. We sat in silence for a long time and were roused from our trances only when we started down a steep grade into a valley where I could see houses and buildings. Many of the trucks began to backfire as the drivers announced their arrival by turning off the ignition and restarting it, a favorite pastime of drivers in trucking battalions. The convoy only slowed a little as we reached the bottom of the hill and rumbled through the streets of the town, but then we stopped abruptly at an intersection where the trucks separated amid many shouts and commands. Our group of six trucks only traveled about a block before it stopped where several officers and noncoms were directing unloading. After stiffly climbing out and shouldering my equipment I staggered along with the others into an alley which led behind the buildings that fronted on the street to an open area about thirty by fifty yards. The snow was at least six inches deep and caused us to slip and slide in our pathetic attempt to line up in formation. I thought we must have been a disappointment to the captain and first sergeant who watched our awkward shuffling without comment.

The sergeant shouted, "Be at ease, men. Captain Doyle will speak to you, and then I'll tell you what to do. My name is Hinkle."

The captain was mercifully brief and reassuringly sincere in welcoming us to the reconnaissance troop of the 28th Infantry Division. He said we were in a place called Ste. Marie in the Vosges Mountains of Alsace, but he knew little else because he too was a new arrival. He turned us over to the sergeant who quickly checked us off against the roster and directed us into a nearby building which had been an inn. He

Leon D. Ostrander, Jr.

told us to put our belongings anywhere and get ready for dinner, an order that sounded like the answer to a prayer. This cordial reception and promise of food and shelter seemed as auspicious a beginning as one could expect for a new trooper in the 28th Reconnaissance Troop.

3

THE TROOP

There was enough room for all the men in the three story building that served as both troop headquarters and billet. George Lane, Dave Morton, and I followed three other men into a large second story room where two soldiers sat on the floor next to their bedrolls and talked. They smiled and introduced themselves to us as Red and Applejack. The smaller of the two had reddish hair, a thin, pitted face and a large hooked nose, so I had no trouble understanding his nickname. The other was a tall, well built, blond haired fellow with a friendly grin on his even featured face. He told us his real name, a tongue twisting mouthful, and laughed as he enunciated its multiple syllables.

"You boys better call me Applejack like everyone else," he said. "Nobody except my folks pronounces my last name right, and let's not even talk about my first name."

As I thought about it, his last name, as he pronounced it, sounded more like Applejack than anything else, so his sobriquet seemed appropriate enough.

After the introductions, we plied our new comrades with questions about the 28th Recon. Red said the division was a national guard outfit from Pennsylvania and reviewed the organization's history from Normandy through the triumphant march through Paris in August to the German border in the fall. Applejack told us that the division had engaged in furious combat in the Hurtgen Forest during November, where it suffered so many casualties that the remnants had been withdrawn from that sector and sent to a supposedly quiet area near Wilz, Luxembourg. The depleted ranks were partially filled with replacements in early December, but before the division could be rebuilt into an effective force, the main thrust of the German Ardennes offensive was unleashed against the 28th and the 106th Infantry Division. The 106th was newly arrived from the states and, like the battle scarred 28th, was thinly deployed along a wide front when the Germans attacked. Only 14 men of the 28th Recon escaped capture, death or injury in the fighting. The handful had been augmented by a few replacements in Belgium, but the troop strength was only about 25 men when we arrived. Neither man said much about the details of the fighting, and I did not think it was my place as a raw newcomer to ask any questions. Still, I was appalled by how few from a troop of 150 men escaped this disaster, and I wondered if there had been anything in particular that had made the 28th victim of such losses.

Meanwhile, George had asked whether there were openings in the troop for armorers, and Applejack said that both had been casualties at Wilz, so it looked as though they needed two. From the veterans' comments it seemed that men were needed in every category, officers, noncoms, and specialists of all kinds.

Finally I blurted out my question about why the 28th had suffered such severe casualties, and I was immediately sorry that I mentioned the subject. Applejack seemed to interpret my query as denigration of the division, and he became both defensive and more than a little incensed.

"The whole trouble is that this is one of the best outfits in the army," he replied heatedly. "We get all the toughest jobs. Here, see this patch?" he exclaimed while pointing to the red keystone insignia on his shoulder. "They don't call it the bloody bucket for nothing; the krauts call us that, they hate our guts 'cause they're scared as hell of the old 28th. Why, do you know, they have spies follow us around wherever we go, and then they welcome us back on the line with leaflets and radio broadcasts. They know more about what we're doing than we do."

I was impressed by his fervent loyalty to the 28th and tried to convince the two veterans that I had meant no offense by my question. They nodded agreeably, so I was emboldened to ask where we really were and what they thought we would be doing. Both Red and Applejack shrugged their shoulders and said they had no idea what the army had in store for us.

After a pause, Red added, "They can't expect much from this outfit for a while. We need to get organized and get you boys worked into the troop. We got all new officers, except for Lt. Dewey, and they're just over from the states too. Hell, this outfit needs so much training that the damn war will be over before we're ready for combat again. It beats hell outa me why they moved us outa First Army and way down here in Alsace. I heard from a sergeant at division that we're really in the French First Army, 'n' we're in reserve for the divisions on the line near Colmar. You never know what the brass will do next, so we might end up just about anywhere."

The conversation was interrupted by a call from the stairs for chow. No second summons was necessary as we eagerly clumped down the stairs for our first hot food in three days. I moved slowly through the line and carefully edged back up the stairs with my mess kit heaped with food that visibly tantalized the hungry men still crowding the halls waiting their turn. After eating I could hardly keep my eyes open as the warm room and a full stomach had a powerful sedative effect. My companions were yawning and glassy eyed with fatigue, so we gave up further discussion of the 28th Recon and spread our bedrolls on the floor. I was asleep almost as I pulled the blankets up and remembered nothing until I was roused by the call to breakfast the next morning.

It was still dark outside as I scrambled up and pulled on my clothes, spurred on by the smell of bacon and coffee. After breakfast we were ordered to assemble behind the building, where there was plenty of room for the hundred or so men of the troop. The first sergeant called roll and then turned the assembly over to Capt. Doyle.

The captain told us that the building we had slept in would remain as troop headquarters while we were in Ste. Marie, but many of us would soon be quartered in a large house on the edge of town. He explained that each man's record was being examined to determine where to assign him. Later that day or early the next morning men assigned to the field platoons would move to new billets. I would soon know whether I was to serve in a line platoon or in a safer and more comfortable spot as a troop armorer in headquarters platoon.

While the captain rambled on, my gaze wandered to the landscape of rounded mountains encircling the town, their slopes spotted with evergreens and the whole scene frosted with a heavy cover of snow. The faint morning light gave the valley a somber look, which was enhanced by the ugliness of the town. The buildings were utilitarian and old, their unattractiveness accentuated by several sooty smoke stacks that rose above the grimy shops and houses. The dwellings were closely packed row houses without adornment or distinction. I was thinking what a melancholy place it was when the authoritative voice of Sgt. Hinkle brought me back to reality. He told us to police up our quarters and stay around headquarters until further orders.

It didn't take long to clean up our quarters, and we were soon standing on the street or walking around the building, about the only pastime that kept us within reach of the first sergeant. A column of troops approached while I was in front of the inn, and at first I took them for Americans. Most of their clothes were American government issue, but on closer inspection I was struck by the shabby hodge-podge of clothing and gear that made up their equipment. One of the veteran troopers told me they were French recruits in basic training, an exercise that consisted of a few weeks of drill and practice fire with their weapons and then assignment to a line outfit. I had grumbled about my clothing, but some of these men had no gloves or hats and their clothes were worn and threadbare. I realized then that I was better off than some of the poor wretches fighting in the war.

The old inn was reasonably comfortable because of stoves spotted strategically throughout the building, and fuel was no problem because the civilians were eager to barter wood and coal for cigarettes, candy and soap. The place had indoor plumbing, but the two toilets would overflow when flushed, so a straddle trench had been dug in one corner of the yard. Boards were laid across the 18 inch wide trough so that 4 or 5 men could squat at a time. Unfortunately snow had coated the edge of the trench and the boards with a frozen crust that made every trip a precarious acrobatic feat. Failure to perform the trick of squatting without slipping was penalized by at least one foot in the feces lined hole. I visited this hazardous latrine late in the morning and was congratulating myself on successful completion of the task, when the captain hurried across the yard, and his expression and attitude were those of a man with an urgent call. He was unbuckling his belt before he reached the trench and almost leaped onto a pair of boards as he dropped his pants. This motion was too quick for the footing, and one foot in its beautifully polished leather boot slid off the board and into the trench. Simultaneous with a loud expulsion of gas and diarrheal stool Doyle uttered what for once were the most appropriate words in the language.

"Oh shit!"

Then as he extricated his foot from the mess, he quickly looked around at me and another man with an air of half embarrassment and half apprehension that we might be laughing at him as he muttered, "Well, I guess that's all you can say about that!"

I stifled my natural inclination to laugh as much out of empathy with a man who had just suffered a disgusting accident as out of fear of my C.O. The other trooper stood mute too, and the captain let a shy smile cross his face, finished his business, and pulled his trousers up.

To his credit, Doyle apparently cleaned the boot himself rather than detail some unfortunate enlisted man to the job, because I never heard another word about the incident. Any man assigned to such an odious task would have griped about it afterwards to his friends, and soon the whole troop would have known.

Dave, George and I had speculated about our assignments, for two of us would probably be armorers in headquarters platoon and one would surely be sent to a reconnaissance platoon. Lane and Morton came before Ostrander in the alphabet, and we had been the three top trainees in armorers' school, but I had been third, so it was no surprise when my name was called the next morning for assignment to the other billet as a member of a line platoon.

Before leaving headquarters we were ordered to turn in to the supply section our duffel bags, extra boots, and second uniforms. We were issued a sleeping bag made of blanket material to fit inside an already fat bedroll of four blankets and a shelter half, a reassuring protection against the cold of the winter nights. This was an immediate and obvious benefit of a mechanized unit, because the foot soldiers could not hope to carry so much gear. I resented having been used as a beast of burden to carry a duffel bag full of clothes to Europe only to have them turned in to the general supply of the troop. At first I had not understood this plan and had asked the supply sergeant if they were going to keep my extra clothes so I would have something to draw on when needed.

He looked at me scornfully and sneered, "Sure, Mac, it's just like a store back in your home town, you want something so you come in here and take your pick."

After our business at the supply half track we formed a column of two's and marched through the town until we were at the outskirts, where we turned into a drive leading to a large house on about a half acre of land. It looked more inviting than the decrepit inn, perhaps because it was out of the dingy part of town. Two jeeps were parked in a space in front of the house that was large enough to accommodate at least twenty more vehicles.

We assembled in formation in the yard, and a Lt. Parker introduced himself in a deep Southern drawl. He was of medium build and height, with glasses, a prominent, almost bulbous nose, thin face, heavy dark brows, and a uniform so new that it looked as though it had never been worn before. He said that he would be our lieutenant and after a few general remarks turned us over to a staff sergeant named Meeker, who had been on the train with us. Meeker seemed very ill at ease while he told us that he would be our platoon sergeant and we could just drop our bedrolls wherever we wanted in the house. For the present we were to march down to headquarters for meals, but after we got more vehicles we could either ride or they would bring the food to us.

The mess arrangement didn't sound very good, but otherwise the house seemed comfortable. It was roomy with enough stoves to keep it warm and even a functional flush toilet in a small closet on the first floor. At least we would not have to do a balancing act on the slippery boards at the slit trench anymore.

There would be plenty of work because equipment of all sorts had arrived and more was coming every day. We were getting new jeeps, armored cars, machine guns, mortars, radios and everything else necessary to make us a functional unit. Meeker took me aside and said that he hoped I wasn't too disappointed at not being one of the troop armorers, but the platoon could use my skills right away. I was probably the only one who could assemble and disassemble all the weapons that had arrived or were expected. He then added that he understood how I must feel, since he was a mess sergeant and didn't know a thing about leading men in combat. I was taken aback by this admission but told him I didn't mind being in the platoon and would do whatever he and the lieutenant wanted me to do. Privately I was dismayed that we might go into combat led by a mess sergeant but thought it best to keep this concern to myself. My discretion was in vain, because Meeker bleated his story to enough men so it was soon common knowledge.

I was very busy, because the machine guns and mortars arrived packed in cosmoline, a thick grease that could only be removed with a solvent. Gasoline was the only material available to us that would remove the thick, greasy stuff, so I had a room to myself where I carefully disassembled, cleaned and reassembled the weapons amid almost overpowering fumes. In spite of the cold I worked with the windows wide open and no fire in the stove and hoped that nobody would thoughtlessly light a match and blow the place up. In spite of the fumes it was good to be doing something useful at last rather than riding aimlessly all over France. Most of the other men were as busy as I, because the new vehicles and radios needed to be serviced and adjusted before they were ready for use.

When we were at headquarters for our evening meal I picked up a copy of "Stars and Stripes", the army newspaper, because I wanted to know how the University of Michigan basketball team was faring. In retrospect this interest seems irrational in light of my situation, but my thoughts were still more in the states than in Alsace. After scanning the headlines and the Mauldin cartoon, I turned to the small type of the sports section until I found what I wanted.

A young man sitting near me on the floor and humming a Hoagie Carmichael melody glanced over and asked, "What're you looking for in there, news that the war's over?"

I replied nonchalantly, "I just found out that Michigan beat Wisconsin two days ago, so that's something worth knowing."

At first he looked at me blankly, and then he broke into a broad grin and replied, "You mean they have basketball scores in that rag? Let me see how Indiana did."

I handed him the paper, and he groaned at the result. "Hell, IU wouldn't lose to Northwestern except for this damn war. You wait 'til next year or whenever the war is over, you'll see what I mean. Just wait until the real Hoosiers get back, then ol' IU will really go."

My new acquaintance's name was Nick Weiner and he hailed from New Albany, Indiana, but he added in a great Hoosier twang, his friends all called him Indy. We were soon talking sports with all the zest of two friendly rivals back in the collegiate circle of the midwest. He gleefully recalled that Indiana had "whipped Michigan's ass" in football the previous fall, a fact I could hardly ignore when every Hoosier I knew delighted in reminding me of it. It was then my turn to assure Indy that Michigan would be back on top in football once the war was over. Later he told me that he was a radio operator and recounted some of his problems in activating his equipment, difficulties much like mine except he didn't have to wash the parts in gasoline.

I was assigned to my first stint on guard duty that night and drew the midnight to 2 AM shift with a man named Hammond. It was hard to get up so soon after going to sleep, but Hammond and I stumbled out to relieve the previous shift. It was a cloudy night, but the snow reflected what little light there was so that we could see the dim outlines of objects in the yard and around the house when we made our rounds through the crackling snow. Guard duty was a necessary but irksome chore because nobody expected anything to happen so far behind the lines, so inevitably our thoughts and conversation drifted to other topics. I had not known Hammond before, but he told me he was a college student from Portland, Oregon, and we soon found that we had a lot in common. For some reason we began to talk of food, good food, such as we had enjoyed at home and in various restaurants with our families. Perhaps it was the total absence of what one could call "good food" that guided our conversation to something so remote from Alsace in the winter of 1945. Hammond described in painfully accurate detail his favorite dishes, and then I reciprocated as we tried to pass the time as agreeably as possible. After a while even food fantasies failed to distract us from the realities of cold, fatigue and hunger, the latter probably aggravated by recollections of sumptuous meals in the past. Time passed at a snail's pace, but when it seemed we would never return to the warmth of our sleeping bags, 2 AM arrived, Hammond left to rouse our replacements, and I made a final tour of the area. The new sentries shuffled out mumbling to themselves, while we returned to our sacks, the only pleasant part of guard duty.

The next day we met with Lt. Dewey, the only remaining officer of the old 28th Recon. We gathered in the largest room in the house when the lieutenant arrived, and I listened attentively to at least the first part of what he said. He was a short, heavy set, unsmiling man, almost grim in attitude, who appeared remarkably ill at ease in his role as teacher. I suppose he said things that were important for men to know before entering combat, but I don't remember any of it. The lieutenant's awkwardness and obvious distaste for his task culminated in a sudden termination of the session as though he couldn't tolerate another minute of such drivel, and we returned to our chores.

At assembly that evening before dinner Lt. Parker described us as looking like a "pack of shaggy cur dogs (pronounced dawgs)" and advised us to get haircuts at a barber shop he had discovered in town. I had learned that Parker was from Georgia and his full name was Charles Rutledge Parker. The other officers called him Rutt, a name that caught on among the enlisted men, who regularly referred to the lieutenant as Rutt behind his back. He loved to appear tough, but I hoped that under his rough exterior he would turn out to be what the Southerners called a "good old boy".

After dinner most of us heeded the lieutenant's admonition and found our way to the barber shop. It was a small affair operated by an Alsatian man and his wife, who spoke no English. They tried to converse with their customers in French or German, but most of the soldiers could not communicate in either. In spite of the language barrier the barbers seemed overjoyed by the bonanza of business when at least 15 men at a time crowded into the little shop. I sat next to the New Englander whom I had met on the train, and I learned that his name was Arthur Robarge and he was a truck driver in civilian life. When Robarge asked me what I did and where I was from, he appeared surprised to learn that I had been a college student at Michigan.

He looked at me quizzically and asked, "How come you're not still in school? Did you quit or flunk out? I thought all of you college guys either stayed in school or went to OCS."

I detected a note of antagonism in his voice, although he continued to smile sardonically as though his question might be just his idea of humor. I could not tell whether he was really irritated about something or this was merely Yankee candor, so I tried to answer him coolly.

"I would still be in school if my vision was better, but I couldn't get into any of the service training programs, so here I am in recon. I'm sure no volunteer, but I'm not complaining either."

My reply seemed to break down some of Robarge's reservations about me, and he confided, "My wife didn't want me to enlist, and I could've stayed home because of my age and I have a kid, but I thought I better get into it, I just thought I could do more in the army than at home. She was great, told me to do whatever I thought was right, but it's been tough on her. She went to work at the navy base in New London, and her mother takes care of the kid. We're from Connecticut, you know."

I didn't know where he was from, and his story was different from that of most of the men his age I had met in the army. I sensed that he was completely honest about his reasons for joining up, and I had not met any others who had volunteered for strictly patriotic reasons. Usually such men would chuckle and say they had gone into the service "to get away from the old lady" or to sow some late wild oats. In an effort to learn more about my companion I asked if he had worked mainly in Connecticut or whether his truck driving had taken him to other states as well.

"I've driven all over New England and New York, been doing it since I was seventeen, and I know all the roads up there with my eyes shut. I never got out to the cowtowns in your part of the country. Where was it you went to school again?"

I laughed and answered, "I guess you never did get to Michigan, we don't have what you'd call cowtowns out there. I went to the University of Michigan in Ann Arbor."

Robarge studied me some more before he responded, "You seem to be a smart young guy; how come you didn't go to a better school like Yale or one of the other colleges in the East?"

That sally took the wind out of my sails, and I hesitated before I replied. I could have taken offense at his affront to my school, but his honesty and forthrightness appealed to me.

Finally I said, "Yale's a great school, I don't even know if I could get in there, and it's so expensive that I don't know if I could afford it anyway. I don't think I would fit in with a lot of rich kids. Michigan is a very good state university and I can afford it."

Robarge thought for a moment and then replied, "Yeah, I think I know what you mean about fitting in. Most of the college guys I've known were pretty stuck up and looked down on working men like me." He paused again before he continued, "Still, I want my kid to go to Yale, and I'm going to do my damnedest to see that he does."

Before the conversation could go further it was my turn to get my hair cut. I drew the man, who was probably in his late fifties and had his own graying blond hair cut in a close brush style so that he looked like a typical movie German. His erect almost military bearing and obvious relish for his task of cutting the soldiers' hair added to his Germanic air. Most of the men were confused by the bilingual culture of the Alsatians and assumed that they were sympathetic to Nazis', a misunderstanding of the sentiments of most inhabitants of the area. Several of the troopers were already joking about getting shorn by a "regular old kraut."

As the barber started on me Robarge exclaimed, "He really enjoys cutting your hair, the Nordic features and short cut make the old bugger think he's still trimming the Wehrmacht."

Everyone laughed at this, and my haircut became the center of banter. When I stepped out of the chair Meeker said, "We'll have to put a sign on you Ostrander, since Fritz trimmed you up like an SS trooper."

I laughed and replied, "I'll keep my hat on so none of you trigger happy guys'll shoot me."

The next day we began to practice patrols on the narrow, snow covered roads leading out of Ste. Marie. Vehicles were forever sliding off the highway, and we gained more experience winching them out of the ditch than in the tactics of reconnaissance. Some of the drivers had little experience with the armored car, which had a particular predilection for the ditch. Several men told me they were not comfortable with their driving assignments, and many had never driven on snow or in mountains. Even my friend Hunk Wilson had trouble driving an armored car. He had driven M8's on the flat, dry terrain of Fort Riley in the summer, and he had some experience with heavy trucks in civilian life, but an armored car does not drive like a truck, and he had never driven on snow. He complained that the M8 was off the road before he was aware that it was slipping. This vehicle had six wheel drive, an underpowered rear engine, and no lateral vision for the driver. Poor traction and insufficient power reduced the driver's ability to halt skids, and as a consequence the ponderous cars were often stranded in snow drifts at the side of the road. Even half tracks and jeeps, vehicles with better handling characteristics than the M8's, slithered into the ditch as a result of the atrocious road conditions and inept driving. Our best hope for improvement seemed to be a thaw, but the chance of such a favorable change in the weather appeared remote.

One evening when we were at headquarters for dinner I laid my carbine and gloves on the floor while I went through the chow line. When I returned, the gloves were gone. At first I thought they had been picked up by mistake, but after an unsuccessful search I concluded that they had been stolen. I went to the supply sergeant with my story and requested a pair of gloves to replace those that had disappeared.

Before I could even finish he interjected, "I don't have no gloves, so you better watch your stuff 'cause a man can get a bottle of cognac or a piece of ass for a pair of gloves in this damn town. You boys better smarten up or you'll lose your shirts."

I was surprised and angry at the theft, but the supply sergeant's indifferent attitude enraged me. I would not have been surprised if the unkempt little man lecturing me snitched articles of clothing himself, but I also realized it was useless to argue with him, so I stalked out determined to get even when the chance presented itself. I was so angry that I hardly felt the frigid bite of the wind on my fingers on the way back to our billet. I continued to fume at my carelessness and the thought that we had at least one petty thief among us. When I told my friends about the gloves, they were as indignant as I, and we decided that we must guard each others belongings.

The story spread, and to my surprise Lt. Parker called me aside the next morning and told me to follow him. When we were in his room he rummaged through his belongings, muttering all the time about "goddam thievin' bastards." He came up with a pair of gloves similar to those I had lost and handed them to me.

"I have these fur lined gloves, I don't need those others unless some son of a bitch steals mine too, so you better take 'em before you freeze your damned fingers off," he said.

I was awkwardly trying to thank him for his generosity when he looked at me fiercely from under his bushy brows and declared, "Ostrander, don't you lose those goddam gloves 'cause I only got the one pair to give you. If you can't hang onto 'em, you'll just have to freeze your fuckin' hands off."

The kitchen started to deliver food to our billet that day, so we no longer had to go to headquarters three times a day for meals. In fact, we didn't go there at all, a great relief, because it spared us the increasingly contemptuous comments of some of the "old boys" of the troop. I could not understand why half the veterans made a point of ridiculing all the new men and even the officers. It wasn't as though we had come into the troop and taken all the choice assignments; it was really just the opposite.

That night PX rations were sent with the evening meal, treats that consisted mostly of candy and Coca Cola, and I consumed all I could lay my hands on after dinner. I was awakened in the early morning hours by severe abdominal cramps and an overwhelming urge to defecate. I sprang from my bedroll and dashed for the toilet, but to no avail as the feces streamed down my legs under the long underwear. Even as I sat down on the commode I was aware of a jet of excreta hitting the floor before I was positioned. I sat in the icy closet until the cramps and stooling decreased, all the while shaking from cold and weakness. At last I felt secure enough to stumble out of the reeking toilet and made my way to the kitchen where I found a flashlight and surveyed my condition. My legs and drawers were a foul mess, so I stripped off the long johns, opened the window, and pitched the stinking bundle into a snow bank. I then washed thoroughly in icy water and hurled the towel out the same window when I had finished. I cautiously returned to my sleeping bag, took my one spare set of drawers out of my pack, and prepared to get dressed so that I could clean up the mess I had made on the floor in several places. As I was pulling on the drawers I broke into a cold sweat, and I felt so weak that I decided I better lie down in the sleeping bag for a few minutes to get warm before I attempted what would surely be a lengthy chore. The last thing I recall was the blessed warmth of the sleeping bag; next I heard angry shouting from the hall.

A loud voice exclaimed, "Jesus Christ, some son of a bitch shit all over the goddam house, he even shit in front of the fucking pot! Why didn't the dumb bastard just stand still if he couldn't hold it?"

Another voice growled, "I'd like to get my hands on the cocksucker who did this. I'd kick his goddamned ass out into the fuckin' snow 'n' let him shit all he wants."

I crawled out of the blankets aghast at my failure to clean up after my monumental case of diarrhea. I was sure the other men would not be sympathetic to my explanation of how I meant to take care of my own filth. In any case it was too late now, and cowardice won out as I contemplated my strategy in this crisis. I dressed quickly and pitched in to help scrub the soiled hall and toilet. I planned to admit my guilt if questioned, but I could see no purpose to a confession if I were not a suspect. It did not seem likely that I would be accused, because several other men had diarrhea the night before, and nobody knew of my early morning problem. My reasoning was correct, I was not a suspect. Poor Hammond, who had been so sick with a combination of diarrhea and bronchitis that Lt. Parker had excused him from duty for a day, was the principal suspect in spite of his indignant denials.

To my relief the furor died down once the house was cleaned and everyone was busy with other tasks. I still felt squeamish, but the weapons were all cleaned, and I was excused from duty because I was scheduled for night patrol. This allowed me to spend most of the day near the stove, dozing and regaining my strength. This was to be the third night of patrolling for the platoon and my first assignment. Men who had participated in earlier patrols had told me of wild rides through the snowy mountains and encounters with French or Moroccan troops who had trouble distinguishing between American and German units. My curiosity about these missions was mingled with apprehension, which was increased when I learned that Sgt. Meeker would be in charge of my part of the patrol. I would ride in a jeep commanded by Meeker, driven by a man named McPhee, and crewed by a fellow Detroiter named Chet Gorlitz. I liked Meeker, who seemed to be a thoroughly decent and honorable man, but I did not trust him in this kind of situation because he never failed to remind one and all that he was really "just a mess sergeant" and knew nothing about reconnaissance or combat. I would have traded him for almost anyone who had even a hint of competence as a soldier.

We left Ste. Marie about 9 PM in a convoy of three jeeps, each with a noncom, driver, and two riflemen. Armored cars were not used on these patrols because of their tendency to slide off the road and the lack of experienced drivers. We drove slowly along the snow covered road which was illuminated only faintly by the blackout lights of the jeeps. The road was used by truck convoys to the front, but they moved mostly during the day. Even against the snow it was difficult to see the other jeeps in the stretches of the road that wound through stands of pine trees, and several times we narrowly escaped a collision with the jeep ahead. In spite of being cold and anxious I could barely keep awake and repeatedly caught myself pitching to one side or the other as I dozed off. I was still feeling the effects of my malaise of the night before in spite of my day of rest. Suddenly I sat up with a start when I heard a loud clatter on the road, and then I realized that my steel helmet was gone and the jeep had stopped. McPhee was recovering my helmet, which had fallen off when I slumped too far to the left in one of my brief snoozes.

As he handed it to me he said in his characteristically grave voice, "Man, I'm sure glad it was just your old piss pot, at first I thought someone shot at us."

Meeker added nervously, "Try to stay awake, Ostrander, 'cause I need all the help I can get on this damn mission. Can we catch up with the other jeeps, McPhee?"

The driver assured him that we could, and we proceeded more rapidly, all the while straining to detect other vehicles or obstructions on the road.

McPhee braked suddenly as we rounded a curve and caught a glimpse of faint shadows on the highway ahead. When we drew nearer I could make out the other jeeps and three dark figures clustered around one of the vehicles. We stopped and Meeker stood up to peer into the gloom before he gingerly climbed out to join a small huddle of men talking in low tones at the roadside. I could now see that the strangers wore dark civilian clothes but carried weapons, and it seemed that our men and the irregulars were having trouble understanding one another. At last my curiosity got the better of me, and I climbed out and joined the group.

When he noticed me Meeker asked, "You speak French, Ostrander? We think these guys are Maquis, but they don't speak English and none of us speaks French, so we don't know what the hell they're trying to tell us."

My negative reply was greeted by a resigned sort of sigh as though the sergeant didn't really expect any good fortune to come his way. For my part, I just hoped we would not stand in the snow all night trying to bridge the language gap, something that more time would not close. At last the Frenchmen gave up and signaled for us to proceed, and I could only hope that they had not been stationed on the road to warn us of some hazard. I no longer had the secure feeling of being miles behind the lines because I could hear the incessant rumble of artillery in the distance, much different from the infrequent faint reverberations one could discern on a quiet night in Ste. Marie. The encounter with the underground men and the sound of artillery brought me to full wakefulness.

After about thirty minutes we again stopped, this time at a cross road. Meeker and the other noncoms conferred, and when the sergeant returned to the jeep he announced that we were to patrol to the left on the side road. As we started up the narrow byway I could see nothing but snow and wondered how McPhee knew where to go. Meeker had a map spread on his lap and gazed at it in the glow of a flashlight with all the confidence of a tourist trying to read hieroglyphics. He announced that we were to travel one kilometer on the road and then take a cross road to a village with an unpronounceable name. However, the relationship of our present position to anything on the map seemed to be a nearly complete mystery to our leader.

The road had no tracks from prior use, there was at least a foot of snow on the level, and much more loomed up in huge drifts, so that McPhee stopped the jeep and looked inquiringly at Meeker. Where we had come to rest the snow was at the level of the front bumper.

Meeker laid down the map, studied the scene, and finally asked, "McPhee, do you think you can get this jeep up the road?"

The driver paused for a moment before replying in his solemn manner, "Well, if you want to try, I'll see what I can do. I've never driven in this stuff until I got over here, but I'm game if you are."

He put the vehicle in four wheel drive and low gear, gently applied his foot to the accelerator as he let out the clutch, and the jeep slowly plowed ahead through the heavy white blanket with only a minimum of slipping and shuddering. Once or twice the engine seemed on the verge of stalling, but he would then back up a few yards and get a running start at a drift. In this fashion we negotiated about 1,000 yards on what we guessed was a road. At that point the sturdy little car shuddered to a stop with its nose buried, in a drift that loomed over the top of the hood. Meeker turned his flashlight ahead illuminating a wall of snow that filled the entire roadway as it curved around the side of a steep hill.

The sergeant looked at his map, thought for a moment, and then muttered, "I don't know how in hell we can complete this mission. If any of you boys have an idea, say so. Otherwise, we might just as well go back, if you can get the jeep out of here, McPhee."

The driver drawled, "I got her in here, I can get her out, but someone will have to guide me when I back up so we stay in the tracks."

Gorlitz and I assured him that we would direct him from our positions on the rear seat. Meeker handed Gorlitz his flashlight, and we did our best to keep the jeep on course as McPhee inched it backwards. It was slow work made worse by a bitter wind that had come up and whipped clouds of icy snow particles against our faces. After nearly an hour of tedious backing we came to a place where the wind had swept the road clear, so McPhee could turn the jeep around and move down the road at a more rapid pace. By this time I was nearly frozen and longed for a regulation GI overcoat that would cover my lower body. The finger tip length canvas coat simply was not warm enough. When we arrived at the intersection where we had started our patrol, I was surprised that neither of the other jeeps was there. Meeker wondered aloud if they had returned to Ste. Marie without us, but after about 20 minutes they chugged into view, and we retraced our route back to the troop. On the way we passed a convoy of heavy artillery moving up to the front. The huge tractors hauling the great guns took up most of the road, so we stopped on the shoulder while the ponderous procession growled past. The Maquis were nowhere to be seen when we passed the crossroad where we had unsuccessfully tried to cooperate with our allies. It was nearly 5 AM when we reached our quarters in Ste. Marie, a cold, hungry, and tired group of recon troopers. I tried to think of anything we had accomplished during a night of driving erratically through the Vosges Mountains, but the only certainty was that Meeker was a thoroughly inept leader.

No palace could have been more welcome than our billet when we climbed stiffly from the jeep and headed for the room with the largest stove. We threw wood on the glowing coals in the potbellied heater and rummaged for C rations to eat while we thawed out.

Chet Gorlitz was a quiet fellow and not one to knock others, but after a few minutes of soaking up the heat and eating he looked at me and said, "Meeker doesn't like being a line sergeant, and I don't blame him. He doesn't know what he's doing out there."

"I know," I replied, "but what can we do about it? There must be someone better than that to lead us. I sure hope they make some changes before we go into combat."

Chet looked at me quizzically, "Do you think they'd send us into combat without more training? I don't think we're ready, except some of the old guys. I wonder why they don't assign one of them to lead the platoon? They've all got jobs at headquarters."

As he said this he looked at me, and I looked back, returning his knowing glance, as he continued, "Yeah, I guess that's the answer, they got the good duty and we got Meeker."

The next morning Meeker pulled me aside and said, "Ostrander, we want you to be a jeep driver. Come on over here, this is your jeep," he continued, pointing to a vehicle parked in the yard. "We'll fill out the rest of the crew when we get more men, but for now you'll drive it without a crew. How's that sound?"

I had little experience as a driver in civilian life and only a few introductory lessons on military vehicles at Fort Riley, but the jeep seemed easy enough to drive, although I had heard that it was top heavy and turned over easily. I didn't know what to say to this proposal, so I ended up smiling, nodded my assent, and mumbled something about being glad to be a driver.

Later that morning we were told to assemble, and Lt. Parker looked uncharacteristically ill at ease as he came out of the billet to speak to the platoon. He said that a deserter from one of the infantry companies of the division was to be executed by firing squad that morning in the courtyard of a large house about 200 yards from our billet. At first I could not comprehend what he was saying, I just could not believe that the American army would execute one of its own men. That was something that happened in movies about the Foreign Legion or the French in the First World War. I thought the whole thing must be some grotesque episode in a nightmare, but the small convoy of military police jeeps that arrived at the compound were authentic enough. About a score of men and officers got out, and I thought I could recognize the prisoner between two M.P.'s, but it was hard to tell at that distance when everyone was clad in olive drab. It wasn't long after the detail entered the compound until we heard a volley of shots. The execution had been conducted in a very business like way, no delay or waste of time, and then back to the war. Most of the group in attendance at the execution left soon after the firing, and the final act of this stupefying drama was played out a few minutes later when an ambulance received the body of the deserter and carried it toward Ste. Marie. Within a day bulletins were circulated to all units of the division announcing the execution and warning the men that like punishment would be meted out to any who shirked his duty. Many years later I learned that I had been witness to the only execution of an American serviceman for desertion in the entire war.

On February 2, we left Ste. Marie in a long convoy of all manner of vehicles. Not only recon but headquarters, one infantry regiment, and many support units of the 28th were on the move. The weather had turned cloudy and much warmer as we wound our way south and east down a long valley. The snow was melting rapidly, so the road was soon bare in places, and pools of muddy water filled all the pot holes. I quickly learned that eyeglasses were a great disadvantage for a driver as droplets of muddy water churned into the air by the vehicles caked on my lenses and rendered me nearly blind much of the time. At last I laid my glasses on the seat next to me and relied on my unaided myopic vision to guide my driving. It was more than adequate for a slow daylight convoy, but I wondered how I would fare at night under blackout conditions.

As the driver of a crewless jeep I had no one to talk to and nothing to do except follow the vehicle ahead of me, a tedious and lonely chore. The monotony was accentuated by the many stops for unknown reasons when we could not even leave our vehicles, and my mind wandered over all the things that had happened during the month since I had left the United States. The trip itself had been such an incredible odyssey that the division seemed a haven of comparative comfort and security. On the favorable side, I was in a cavalry unit, I liked most of the men I had met, and the officers seemed all right too. I still cringed at the thought of Meeker leading us in combat, but at least he was a decent, honest guy, so maybe that would turn out all right in time. I realized that I had adjusted enough to my new duties and surroundings so that even my vivid dreams of home had faded. While hardly a veteran, I now felt like a member in good standing of the 28th Recon. On the other side of the ledger, I could not understand the continued contempt and hostility of some of the "old boys" toward us, the newcomers. Then, the execution of the deserter bothered me, but fortunately I did not know at the time what a truly extraordinary event it was. Although many of my fellows still clung to the idea that we were slated for more training or at worst a reserve role, I believed we were headed for a front line assignment, a task that seemed daunting considering our patchwork organization. Still, weighing it all I felt more optimistic than downhearted; indeed, I had a curious feeling that could best be described as calm anticipation of new activities and scenes, something short of euphoria but decidedly more positive than fear or dread.

4

COMBAT

The convoy curled along the highway as far as one could see in its slow descent from the snow covered valley onto a soggy plain where muddy fields were dotted with mean little hamlets. Each settlement consisted of a few hovels huddled together along a street lined with waist high mounds of manure. The dwellings were not flimsy like the shacks in some rural areas of the United States, but in spite of masonry construction they looked as squalid as any houses I had ever seen. It was obvious that they had no indoor plumbing or electricity, and some windows had no glass but were covered by cloth in an effort to keep the places warm. Later I found the interiors of such farm houses just as primitive with little furniture and sometimes a dirt floor. Domestic animals and fowl rooted in the filth and seemed to have free run of the dwellings as well. We had stopped near one such village when Hunk Wilson climbed out of his armored car and started walking from one vehicle to another.

As Wilson approached me he yelled, "Hey, Leon, ya got any water? I'm thirsty as hell, but I'll be damned if I'll drink that treated shit!"

I grinned for I knew what he meant; much of the army water tasted like an iodine cocktail. In case we could not get GI water, each man was supplied with halogen tablets to treat local water, but this process conferred such a strong iodine taste that one could barely choke it down.

I replied, "My water's the same as yours. It tastes awful, but I guess that's better than getting sick."

Hunk laughed and chided me, "Oh, you city boys are too scared of a few germs. After you've been cutting down trees you're not so fussy, why hell, you'll drink right out of a stream if you're thirsty. It's never made me sick. All this crap about the water is just like the army bull shit about gas attacks, trench foot, and all that other damned stuff they're always talkin' about." Pausing, he looked around and then continued, "That house over there has a well," pointing to a nearby dwelling, "and I'm gonna get some water if the frog doesn't sick his big mutt on me."

He walked toward the house, keeping a wary eye on a large mongrel dog which seemed engrossed in sniffing some exotic aroma from a pile of chicken feathers next to a heap of manure in the front yard. As Hunk approached, the cur looked up and seemed to growl but then returned to its rooting in the debris when a man came out of the house. Apparently he had said something to the animal before he greeted Wilson. I could not hear the conversation, and I doubt if either understood the other's words, yet I could read the gestures and smiles as the two walked to the well. Wilson eagerly accepted a pail of water and drank deeply while the little Frenchman beamed up at him. Hunk then emptied the halogenated water from his canteen and replaced it with well water. He motioned for the farmer to wait while he hurried back to the armored car, rummaged in his musette bag, and then returned. The little farmer smiled even more broadly as Hunk gave him two packages of cigarettes in appreciation of his hospitality.

Wilson sauntered over to my jeep and held out his canteen, "Here, have some real water. We oughta empty all our water cans and fill 'em at that well. The little frog is so happy with the cigarettes that he'd almost give us the damned well."

I declined, "Thanks, Hunk, but I'm still a scared city boy, and I'm not taking any chances. The water may be OK, but I just don't trust it."

Wilson retorted in a sneering tone, "The Frenchman drinks it, doesn't he? He looks as healthy as any of these frogs. Jeez, it's going to be a long war for you if you're so worried about dirt and germs."

He then turned away and offered the water to other troopers, but none accepted, so I felt better for not being the only sissy. I was pondering what sort of disease one might contract from well water when the roar of engines told me that we were about to move on.

Although the journey consumed most of the morning, we had probably traveled no more than 20 miles when we came to the first town of any size since Ste. Marie, a place named Lapeoutroie. We halted and sat in our vehicles at the edge of town until word was passed that this was our destination. I looked at the town with more interest then and tried to discern any favorable features, but Lapeoutroie was as drab as Ste. Marie and even lacked the latter place's mountains.

While scrutinizing this unappealing place my gaze was suddenly riveted on five men who stepped out of a house but might just as well have come from the Arabian nights. They were tall and powerfully built with Negroid features and dark complexions and were clad in heavy brown robes that reached nearly to the ground. Each man's head was wrapped in a dirty turban, and two of them wore steel helmets atop the turbans, a feature that would have seemed droll were it not for their fierce demeanor. They were heavily armed and moved with the bearing of proud, barbaric warriors. I recognized them as Moroccans, natives recruited from North Africa to serve in the French army. I had heard that they were ferocious fighters, a reputation I was ready to accept on appearances alone. I watched them until they were out of sight, fascinated by even a brief glimpse of warriors who looked as though they had stepped out of a Hollywood movie. I hoped to see more of the Moroccans, for they lent a little color to the drab town.

At last we moved into Lapeoutroie, where we were directed into a large parking lot next to a small factory. Amid shouts, curses, and vigorous arm signals by the noncoms we parked the vehicles with fair military precision and assembled in front of a very large house on the opposite side of the street. Sgt. Hinkle announced that the entire troop would be billeted there, but first the building had to be cleared of debris. He assigned particular tasks to various sergeants, who then selected men to help them. Robarge was to haul trash from the house to a dump outside the town, and he selected me and a man named McHale to help him.

We took a jeep with a small trailer to the door of the house and loaded it with the refuse the cleaning crews were throwing out of the building. A German unit had occupied the place before us, and most of the trash consisted of papers, ration boxes, discarded clothing and broken equipment. A few souvenirs were uncovered by men working in the house, such as pictures of leading Nazis, swastika flags and arm bands, and one decorative dagger and scabbard, but mostly the place was full of useless junk. The former Wehrmacht occupants had been anything but stereotypes of tidy German soldiers.

We made numerous trips during the gray, drizzly afternoon, and I became better acquainted with the sergeant, who sat in the front passenger's seat while I drove, and McHale occupied the back seat. In spite of the weather and menial task Robarge and I were having a good time, laughing and joking as he recounted one funny story after another from his experiences as a truck driver in New England. McHale, a lugubrious fellow with a long nose that always seemed to support a drop of snot at its tip, said nothing at all and stirred only to help load or unload the trailer.

On our last trip to the dump, as Robarge was regaling me with yet another hilarious tale, McHale's plaintive whine penetrated our mirth. " 'Scuse me, Sarge, but your shit's falling out."

We turned around and simultaneously burst forth in almost hysterical laughter as we saw a trail of trash for a quarter mile behind us, the result of the tailgate falling open.

I stopped the jeep, and McHale blinked, appearing dazed by our reaction to his announcement, but then he continued, "Ya wanted me to tell ya, didn't ya?"

Robarge controlled his laughter enough to reply, "Sure, Mac, you did the right thing, but when did you notice we were losing the stuff?"

McHale shrugged his shoulders and slowly answered, "Oh, I guess it was back there a ways, but I didn't wanta butt in to what ya was sayin', but then I got thinking' maybe ya wanted me to, so I did."

Robarge and I dared not look at one another or we would have started laughing again, but the sergeant controlled himself enough to reply, "You're OK, Mac, but are you ever more lively? I hardly heard you when you did speak up. You feel all right?"

McHale looked at him with a flat expression and mumbled, "Jeez, Sarge, I'm cold all the time, and I guess I'm just sorta froze up. You ain't sore at me, are ya?"

We were all getting to the "froze up" stage when we had recovered most of the load and finished the job. I hoped that the cooks were preparing a hot meal and that the newly cleaned house was at least warmer than the out of doors, but I need not have worried. The quarters in Lapeoutroie were more than satisfactory; they were opulent by ETO standards. The house was even roomier than it appeared from the outside, the windows were intact, there were stoves in most rooms, and there were generous supplies of firewood close at hand.

I tossed my bedroll into a room where five other men from first platoon had already staked out spots. Hunk Wilson, his two radio operators, Hovanesian and Johnson, another crewless jeep driver name Panos and a little balding technician 4th grade named Merrick didn't nearly fill the room. It seemed to be a congenial group, although I only knew Hunk Wilson well. Hovanesian and Johnson were close friends who had gone through basic training together, but the others were only casual acquaintances at best. "Hovey" was a big man with a round face and a ready smile, very much the extrovert, while Johnson was almost the opposite, a lean little fellow with a meticulously trimmed mustache, quiet and reserved almost to aloofness. Merrick was older than the rest, but he was neither condescending nor domineering like some of the older men who were thrown in with eighteen and nineteen year olds. Al Panos was a quiet but friendly young man who had gained his jeep driving job about the way I had.

Hunk and Hovey set the tone, a pair of West Coast boosters who joyfully razzed the rest of us unfortunates from "back East" about everything from weather to sports. The food turned out to be tasty and hot when chow was called. Putting it all together, I was developing a more favorable view of Lapeoutroie and began to hope that we would stay for a while. Division headquarters was in the town, but, unlike Ste. Marie, the rumble of artillery was clearly audible most of the time, and a constant stream of military traffic passed the house. All signs pointed to an early advance, but I was too green to recognize the obvious.

The next day was cold and dark, and an icy wind nipped at my fingers as I serviced my jeep and checked some weapons in the motor pool. I was inspecting the .50 caliber machine gun on Hunk's armored car when I heard a distinctive and familiar voice.

"Where's that little schmuck?"

I looked down to see Ed Glowacki, a voluble and cantankerous radio operator, who, at 25, looked middle aged with a deeply lined face and receding hair line. He was peering around the fender of the armored car as though the object of his search might be hiding there, and I thought he was unaware of my presence above him in the turret.

When there was no reply to his question, he looked up and said in his nasal New England twang, "I asked you a question, where's the little schmuck?" I must have looked blank, for he added, "That little bastard said he had a cable for me. Where is he?"

I finally replied, "I don't know who you're looking for. Hunk's the only guy I've seen in the last few minutes."

Glowacki looked at me in disgust and exclaimed, "Christ, I'd think you'd know, there's only one little heeb in this fuckin' outfit!"

In irritation I snapped back curtly, "Tell me the guy's name, I don't know who you're talking about."

He looked at me in disbelief and sputtered, "I'm looking for the little kike friend of yours, Weiner. Where're you from anyway? Dontcha know a heeb when ya see one?"

I was irritated and offended by the man's crude and insulting inquiry, and I replied gruffly, "Whatever Indy is, he isn't here, and I haven't seen him in the last half hour."

Glowacki gave me one more contemptuous glare and stalked off muttering, "You smart assed babies better wise up over here, or you'll all end up dead or basket cases. Bunch of wet behind the ears kids, it's like a fuckin' nursery."

He continued this monologue as he stalked out of earshot, and then I realized that I was almost as amused as irritated by our ridiculous conversation. Glowacki was a character whose life story was soon known to every man in the platoon. He talked incessantly of the radar unit in which he had served before he was transferred to cavalry. When he wasn't talking about radar, he bragged of his close ties to a petty hoodlum named Butch Reiman in his home town of Worcester, Massachusetts, and his sexy girl friend, a woman named Nora. His adventures with the latter were recounted in intimate detail and justified by his wife's alleged frigidity ("she's a once a weeker, and even then she acts like she's doin' me a favor."). It was inevitable that he became a laughing stock, and soon half a dozen men could mimic his monologues so well that I had to look to tell if it was the real Glowacki or one of his imitators. Because all of his impersonators and most of the other men in the platoon were eighteen year olds, he retaliated by ridiculing us as babies and rarely failed to allude to the possibility that we would go home as "basket cases", a fate that had a morbid fascination for him. He regularly referred to men in the troop by ethnic epithets, a puzzling habit for a man of Polish descent who had probably been the target of such slurs. Glowacki was a character who unwittingly provided comic relief, but the humor was appreciated most by those who were not constantly exposed to his palaver.

The rest of the day was uneventful, and my favorable feelings about Lapeoutroie were reinforced by an announcement at dinner that a movie would be shown that evening in the factory building next to the motor pool. Men crowded into the shop from the different units in the town, filling all the space until they were sitting on machinery, benches, and a few chairs and standing around all the walls. I remember nothing of the film except that it was a temporary escape from Alsace to America, but about half way through the movie a shout from the door brought me back to France in an instant.

"All men of the 28th Recon, report to your unit immediately. You got that? All recon men, back to your troop."

About 25 to 30 men began to grope their way toward the door amid grunts and curses as we stumbled over objects and jostled other men in the dark. Outside, several men with hooded flashlights were moving about the motor pool, and a sliver of light shone briefly from the door of the house whenever anyone entered or left.

The place was in turmoil as everyone scrambled to pack gear and roll up bedding. I hurried upstairs to get my belongings together and found Lt. Parker talking to Panos.

When he saw me Parker said, "Ostrander, pack up your gear and load your quarter ton (Parker's accurate but unusual term for a jeep) and be ready to leave in ten minutes. Applejack will ride with you; you're part of the recon advance party into Colmar. The captain is going to lead it himself."

I was surprised, excited, and a little nervous to be part of this mission. As far as I could learn from others, Colmar had just been captured by the 109th Infantry Regiment of the 28th Division, but it was still a hot spot. I had loaded my jeep and was ready to go in less than the ten minutes allowed and well before the arrival of a strangely silent Applejack. I could not see his face in the dark, but he climbed into the jeep muttering something and sank down in the passenger's seat as though he wanted to shut out all conversation. The captain stopped at each jeep and warned us to stay close together because the whole trip would be under blackout conditions due to the proximity of the front lines.

We drove slowly out of town on a paved road, but after a short time we turned onto a deeply rutted dirt trace. It was wet, the mud as slick and treacherous as grease when one tried to stop or turn. I could see just enough to stay in the wheel tracks as we chugged up a long grade. I could hear the engine sounds of many vehicles, but my only visual contacts with the others were the tiny red blackout tail lights on the jeep ahead. We stopped so frequently that we spent a great deal of time covering what was surely a short distance, but throughout the drive my passenger remained taciturn and almost uncommunicative. At first I thought he was uneasy about my driving, but he denied it and rejected my offer to let him drive. Gradually I realized that Applejack resented his assignment to enter Colmar in the advance party. When he said anything at all, it was to grumble about his bad luck in drawing duty with a stateside officer on such a dangerous mission.

After we had crested a long hill and were far down the other side, we entered an area where the ruts disappeared and we seemed to be in a plowed field of muck. I put the jeep into four wheel drive and low gear range and was able to churn through the slimy goo. I caught sight of men ahead directing traffic with baton flashlights, and soon I was following the line of vehicles onto a Bailey bridge while the MP's shouted and waved their lights to guide us. This temporary span consisted of two tracks similar to those on a service station grease rack, which were supported by portable girders. The jeep barely straddled the gap between the tracks, but once on it could not slip off because of high flanges on the treads. The key to a successful crossing was to hit the tracks accurately, for once on the bridge the vehicle was secure. The exit from the bridge was a quagmire at least as bad as the approach, but after about 100 yards of wallowing the wheels suddenly gripped pavement and we were on a road. Here the hazard was shell craters, gaping holes in the pavement that were almost invisible in the dark. At times I could discern rows of trees along either side of the highway when flashes from the distant artillery were particularly bright. Both the sound and the light from the guns increased as we got closer to Colmar.

I could not see my watch, but it seemed we had been driving all night when we stopped once again and a man came alongside the jeep to warn us that the road ahead was the target of a German railway gun, a monster artillery piece carried on a special flat car.

I didn't know the proper response to this news except to continue following the jeep ahead, so I asked Applejack, "What are we supposed to do? What good is it to know that thing's firing at the road? You can't dodge the shells can you?"

My passenger said nothing at first but after a moment exclaimed in a tense voice, "They tell us that so we're not surprised when the convoy is hit. You can't do anything, it's like all this shit, when your time's up, it's up. Like I told you, the 28th gets all the shitty jobs, but you gotta do what they say, or they'll have your ass for sure."

No shells landed anywhere near the road, and soon we entered a town which had to be Colmar. We passed lines of parked tanks, artillery, and trucks as we wound through the narrow streets; all the military traffic in Alsace seemed to be trying to go through the place. Suddenly a massive shape crowned by a turret and a long gun loomed in front of me, and I swerved right just in time to avoid being crushed by a tank moving against the traffic on the crowded street. The jeep did not escape unscathed, for the monster's track smashed the shovel loose from its attachments on the left side of the vehicle and ground it into the pavement. I was sure my musette bag was gone too, but miraculously the track had merely flipped it into the back seat where I found it later.

Suddenly the jeep ahead stopped, and I pulled up behind it. We sat for a short time while a figure I took for the captain talked to some other shadows at the side of the street, and then we moved ahead and around a corner into what appeared to be a narrower byway that was flanked by three or four story buildings. We had only gone a short distance when we again stopped in front of a large house or apartment where an impressive array of military police stood guard. After parking we clustered around Capt. Doyle, who said we were at division headquarters. He was going inside to a meeting but would send Panos back to let us know if there was a place in the building where we could rest and get warm while we waited.

It was good to get out and move around, but without my attention on driving I suddenly realized how cold, stiff, and tired I was. The noise of artillery fire was awesome and seemed to come from every direction, the muzzle flashes lighting the sky so that buildings, vehicles and people were abruptly thrown into silhouette, as in a violent thunderstorm. While I stood gaping at the pyrotechnic display, a great roar and flash erupted from a point only a few blocks away where all had been silent before. I turned to ask Applejack what it was, but he was gone.

I called, "Hey, Applejack, where are you?"

There was no answer, and then I noticed that the MP's had disappeared as well.

I called again, and finally a voice from under a nearby half track snarled, "You better get your ass under somethin' 'cause that's incoming mail from that damned railway gun."

As I began to look for shelter Panos returned and said, "It's OK for us to sit on the floor inside the house, just so the captain can find us, and we don't get in anyone's way."

On entering the place we joined a huddle of other men, mostly drivers, sitting on the floor of a dimly lit hall. I had hardly sat down before I was asleep, but it seemed that I had just shut my eyes when I heard someone calling my name. I struggled to my feet, still groggy and half asleep, and was introduced to a Col. Cohen and a Capt. White.

I seemed to hear Capt. Doyle from a great distance as he declared, "Ostrander will drive you back to Kayersberg."

I was still in a fog when the two officers and their driver climbed into my jeep, but the cold air quickly revived me. The colonel sat in the front passenger seat, and the other two perched in the back. Col. Cohen was friendly and talkative; indeed, he was almost too loquacious as I tried to concentrate on threading the jeep against the flow of traffic and around shell craters on the dark road back toward Lapeoutroie, for Kayersberg was a village near our previous billet.

The colonel asked where I was from and then inquired about my age, occupation, and length of service overseas. When my passengers learned that I was an eighteen year old college kid who had been in Europe less than a month, the backseat driving began in earnest. This was quite literally true, for Capt. White was far more apprehensive than the colonel, seeing shell craters and other hazards even when they didn't exist. Part of his nervousness stemmed from an accident earlier in the night when his driver damaged their jeep in a shell hole, necessitating the ride with me. Cohen remained calm, chatted cordially, and learned everything imaginable about my background, perhaps normal behavior for the chief of division intelligence. By now I was awake enough to appreciate the gravity of my assignment. Never before had I so much as spoken to a colonel, but now I was chauffeuring one along with the division commander's chief aide!

When we were past the convoys I drove a little faster, while constantly squinting into the darkness in an effort to spot the turn to the Bailey bridge. Capt. White urged me to speed up one moment and to slow down the next, depending on whether he was thinking about his business at division rear or the craters in the road. The artillery flashes were more distant and afforded even fainter glimpses of our surroundings as we got farther from Colmar, and with the diminished visibility the captain became increasingly apprehensive that I had missed the approach to the bridge. Col. Cohen didn't think we had reached the bridge, and White's driver voiced no opinion for he had fallen asleep. When it seemed that the issue had grown nearly to a crisis, I spotted the turnoff, an unmistakable sea of churned mud stretching away into the darkness on the left. I shifted down and put the jeep into four wheel drive and turned into the muck while peering into the dark to catch any signal from the MP's who were supposed to guard the bridge. The captain was sure we would get stuck and cursed the absence of a man to direct us, the colonel said nothing, and I struggled to keep the jeep moving without going so fast that I could not control it when we were about to drive onto the narrow treads of the bridge. Suddenly we lurched up an embankment, and I knew immediately that we were about to plunge into the swirling water of the swollen river. I stopped just in time to avoid a nose-dive into the torrent, triggering a stream of curses from the captain and a few choice comments from the colonel as well. Just then an MP approached and belatedly signaled us to a point about 25 yards downstream where the bridge lay. Capt. White lost no time identifying himself to the hapless guard, who admitted that he had dozed off after the last convoy had cleared his post. White threatened him with every punishment short of execution for this dereliction of duty and was still sputtering as I eased the jeep onto the treads of the span. We negotiated the slick hill beyond the bridge without incident and drove into Kayersberg as the first faint streak of dawn tinted the eastern sky. I delivered my passengers to division rear, where the captain hurried into the building without a word to me, his driver yawned and sauntered away, and the colonel thanked me for the ride.

Almost as an afterthought, Cohen said, "Park your jeep by that building," pointing to a small factory, "and go in there and get some sleep before you try to get back to your outfit, and good luck, soldier."

I thanked him and lost no time in obeying his order. In the light I could see that the jeep was covered with mud and I had my share as well, but none of that mattered as I lugged my bedroll into the factory where I could make out a few work benches in the gray half light. I crawled into the sleeping bag and was asleep instantly. I have no idea how long I slept, probably no more than an hour, before I was roused by a tremendous series of explosions which shook the building. The noise came in salvos, and when I looked out of a grimy window I saw the source, a battery of 155 mm "Long Toms". More important than the guns, I noticed that the battery's mess was still feeding, and I realized that I was more hungry than tired. I hurried to join the artillery men for a hot breakfast, and the cooks even gave me a supply of C and K rations to take along when I headed back to Colmar. I felt very well after eating and, buoyed by the meal and excitement from my night's missions, turned the jeep toward Colmar.

The return trip was easy until I was in the city, where I was soon lost with no recollection of where I had been in the dark of night. The streets were narrow and winding, more like a maze than thoroughfares, and I looked in vain for a sign pointing to either recon or division headquarters. To make matters worse, many streets were barricaded creating numerous cul de sacs. Finally I saw a jeep with headquarters company, 28th Division, on its bumper, and I managed to follow it through the labyrinth to division headquarters, which had moved to a large house on a sizable plot of land. I parked the jeep and walked toward the mansion, now guarded by half a dozen MP's. I asked one if he knew where the recon troop was, but he only shrugged his shoulders and said he didn't know. As I was turning away, he suggested I go into the headquarters to a particular room where "they know how to find every damn man in the division."

I followed his directions and found myself in a room that was a beehive of activity, full of officers and noncoms. I timidly approached a staff sergeant who seemed less frantic than the others.

"Pardon me, sergeant," I said, "I'm from the recon troop and I'm trying to find my outfit. Can you tell me where the troop is?"

After a pause he looked up from a pile of papers and snorted, "How the hell did you get separated from your unit, soldier? Are you alone? If you're pullin' somthin' funny, think again, 'cause the old man's in no mood for any shit."

I retorted angrily, "I was ordered by my CO to drive Col. Cohen and Capt. White back to division rear early this morning, you know who they are, don'tcha? Now I'm just trying to find the troop; can you help me or can't you?"

The sergeant looked up and laughed at my indignation. "You must be OK, hell, no damned deserter comes in here looking for his outfit, but funny things happen in this war. Just a minute and I'll see what I can do."

He stepped across the room and spoke to a major and a master sergeant who were studying a wall map. All three turned and looked at me and then turned back to the map. I wondered what they thought, because I must have been one of the dirtiest GI's in the ETO. Not only was I covered with mud, but I hadn't shaved or even washed my face. The staff sergeant returned with directions to the reconnaissance troop or at least where it was supposed to be according to the big wall map. I repeated the directions, thanked the sergeant, and left hoping to catch the troop before it moved again. I confidently drove through the torturous streets until I came to a thoroughfare on the outskirts of the city where the curbs were lined with army vehicles. I slowed and watched for the recon troop and was rewarded when I came to where the familiar M8's were parked along the side of the street and I recognized several men loafing on the sidewalk.

Meeker accosted me outside the house that was being used as troop headquarters and asked, "Where have you been, Ostrander? The captain was just asking about you, he wants to see you right away."

I was taken back by his accusatory tone and replied, "I got lost coming back from Kayersberg and had to get directions at division headquarters."

I was afraid that Doyle would reprimand me for being late, but he was cordial and apparently thought nothing about my tardiness.

"Ostrander, you know the road to Kayersberg pretty well now, don't you?" he asked.

"Yes, sir," I replied. "The worst part is in Colmar; the rest is easy."

The captain nodded, apparently satisfied with my reply and then continued. "I have to ask you to go back there again. Applejack is sick, and I'm sending him back to division rear. I want you to drive him. I think you can get there without going through Colmar. Robarge will show you how on the map."

The sergeant gave me a map with the route marked and told me to return as soon as possible. It was nearly noon, and I had hoped for a hot meal, but the kitchen was loaded and ready to move, so I could choose C or K rations. Applejack appeared looking dejected but otherwise no different than usual. He grunted a greeting as we got into the jeep but remained silent and withdrawn as we started the trip to Kayersberg. He was no help in finding our way, but I was confident that I could follow the route on the map. This assurance began to evaporate soon after when I realized that we had not seen an American soldier or vehicle for a while, nor were there signs that our army had passed that way. We drove through two badly damaged hamlets which appeared deserted and approached a larger village that also bore the scars of bombs and shells. The streets were strewn with rubble, and fires were still burning in some of the shattered buildings.

Applejack roused from his torpor as I steered cautiously through the debris on the road and exclaimed, "Jeez, we could be between the lines. It would be just like that stateside CO to send us to some damn place like that. We oughta see some GI's, but we're more likely to run into some krauts, or maybe not even see them and get ourselves shot.

Are you sure this is the right way?"

I stopped the jeep and we studied the map. We were on the road that Robarge had marked because the village names matched those on the map, but that did not ease our anxiety. The area had an ominous, brooding atmosphere, as though some danger lurked in the strangely deserted dwellings, so we drove on as quickly as possible with growing fear.

I asked Applejack when he got sick, as much to take my mind off our possible peril as out of curiosity. He shot a quick glance at me and then settled back as though he would ignore the question, but then after a long pause he replied, "Hell, I don't know. I guess it's been coming on for a while, but now I feel like shit, and the captain thought I better go back and see a medic."

His evasiveness warned me to drop the subject. I was quite hungry by now, so I told Applejack that there were rations in the back of the jeep. He came to life and eagerly rummaged through the little bag that had once contained a gas mask, but like almost all such containers had been converted to a second musette bag. There were gas masks scattered all over France by GI's who refused to carry what was universally perceived to be a worthless piece of excess baggage. Applejack found a couple of reasonably palatable rations and we were finishing them when we heard the welcome sound of a truck convoy ahead. We came out of a wooded area at an intersection with what appeared to be a main highway with many signs of heavy truck traffic. There were deep ruts in areas where the pavement had disappeared, and the refuse along the road told us that American soldiers had passed. There was also a rude sign pointing to Lapeoutroie. There seemed to be no more direct route to Kayersberg, so we turned toward the larger town confident that we would soon reach our goal. The going was slow due to the bad condition of the road and the heavy truck traffic, and the distance was farther than it appeared on the map. It was 3:30 when I left my passenger at division rear and hurried back to Colmar in an effort to join the troop before dark.

In spite of my good intentions it was getting dark when I entered Colmar, and I knew that I would never find the troop at night. I found my way to division headquarters but somehow ended up outside of the barricades in a cul de sac at the rear of the mansion. I was afraid that I would get lost again if I reentered the maze to reach the motor pool, so I left the jeep and walked to the building. I met a group of soldiers headed for a mess line, so I asked a sergeant if it was all right for me to eat and sleep there for the night. It must have been a common practice because he directed me to a room in the house where I could sleep and told me the chow line was open to any GI.

I fetched my bedroll and entered the house, a more elegant building than I recalled from my earlier visit. To my surprise the place was heated, and there was electricity and running water. It was luxury, a hot meal, a place to wash and shave, and a warm room in which to sleep. Fatigue made the floor of that house seem like the most comfortable bed I had slept on since I arrived in Europe.

In spite of exhaustion and a full stomach I could not fall to sleep when I first laid down. Images of all that had happened in the past 24 hours flowed through my mind like a vivid motion picture. In each scene I was driving in the dark, straining to avoid shell craters and to stay on the road, and peering into the night to watch red dots which danced erratically before me. I would suddenly wake with a start, gripping an imaginary steering wheel and stepping on phantom brakes. As soon as I realized where I was I would relax enough to drift off to sleep only to have the entire sequence repeat. I don't know how long I laid there, uneasily suspended between sleep and wakefulness, when I heard voices. At first I thought someone was calling me, but when I woke more completely I realized that I was overhearing a loud conversation.

One voice cried, "You can call me a communist if you want, but this damn war is all wrong. What the hell are we doin' here anyway? When you see all them guys killed and wounded it just don't make no sense. Someone must be gettin' rich off this fuckin' war, or we wouldn't be in this hell hole!"

After a brief pause a different and more slurred voice took up the theme. "You're fuckin' A well right, Marty. This damn war makes me want to puke. You know what gets me the most, you know what damn near kills me? It's them young kids, the ones they're sendin' up now, jes kids, don't know shit, and they get killed before they've even had their first piece of ass! Ain't that a bitch? A kid gets sent over here, never even had a fuck, and gets himself killed. It jest ain't right."

After another pause the first voice replied, "Christ, I never even thought of that, but you're right, a lotta them 18 year old boys never even have their first pussy before they're dead. What the hell kinda shit is that?"

The two drunks continued in this vein until they had wandered out of earshot, but their prattle tickled some macabre side of my sense of humor, and I chuckled to myself as I fell into a deep sleep. It was dawn when someone poked his head in the door and yelled for everyone to get up for breakfast.

As I went through the mess line I recognized two men from the recon troop in line behind me. I was elated because they could direct me to the troop or let me accompany them if they were going there themselves. They were "old boys" assigned to Lt. Dewey, now the liaison officer at division headquarters, but I had no reason to doubt that they would assist me. I introduced myself and told them what I wanted, expecting at least a civil response. The pair looked at me with malicious contempt, and one, a shaggy looking man with a drooping handlebar mustache and the affectations of a frontier gunfighter including a revolver in a holster, snarled a reply.

"Oh, you wanta get back to that half assed outfit, eh. We might be able to help you if the lieutenant is going that way, but we'd just as soon stay away from that bunch of fuckups. I don't even know if we can find 'em, they're probably as lost as you."

At that moment Lt. Dewey joined us, looking sullen as usual, and snapped at the two "tough guys", "Get the jeep, we have to go to the troop. I hope that stateside CO hasn't fucked up too much." Then looking quizzically at me, "Who the hell are you?"

I came to attention, saluted, and explained who I was and my predicament. My proper military reply to the officer's question evoked smirks from Dewey's subordinates, and I felt my face flush. I was angry that this trio were so hostile to me, a man they didn't even know, and for no apparent reason. It was almost as though we were not in the same army.

Dewey looked at me as he might at an offensive beggar and then snapped, "Follow us, soldier, and we'll get you back to your outfit. Where's your jeep?"

When I told him it was parked outside the barricade, Dewey snarled, "Why the hell didn't you park it inside where you're supposed to? We'll meet you where the streets come together in 5 minutes. If you're not there, you can find your own way to the troop."

The lieutenant didn't wait for a reply but turned on his heel and resumed his conversation with his two surly companions. I lost no time gathering my belongings and hurried to the jeep, which was standing where I had left it. As soon as it started to move my heart sank; it had a flat tire. I was seized by rage mixed with fear to the point that I almost lost my breakfast. Swallowing hard I ran from the jeep to where Dewey had been parked, but the three men were just pulling away as I dashed into the motor pool. I shouted but to no avail, so I raced back to my jeep and changed the wheel in what must have been record time, but all my efforts were in vain. At least 10 minutes had elapsed, and there was no sign of Dewey's crew when I reached the rendezvous; the lieutenant had said 5 minutes, and he had waited no longer. Afterwards I even wondered if they had waited 5 minutes, they seemed so eager to prove that any new man was a hopeless misfit.

I could not bring myself to return to the operations room in division headquarters, where they would surely think there was something suspicious about a man who was separated from his unit for the second day in a row. I decided that I would find the troop if I had to drive all day and cover all of Alsace. When I reached the outskirts of the city, I followed the flow of traffic, reasoning that ultimately I would reach some contingent of my unit. The idea seemed sensible except that the traffic soon divided, and I had no way of knowing which stream to follow. I stopped to devise another plan, and while pondering my dilemma, I noticed two men from signal company stringing wire nearby. I thought they might know where the recon troop was, even though most cavalry transmissions were by radio rather than telephone.

I picked the right men, for they had just strung a line to a hamlet less than a mile away for a battalion of the 109th Infantry Regiment, and at least part of the troop had been there. The directions were easy, and I sped away with a sense of relief that I would soon rejoin my outfit. I had some concern about what sort of tale Dewey and his henchmen might have told about me, but it was submerged by the jubilation I felt when I drove into the hamlet, a miserable collection of hovels in a sea of mud, and saw the familiar M8's and jeeps tended by some of my friends.

I reported to Lt. Parker and Sgt. Meeker, who were quartered in the best house in the village, and they were cordial and made no comment about my tardiness. I then joined other members of first platoon, who were sitting on the dirt floor of an adjacent room which served as pantry and kitchen for the house. A pot bellied stove radiated welcome heat, and at first I thought everyone was subdued and drowsy from the comfort of the warm chamber. When I got only dull stares in response to my cheerful greeting, I sensed that something was wrong.

Panos turned to me and said, "You heard about Johnson, didn't you?"

I looked at him quickly and shook my head, "No, I haven't heard a thing, what about Johnson?"

Panos sighed and mumbled, "He's dead. He ended up under his M8 when it turned over at a bridge going to Colmar. I don't know whether he was crushed or drowned, but he's dead."

I felt sick at this news and asked, "What about the others, Hunk and Hovey? Are they OK?"

Panos nodded, "Yeah, they got wet and shook up, but they'll be all right. I hear Hovanesian is really mad, he and Johnson were buddies, and he blames Wilson. I guess Hunk feels real bad and blames himself too. Everyone feels lousy, it's not even like he was killed by the krauts, it was a damn accident."

I sat down next to Panos and basked in the heat from the stove. It seemed that getting warm, finding food, and grabbing sleep whenever possible had become my main concerns. Beyond that, it seemed to be just luck that determined one's fate in the war business.

While these somber thoughts were running through my mind Meeker came into the room and exclaimed, "All out, you guys, we have a mission. All jeeps, no M8's, three men to a jeep."

We scrambled out with our weapons, climbed into the jeeps, and formed a line behind the lead vehicle. Indy and a man named Williamson rode with me as we chugged out of the hamlet, a procession of 5 "quarter tons" as Parker would say. A faint sun shone through the overcast and relieved the drab landscape as we bumped along the rutted road to another village almost identical to the one we had left. The crackle of small arms fire was mingled with the rumble of artillery when we stopped in the cluster of houses, but the place looked deserted. We conducted a quick reconnaissance of the area and then moved out on a road built on top of a 10 or 12 foot embankment. The land was flat in all directions, broken only by a few lines of trees along the fences. The lead jeep set a faster pace on this leg of the mission, perhaps because of our exposed position on top of the dike.

Part way through a leftward curve my jeep started to skid to the right in the mud. Instinctively I pulled the wheel to the right halting the skid but sending the vehicle hurtling down the embankment into a soft, muddy field. More by luck than skill I gunned the engine to avoid getting mired and arched to the left and up the dike onto the road where I fell into line behind the other vehicles. When we reached our immediate objective my petrified passengers and I were the center of attention. Parker and Meeker seemed to think that my successful completion of the wild maneuvers on the dike marked me as a superlative driver, but I knew that inexperience and lack of skill were responsible for the skid that could have ended in death or serious injury.

A search of the target village turned up nothing, and we were soon ordered back to our starting point. By this time it was late afternoon and I was hungry, a feeling apparently shared by others. As we clustered around the stove in the farmhouse, someone asked Meeker whether we would have hot food for dinner. He conferred with Parker and an inquiry was sent to troop headquarters. The mess sergeant replied that he could not send us hot rations, but we could have more C rations if we sent a jeep to pick them up. This seemed but one more example of the "old boys'" callous disregard for us. While it would not help right away, I thought that Parker's rage at this insolence would have effect later.

A tank company headquarters had moved into the village, and their mess moved with them. Not only did the mess get close to the front, but they regularly sent hot meals to outlying units, a fact not lost on any of us as we talked to the new arrivals. Parker disappeared into their command post and returned with a sly look on his homely face.

"If our fuckin' mess won't feed us, the tankers will. You all just get into their chow line. Their captain is from Augusta, and we're welcome to anything they've got," he declared.

The tankers' food justified their reputation as the best fed troops in the army. We had hardly finished our meal when we received an order to load up and be ready to move. It was dark when we left the village, and I soon had to remove my mud spattered glasses to see the blackout lights on the vehicle ahead. We moved very slowly, and after what seemed like hours but was probably 45 minutes, we entered another village where the houses loomed as dim, lifeless shadows with no sign of human occupancy. Small arms fire was more sporadic than in the afternoon, but the artillery continued its intermittent rumble and lit the sky with flashes that threw the landscape into ghostly silhouette. We halted in the center of the village, where Parker, Meeker and Robarge huddled in the street and then approached one house. After repeated loud knocks on the door, it opened and they entered the dwelling.

They returned soon and Parker said, "I'm setting up platoon headquarters in that house, there's room for all of us in there if you include the shed alongside it. Sgt. Meeker will assign guards; radio operators will rotate on duty. Everyone better know the password and countersign, or you might get shot. If anyone approaches and doesn't know the password, it's probably a kraut patrol. And don't wander off, we may have to get outa here in a hell of a hurry. You all understand?"

I drew the first stint on guard, a welcome assignment because then I could sleep afterwards for the entire night without interruption, unless we were ordered out on a mission. I moved about in the shadows and checked a few men on the street, but after a half hour all was quiet except for a faint light and some crackles from the radio in the communications M8. My two hours passed uneventfully, and I retired to the shed attached to the house. The place had no floor, the ground was hard and uneven, and animal smells permeated the air, but at least it was a roof, and I soon fell to sleep.

I woke to the crowing of roosters and saw a faint gray light in the east when I emerged from my fetid sleeping place. It was good to get outside, even though it was a cold, damp day. Even a despised K ration was welcome for breakfast, and I munched ravenously while I watched the dawn gradually illuminate the village. It was slightly larger than those we had visited the day before, but the houses and manure piles were the same. For several hours we did minor maintenance chores, loafed, and waited for further orders. There was a community hydrant where we could wash and shave, if one could stand scraping the whiskers off with a dull GI razor blade rinsed in cold water.

At about 10 o'clock we were ordered to move out, the start of a series of missions that blend into one another in my memory. I recall one village where the entrance road passed through a massive log gate topped by a sign that read: "Tod zu den Zerstörern Europas" (death to the destroyers of Europe), a chilling reminder of our foes' warped sense of reality. The radio operators constantly picked up German broadcasts describing the movement of American units, including our own, and predicting death for all of us. It was obvious that the enemy had many spies, for the information was startlingly accurate and detailed.

Late one afternoon, we entered a larger town with a few substantial houses, a handsome church, and a paved main street. The place was called Hattstatt, a vaguely comical name to my ears, but the atmosphere was more foreboding than humorous. Troop and platoon headquarters were established in a large house with a yard big enough for the communications half track and several jeeps, and at the rear of the yard there was a sizable barn without the usual foul manure pile in front of it. The captain, executive officer, and Lt. Parker were quartered in the house along with key members of the headquarters staff, while Panos and I, who were to serve as couriers and guards for the headquarters, were to sleep in the barn. Most of the troop was situated in a nearby village, and I have never quite understood this odd separation of the command from the troops. The chatter of small arms fire could be heard in the distance, and, as if to emphasize the gloomy air of the place, a dead German soldier lay sprawled at the side of the road less than 100 feet from our command post. As night settled the eeriness of the location was heightened by the incessant howling of the family's large shepherd dog. The creature was chained to the barn and seemed to resent our invasion of his territory.

Panos took the first turn on guard, and I tried to sleep on a pile of hay, but the early hour and the noise of the dog kept me awake. As I started my first stint on guard, the door of the house opened and Lt. Parker stormed out.

"Who the hell's on guard here?" he bellowed. "Can't you make that goddam dog stop yowling?"

Parker's anger struck a responsive chord in me, and I replied, "It's me, Ostrander, lieutenant. I wish I could make him stop, but I don't know how to shut him up. Maybe the old people who live here can quiet him down."

"Those damned people don't speak a word of English," he replied. "Anyway, I think the old son of a bitch is more kraut than French. He won't do anything for us."

"Do you want me to speak to him in German?" I asked. "I know enough to ask him to make the dog stop howling."

I could not see the lieutenant's face in the dark, but his tone conveyed his surprise. "Ostrander, I didn't know you could talk German. Where'd you learn that?"

"I had a year of German in college. I'm not very good, but I think I can make them understand simple things."

Parker interjected, "Well, you can tell that old kraut bastard that you'll shoot his fuckin' dog if it doesn't shut up. I'll give you a direct order to shoot that cur if the old Nazi doesn't make it stop yowling."

He continued a grumbling monologue about the old couple as he led me inside the house to a room where the pair sat on a large, old fashioned overstuffed sofa, which made them look like two frightened elves on a hill. They brightened a little when I spoke to them in German, but the old man's answers came in such a rapid torrent and in an accent so different from what I had learned that I could not catch the meaning.

While I tried gently to slow him down so I could understand, Parker became increasingly impatient and finally exclaimed, "Jesus, Ostrander, just tell these damned people to make the dog shut up. I don't care about their life stories."

I turned and said, "These people aren't Nazis; they hate the Germans. The krauts shot their cows right in the stall and threatened them only a coupled of days ago. You don't want me to say that we'll shoot their dog, do you?"

He looked at me with mixed disgust and skepticism and muttered, "Damned krauts must have been deaf; they shot the wrong animals. Look, Ostrander, can't you cut the bull shit with them and just get the old bugger to take care of the dog?"

I explained that we would not harm him or his wife, but we wanted him to make the dog stop barking. As we walked into the yard the old man continued to talk at a rapid pace, and I could only catch part of what he said. At sight of his master the shepherd stopped howling and whimpered affectionately. So far as I could understand, the dog was hungry, but they had nothing to feed it. The old man seemed to say that the shepherd would howl until he had something to eat.

After I explained this to Parker, the lieutenant retorted, "Hell, give the damned mutt a can of rations, they're about the same as dog food, but if he still howls, you're to shoot him!"

The shepherd gulped a can of corned pork loaf in one swallow, then curled up next to the barn and seemed to go to sleep. With the apparent success of our strategy the old couple relaxed enough to force a little smile, and even the lieutenant managed a sardonic grin. The rest of the night was cold and monotonous as Panos and I took turns on guard, but at least the dog was quiet. Hot food was delivered at dawn, thanks to the trio of officers in the house. The mess sergeant made the effort grudgingly I'm sure, but he knew the limits of his intransigence.

As soon as I had eaten I was summoned to the house, and Parker gave me a packet of papers to deliver to Meeker, who was in charge of the rest of the platoon in the other village. I was elated to do something besides wait in the barnyard, and I wheeled the jeep onto the road where I drove as fast as the craters in the pavement would allow to the next village, a place called Rouffach. I found the platoon in a school house next to the road which was lined on both sides by a column of muddy GI's of the 109th Infantry trudging toward the crackle of small arms fire.

As I entered the building I nearly ran into my friend D. J. Caulkins, who exclaimed, "You wanta see somethin' good? Look out behind there."

He threw wide a heavy door to the schoolyard in the rear of the building where three troopers were guarding at least 75 German soldiers who stood around impassively. Like all POW's they were stripped of helmets and arms so that I got a good look at them. They appeared to be first class troops, not oldsters or teenage boys as one might expect of a nation nearing the end of its manpower.

D. J. laughed at my gawking and added, "The war's over for these boys."

I was impressed and asked, "Did you guys capture them?"

"Cob no," he chuckled, "Some old boys from the 109th left 'em here; we're watching 'em until the MP's take 'em away. I don't know what we've been doing except wandering around. What've you been doing?"

When I told him about Parker and the dog I didn't think he would ever stop laughing. D. J. and I had been friends since we met. He was a lot of fun, very bright and witty, but at the same time very religious and morally upright. His strongest epithet was "Cob," whatever that meant.

When I asked where Meeker was he pointed to a door and said, "I know where he is, but I don't think he does. That old boy leads you on a lot of wild goose chases, but you don't even see the goose."

I walked to the door and knocked. Meeker shouted for me to come in, and I could hardly keep a straight face as I entered what appeared to be the principal's office, now the headquarters of our sergeant who was seriously scrutinizing a map that he probably couldn't read.

"I have these papers for you from Lt. Parker," I said. "He told me to stay here and do whatever you wanted me to do."

He looked at the packet and then at me with a perplexed expression and then muttered, "Oh, thanks, Ostrander. Why don't you go out with the others, but stick around, I may need you."

When I rejoined my friends they were examining a pile of German arms and equipment in one room of the school house. I had just started to look at this souvenir material when Meeker shouted my name, and I saw him come out of the room with his perpetual bemused and worried expression. He handed me a message and told me to deliver it to Lt. Parker. I wondered why they didn't communicate by radio but refrained from any wise comments. It was clear that my job was to obey, not to make suggestions.

As I drove off D. J. called after me, "Feed that dog so Rutt can get his sleep."

I grinned under my grime and accelerated on the muddy, shell pocked road. I had only gone about a kilometer when I had a flat tire. I had no spare after using it in Colmar, but fortunately I was near an artillery battery where a friendly sergeant swapped a usable spare for one of my flats. In the process of changing the tire I acquired an additional coat of mud, particularly on my feet and arms. My face and chest were already covered with caked dirt, so now I was about as filthy as one could be.

When I reached my destination in Hattstatt I knocked on the door, and a familiar gruff voice shouted, "Come in dammit. This ain't no hotel room."

I opened the door just enough to call, "I better hand this message in, I'm so muddy I'll mess up the house."

Parker roared, "Jesus, Ostrander, you think you're home, and your mother'll give you hell for getting the floor dirty? This damned old kraut bitch can clean it up, it's no skin off my ass." Then at the sight of me, "God damn, what happened to you? Did you fall in a river or take a nap in the ditch?"

I explained what had happened and took off my coat and boots so they could dry next to the kitchen stove while I washed at the sink. The old man produced a basin of warm water, so I managed to shave before the order came for us to move out. My coat and boots were not dry, but damp had replaced wet, a distinct improvement. We joined the rest of the troop at Rouffach and began a series of missions that run together in my memory. The next several days consisted of a jumble of wretched villages, patrols, C and K rations, short periods of sleep in sheds, barns or hovels little better than stables, stints of guard duty at all hours of the night and sporadic road reconnaissance at any time of day or night.

I recall one embarrassing episode when we were in a line of vehicles waiting to advance to another of the seemingly endless little villages in the area. The day was raw and cold with a penetrating dampness that made me shiver. It seemed that we had been parked all afternoon, and I was not only chilled to the bone but increasingly uncomfortable because of a mounting need to urinate. Unfortunately, my part of the convoy was in the very center of the hamlet where a few women and children were moving about. Several other men had the same discomfort as I, and we groused to one another that it was just our luck to halt at the one spot for several miles where civilian women and children were observing us. Finally the old crone who lived in the house closest to our column screeched something to a younger woman, apparently her daughter, who in turn called several children, and then the family entered the house. At that moment the street was clear of civilians on the right side of the armored car, so Robarge and another man climbed down and started to urinate in the shelter of the M8.

"You better take a leak while you can, Ostrander," the sergeant called, "You never know when you'll get another chance."

With this encouragement to overcome my modesty about relieving myself on a public street I lined up to water the armored cars underside. My friends had finished as I started, but before they could climb into the car I heard the old hag of the house bawling something at us. I turned my head to see her cackling, laughing and gesturing like a mad witch; so far as I could tell she was tremendously amused by the sight of the soldiers urinating in front of her home. My initial reaction was embarrassment that was replaced almost immediately by indignation that the horrid old biddy would deliberately ridicule me. I finished my business with the wretch practically on my elbow while my friends laughed uproariously.

"Hey, she likes you, Ostrander, you can score with her," someone yelled.

"If I score it'll be a bullseye with my carbine," I replied angrily. "She's the worst old bitch I've ever seen."

I was saved from further taunting when the column at last began to move, a procession of jeeps, armored cars, and six-by's loaded with infantry heading out of the squalid village and bound for others of the same sort until we would finally complete our mission in Alsace. I had at least learned that modesty had no place in war, and calls of nature must be answered regardless of the neighborhood.

On the final morning of this campaign, although I didn't know it at the time, we were ordered to another name on the map, a hamlet indistinguishable from scores of others except that here the small arms fire was particularly close and intense and occasional geysers of earth erupted with a roar in fields around the village, the hallmark of mortar fire. We gained the partial shelter of the buildings after parking the jeeps and two armored cars in the lee of a wall. Lt. Parker shouted for us to take cover when a mortar shell exploded 60 yards up the street. Caulkins and I squeezed into a narrow space between two houses to wait out the shelling, which was probably in response to our arrival.

Tanks and armored cars always drew fire, although we didn't realize it at first. As we crouched in our cramped refuge occasional pieces of tile or plaster fell near us after bouncing off the roof above. A gust of wind blew a paper between the buildings and Caulkins grabbed it and started to read in the dim light of the cranny.

"Oh Cob, look at this," he exclaimed as he handed the paper to me. "I wouldn't believe this if I didn't see it."

The paper was a handbill which the Germans had printed for American consumption, and it was truly an incredible piece of crude propaganda. There were sketches of Negro and Jewish stereotypes and a bit of doggerel that concluded with these verses:

"If you take time to piss,
You'll a German miss,
If you take time to crap,
You'll not get a Jap.
So piss in your pants,
And shit in your shoes,
And win the war
For the God damned Jews."

It was so bad that I started to laugh, but then I became angry to think that the Nazis not only wanted to kill me but thought I was stupid as well.

Our wonder at the leaflet was interrupted when the lieutenant shouted for us to assemble by our vehicles; we had a mission for jeeps only. We were to make a reconnaissance patrol to a village on our flank. Parker ordered the jeeps to stay 20 yards apart and cautioned us about mines on the road. I was third in line as four jeeps moved from the shelter of the hamlet toward another cluster of hovels about half a mile away across the muddy fields.

About a third of the way to our destination the lead vehicle stopped, and Parker got out and inspected the road. He then signaled for the jeeps to proceed along the left side of the pavement. When I reached the lieutenant I could see uncovered mines lying in potholes on the right side of the road. Either the Germans had been in a hurry and had not had time to cover the devices, or they had concealed other mines more cleverly and used the obvious charges to channel traffic toward the hidden explosives. Jeeps were maneuverable enough to avoid most suspicious spots on the road, but thoughts of instant annihilation from an unseen mine created an eerie tension. Soon after clearing the first minefield we reached a second more extensive cluster. As we cautiously negotiated the ugly devices, an explosion and shower of mud in the field to our right froze us. The sharp crack of the muzzle blast reached us after the shell had landed, a sign of a high velocity artillery piece, probably the notorious eighty-eight. Before we could do anything a second shell landed to the left, and even green replacements knew they were bracketed, and the next shell should land on or close to the patrol. The mines had served their purpose by halting the jeeps in sight of the German gunners. Instinct told us to race to the shelter of the nearby village, but there was no choice but to continue our cautious passage of the minefield and hope that the German gunners had a bad day. I tried to remain calm as I waited for the next shot, but the blast never came. We cleared the mines without damage, a seemingly miraculous escape. When I glanced back I saw two tanks scuttling for cover in the village we had left and from which they had sallied forth at the critical moment to save us. The Germans could not resist turning their attention from a few jeeps to more tempting targets.

When we reached our destination, a mean hamlet without a sign of life, I tensed expecting fire from concealed Germans, but our only greeting was the wagging tail of a whimpering cur dog, an animal so thin that every rib stuck out of his mangy hide. We cautiously entered one house after another but found no friend or foe. The results of the patrol were reported by radio while we waiting for further orders. I hoped division would tell us to occupy the place, which seemed more attractive now that we knew it was free of enemy troops and did not seem to draw fire.

It was not long before we were ordered back to the village from which we had come, and I tried not to think of the mines or eighty-eights when we started to retrace our route. We made it without incident, because the Germans were fully engaged by the American infantry, who moved across the fields toward a treeline where flashes marked the enemy position. The firing was intense and soldiers fell, an everyday occurrence for the infantrymen. It was easy to see why infantry companies had a three or four-fold turnover in personnel if they were on the line for a long time.

When we regained the shelter of the village, the mortar fire had also been redirected to the infantry, and the streets were quiet. Parker said the captain had arrived and would personally lead the next reconnaissance, a patrol to ascertain the progress of the infantry. The goal was to drive the Germans beyond the Rhine-Rhone Canal, the last defense line for the enemy west of the Rhine River. While Parker and Doyle conferred in the house, the rest of the platoon stood around in the street.

When the lieutenant and the captain returned they said that the patrol would consist of two jeeps, the captain and Panos in one and

Robarge and Merrick in the other. The rest of us were to wait where we were, a welcome assignment now that the mortar fire had stopped. Like so much of the time, this was a period of boredom and yet I felt a peculiar nervousness about the place. I thought it was the memory of the close call with the artillery fire on the road that morning and tried to dispel my anxiety by talking to some of the other men. I walked over to an armored car where Hammond sat in the radio operators seat and shook with a chill. I asked him what was wrong, and he said he was sick again, a fact that was quite obvious. I urged him to report his problem to Lt. Parker before it got worse, but he was reluctant to complain. I understood his reluctance, nobody wants to be thought a weak sister, but there was no question that he was very ill. Any talk tended to be strained and brief, and I sensed that the others shared my mounting uneasiness as time passed and our comrades did not return. I started to eat some rations, but for once my appetite had vanished.

At last one jeep returned, and Robarge and Merrick got out and strode into the house where Parker waited. I knew something had happened when the others did not appear, and suspected the worse.

When the door opened I heard Parker say to Robarge, "Go ahead, try if you think you can do it. Take anyone you want."

"I'll go with Robarge," Merrick interjected. "We know where he is and can do better than a bunch who'd just draw fire."

Parker nodded his assent, his long face grim and worried as he watched the two men get back into the jeep and drive toward the firing.

The lieutenant then turned to us and motioned for us to gather around. "Bad news, men," he said. "Panos was killed by an eighty-eight shell, and the captain was hit too, but he may still be alive. Robarge and Merrick have gone back to see if they can bring him in to the aid station."

This news should have been no surprise, and yet I was stunned to learn that my worst fears had been fulfilled. Any of us could have suffered the same fate that day. I thought how I might have been assigned to go with the captain, because Panos and I had been performing similar tasks since the night we entered Colmar. Now I wondered if we would ever see Robarge and Merrick again, but at last they returned with Merrick driving and Robarge cradling the captain in his arms in the back of the jeep. They stopped at the aid station, where the medics helped them carry Doyle into the hovel used for triage of the wounded, and then returned to report to Parker.

While Robarge talked to the lieutenant in the house, Merrick told us about the ill fated patrol. Soon after leaving the village they had encountered heavy fire which forced them to leave the jeeps and hike across the fields toward the German line. A shell landed directly in front of Panos, killing him instantly, and showered fragments into the captains belly. The fire was so intense that Robarge and Merrick could do nothing but crawl back to the jeeps. When they returned later for the captain the infantry had advanced far enough so that the firing was sporadic and more distant, and they were able to carry him to the jeep.

We stood in the village street waiting further orders, a quiet, grim, and sobered group of men. I can only recall a feeling of numb resignation, as though all normal emotion had been drained from me. I didn't feel like crying, and yet I was sad, I didn't feel particular fear, and yet I had every right to tremble. Indeed, I was surprised that I did not feel much of anything, it was as though my very humanity had been muted. My sadness seemed somehow shallow and inadequate, but the events of the day appeared as the expected and normal outcome of the impersonal slaughter that was going on all around me. This sort of grim fatalism, which seems callous and unsympathetic in retrospect, was probably a necessary armor for a man in my situation. If one was too deeply affected by casualties he would surely suffer some sort of emotional collapse.

Dusk was settling when we were ordered to move again, this time to a place called Oberhergheim. It was farther behind the lines and larger than the hamlets where we had spent the day. The entire troop was quartered in a spacious upstairs room of a schoolhouse, but the atmosphere was somber, a mood matched by the drab gray color of the town in the twilight. Hot food was the treat of the day, but while eating my dinner I was assigned to guard duty from 10 to midnight.

I laid on the floor trying to get some sleep before my stint as a sentry, but the events of the day flashed through my mind. Then I heard Weiner singing "When the Roll is Called Up Yonder" from the other side of the room. He was soon joined by other men, who seemed to draw comfort from this and other old gospel hymns. For me the singing seemed to emphasize the mournful atmosphere of Oberhergheim, and I was enveloped in melancholy and pessimism.

I must have fallen to sleep for a while because all was quiet except for snoring when my predecessor wakened me for guard duty. A few soldiers were still prowling the town looking for a different kind of excitement, an occasional rooster crowed, and dogs barked, but for the first time in a long while I heard no artillery. It could only mean that the Germans had been driven across the Rhine, and the campaign in Alsace was over. It seemed harder than ever to stay awake, so I passed the time trying to figure out the date. At last I decided that it must be February 11, and by that time my turn was nearly over and I could look forward to a warm bedroll.

In the morning we joined a long convoy of 28th Division vehicles rolling back through Colmar to Lapeoutroie where we were billeted in the same place we had left 10 days earlier. At least we did not have to do a major cleaning job on the house, and this time we had no illusions about a long stay. Rumor had it that we would move north to rejoin First Army.

The troop was reorganized with Lt. Collins, the rotund executive officer, now in command, and the platoons were realigned so that there were only two active field units, the second and third. Even then we were under strength, but at least we had two functional units. I was assigned to third platoon as a mortar gunner in a jeep driven by Hunk Wilson. Lt. Parker was platoon leader, a Sgt. Samuels was the platoon sergeant, and Robarge was my section sergeant. Our machine gun jeep was manned by Caulkins, Henry, and Gorlitz, and the armored car was driven by a feisty little Ohioan, Mike Reardon. Weiner and another Hoosier named Hilton were the radio operators. I knew most of the men and all seemed to be congenial and competent. Except for Robarge we were all eighteen and nineteen year olds, and I was glad we had no overbearing older men like Glowacki in the section. I liked and respected Robarge, so I felt fortunate in my new assignment

Meeker had been designated troop baker, a move that pleased him and everyone else when we had a chance to taste his culinary creations. Hammond was sent to the hospital, and I never saw him again.

The mood of the men became more optimistic and even euphoric with the reorganization, which generated a feeling of confidence in their leaders and themselves. As a result of this exuberance some of the men raided a local winery and carried their booty away in five gallon jerry cans. The ensuing party was spirited, indeed raucous, until someone noticed that part of the wine had been carried in gasoline rather than water cans. I don't know whether it was the wine, residual gasoline, or just the quantities consumed, but the next morning dawned dark and dismal for some of the troopers. One celebrant had walked straight off the porch of the house and flipped over on his head as he struck the cement of the front walk 6 feet below, but fortunately he suffered only a large goose egg on his forehead and a headache as reminders of his mishap. The rest of the revelers recovered too, but most had monumental hangovers. Instead of a day of rest that would have allowed an easy recovery for the woozy men, we were worked harder than usual in preparation for an evening departure for an unknown destination.

    The move was supposed to be secret, so much of our time was spent painting over all identifying numbers on vehicles and helmets and removing division patches from our clothing. The night departure was another attempt to conceal our whereabouts, but these elaborate precautions seemed ludicrous when German broadcasts announced that the Wehrmacht would be waiting to kill us on the German-Belgian border.

5

THE BIG MOVE

As we left Lapeoutroie I felt enveloped by the blackness of the night, a darkness that seemed dense and impenetrable and was unrelieved by the faintest glimmer of moon or stars. The convoy must have stretched far along the road, but the occupants of each vehicle could barely maintain contact with the car ahead and were visually disconnected from the rest of the procession. We used blackout driving lights, hooded lamps on the front of each vehicle, which cast a faint beam onto a small segment of road immediately before the car, but two pairs of tiny red dots were the only markers on the rear of each conveyance. Secrecy and security from air attack were the reasons for the blackout, but lack of visibility slowed the convoy and increased the chance of accidents. Still, we had no choice but to obey and to try to avoid mishaps. It promised to be a tedious and grueling night, and Hunk and I had agreed to share the driving so that each could get some rest.

We stopped repeatedly for no apparent reason, and the drivers had to be alert to avoid collisions. Our jeep followed the armored car, so that we could scramble out at each stop and warm ourselves next to its radiator. We talked about our favorite topic, sports, until fatigue and cold reduced conversation to occasional grunts and terse gripes.

During one stop, when we had been on the road for about two hours, Hunk exclaimed, "Leon, can you drive for a while? I don't feel so hot, I gotta take a shit in the worst way. I'll squat next to the jeep and climb in when the convoy starts."

While Hunk descended into the shallow ditch, I got into the driver's seat. I had expected to do my share of the driving and at first thought that this excuse was his way of getting relief without admitting that he was tired. Hunk was never willing to concede that he was not a superman who could do things that daunted lesser men. I didn't mind driving at all; I had not been able to fall to sleep anyway and had been keeping an eye on the lights of the M8 in case Hunk should doze off. I had not been able to get comfortable in the passenger's set of the jeep, because the windshield was down, standard practice in a combat zone, and my knees were getting colder by the minute. I had barely gotten settled behind the wheel when I heard gears shifting and engines roaring ahead as the convoy started to move.

"Snap if off, Hunk, pull up your pants and get in," I called. "The train's leaving and we better not miss it."

"Jeez, I feel like I gotta take a crap, but nothing happens. Maybe it's that damned Spam the Greek dished out at dinner," Hunk grumbled as he clambered into the jeep.

Soon he muttered, "Damn, I gotta shit for sure, can't we stop for just a minute?"

"You know we can't stop," I replied in some amazement. "The convoy won't wait, can't you hold it a little longer? Everyone will stop soon for sure."

Hunk mumbled something and fortunately we stopped again after a few minutes. He sprang out of the jeep and squatted while I got up close to the armored car's radiator to thaw out, and all the time I wished that the heat could reach my knees, which felt as though they had been bent at right angles and wrapped in ice. Over the rumble of the engine

I could hear Hunk grunting and half moaning, apparently stricken by a super case of GI trots. I was sympathetic, thinking back to my experience at Ste. Marie, but the consolation was that it usually lasted but a short time. I was confident that Hunk would feel better soon and we would laugh about it in the morning. When the convoy started Hunk was still straining and reluctantly climbed aboard with his pants half down as I shifted into gear.

"You feel any better?" I asked. "You shit over half of France."

He groaned, "Jeez, it's the worst case of shits I ever had. I just can't seem to take a good crap; if I could I'd be all right, but I feel like I gotta and nothing happens."

We continued this way for a long time, and I became alarmed when Hunk seemed to be getting worse rather than better. He complained now of chills and nausea as well as cramps and the urge to defecate. At the next stop, I hurried ahead and found Robarge.

When I told him of Wilson's plight he exclaimed, "Jesus Christ, this is a hell of a time for him to get the runs. I'll talk to him."

He strode back to where Hunk supported himself by holding on to the rear tire of the jeep while groaning in pain as he strained. Just then we heard the convoy starting, and the sergeant said, "Hunk, get into the jeep; hang your ass over the side if you have to go, but we've got to move."

"OK, Sarge, I'll keep going. I'll be better, maybe it's a little better now," Hunk replied as he crawled aboard the jeep.

I added, "Hunk, why don't you pull a blanket out of your roll and wrap up in it. Try to lie down in the back and get some rest, maybe that'll help."

The next couple of hours seemed like an entire night. We drove slowly but steadily with only a few stops that were no more than pauses. Poor Hunk lay groaning in an uncomfortable sprawl in the back of the jeep. Twice he tried unsuccessfully to relieve himself over the side as Robarge had advised, but when he nearly fell out the second time I told him to lie down and shit in his pants if necessary.

I was very tired by now and caught myself nodding off more than once when the hypnotic red tail lights seemed to fade away. Perhaps my stiff, aching knees were a blessing, a critical stimulus that kept me awake. I could just make out the name Epinal on a road sign which marked our arrival in what appeared to be a good sized town. I recognized a railroad to the left of the road by the dim shapes of box cars, and then I heard the shriek of a locomotive whistle. Soon a passenger train rolled by, the sides of the cars emblazoned with red crosses that were illuminated by light reflected from a few lanterns and signals in the yard. It was a hospital train evacuating casualties, a place of comfort and healing in a hostile world. A crazy thought flashed through my mind: if only we could stop the train we could put Hunk on board where he would get the care that he so desperately needed. I knew it was ridiculous, but the proximity of the well equipped train and Wilson's misery in the jeep seemed a cruel paradox. By now my friend did not even try to get up but lay in the back of the vehicle whimpering and groaning.

By this time Robarge had told Lt. Parker of Hunk's condition, but the platoon leader had no idea of how to care for him. Just when it seemed the awful night would never end I glimpsed a faint light to the east and then looked up to see cold, bright stars glimmering across the vault of sky. The light of dawn spread quickly, a golden horizon heralding a bright sunrise. Then I heard a roar and saw half a dozen fighter planes rise from a nearby field and turn east to attack our enemies.

As the sun's first rays shone across the fields we stopped in a village somewhat larger and more prosperous looking than those in Alsace. Word was passed that this was our destination, a welcome end to our all night ordeal. Parker, Samuels, and Robarge gathered around my jeep where Hunk lay groaning almost incoherently about the pains in his guts. Division medics had been summoned by radio, and an ambulance from a hospital in Toul arrived in the center of the village soon after we did. The medics looked him over briefly and then gently lifted him out of the jeep and carried him to the ambulance. As a crowd of red eyed recon men gathered and gawked and asked questions the ambulance sped away.

I must have stood gazing after the departing vehicle and was only brought back to problems of the moment when the familiar voice of Robarge broke into my reverie.

"Ostrander, are you going to stand there looking after that ambulance all day?" the sergeant asked. "Why the hell don't you grab your fart sack and go into the school house and get some sleep? I'll wake you up for breakfast; if you don't lie down soon you'll fall down."

I needed no further urging to hoist my bedroll and enter the stone building that was to be our billet. As I pulled the boots off my strangely numb, yet painful feet, I realized that it was February 14, my nineteenth birthday. I crawled into the sleeping bag convinced that a long nap would be the best gift I could possibly receive that day. Robarge woke me for breakfast and then insisted that I go back to sleep until lunch when he again roused me to eat. I thought how odd it was to sleep away the clearest day in weeks, but rest was more welcome than blue sky and bright sun.

By afternoon I was ready to explore the little town. The school, the most substantial structure, was situated on the town square across from a low stone building with open sides that housed the community hydrants and stone slabs where women congregated to wash clothes. The manure piles in front of the houses were tidier than those in Alsace, and the place had a more prosperous and progressive appearance than the dismal communities we had left.

Our use of the school caused a suspension of classes to the apparent joy of the children who followed us about as though we were a company of Pied Pipers. The women in the wash building were a jolly lot, enjoying their jokes and comments about the soldiers. Few of us could even begin to understand French, but Robarge was amused by what he overheard as the peasant women gabbed about the Americans. At first they did not know that anyone understood what they said as they characterized various men in earthy and indeed ribald terms. The sergeant told me that he had a hard time controlling his urge to laugh at their conversations, but I doubt that the French women would have been embarrassed if they had known that he understood them. They did not restrain their crude discourse much even after they realized that he could understand most of what they said. The children were sharp little urchins too, always figuring ways to get more cigarettes or candy from the amiable foreigners.

During the few days we spent in the village the weather was sunny and mild, which allowed us to clean and service our vehicles and equipment. We made little deals with the women to wash our clothes in exchange for cigarettes, candy and soap. I'm sure we overpaid for these services, but we did not comprehend the value of such items to people who had been without them for years. I looked in vain for a bath or a shower, but the people had no idea what I was talking about even with Robarge's help as an interpreter. We gave up and settled for sponge baths and were consoled by the knowledge that we were cleaner than at any time since the icy showers at Fountainebleau.

Two days after our arrival we learned that Hunk was critically ill with amoebic dysentery, apparently from drinking contaminated water. Perhaps the Frenchman's well on the road to Lapeoutroie had done its damage. If he recovered, it would be a long time before he could rejoin the troop.

About noon of our third day in the village, we were surprised to see a six by six from a trucking battalion roll into the village square and stop in front of the schoolhouse. The town was off the main highways, so we had seen few vehicles except those of the recon troop. The arrival of a strange truck attracted the attention of the men loafing about the square, but idle curiosity quickly changed to speechless shock. The driver of the truck, a Negro, said nothing to the watching men but strode straight to the little apartment in one corner of the school building where the attractive teacher lived. She must have been expecting him, for she flung open the door before he reached the stoop and threw her arms around the smiling driver. The two embraced for what seemed hours, while the recon men gaped in a stunned silence which was only broken when the lovers withdrew into the building.

I was standing near a Mississippian, who snarled, "Waal ah'll be damned if that black sonofabitch ain't got hisself the best white pussy in this whole fuckin' town. Don't that beat all! Maybe ah'm jest lahk ta do somethin' 'bout that!"

Like a gathering storm, similar expressions of amazement and anger rumbled around the square and swelled to a constant hum of conversation as witnesses to this shocking event told their buddies who had just appeared for the noon meal. I feared that the trucker would be seized and lynched within the hour by the enraged soldiers; there did not seem to be a man in the entire troop who did not feel revulsion at this breach of an old and hallowed American taboo. I doubt if any man there had ever seen a black man kiss a white woman. In 1945 blacks were "kept in their place" everywhere, and the army was as segregated an institution as one could find. Most blacks were in service units such as trucking, road maintenance, quartermaster, and the like, usually with white officers. They were not considered capable of success in combat and were treated like servants in uniform for the superior whites.

Robarge had come up beside me and murmured, "I wonder if that colored guy knows how much trouble he's in? He'll be lucky if they just tar and feather him."

But then Lou Cook, sergeant of the second platoon and a native of Texarkana, took charge of the increasingly irate crowd and exclaimed, "Now you boys jest hold on a minute; ol' Lou's got an idea how to take care a' that black sonofabitch. Looky heah, he left his truck fulla' supplies fo' ol' Gen'ral Patton jest astandin' heah unguarded while he gets hisself a piece a' French ass. Now ah jest wonda' what the ol' gen'ral's gonna do if'n he don't get his supplies? Maybe he'll jest shoot the damned nigrah. Any a' you boys wanna take a ride with me in a six-by?"

The men responded enthusiastically to Cook's proposal, and almost before he finished speaking the truck was rolling out of town followed by boisterous troopers in jeeps. Others waited expectantly in the square for the driver to complete his tryst with the teacher so they could see his reaction to the loss of his truck.

When he emerged from the apartment the driver suddenly stopped and his face contorted in fear as he realized that the truck was gone and he was at the mercy of a mob whose malicious glee was all too evident.

He paused for a moment and then stammered, "Where'd you boys hide mah truck? Come on now, we's all Americans, ain't we? You knows ah's gonna get mah ass in trouble if'n ah loses that six-bah, c'mon now, have a haht—"

"You damn black sonofabitch, find it yourself," said Mike Carey, one of Cook's section sergeants. "I hope old Georgie Patton hangs you by the balls. You ain't gonna find that six-by, and if you know what's good for you, you'll haul your butt outa' town before someone finds a rope."

The driver looked about him like a cornered animal and then put his head down and walked rapidly down the street, steering away from the recon men who glared malevolently and shouted abuse. I relaxed when he was out of sight and felt a wave of relief that I had not been the unwilling witness to a lynching. I must admit that I was shocked by the black trucker's affair with the white woman, but my disgust stemmed as much from prudishness as racial bigotry. I justified my antagonism by telling myself that the black trucker had neglected his military obligations for this dalliance with the teacher, a clear case of duty versus illicit sex, a sin that justified his punishment.

Robarge said, "That colored guy's been over here so long he forgot he's not supposed to screw a white woman. He's lucky he's just facing court martial and not burial. I bet he's been supplying her and her friends for a while; it was a good deal for both of them, but he was dumb to go in there today. I gotta hand it to Cook, he knew how to keep that bunch happy without killing the colored guy. I wonder where the truck will end up? I bet Lou and his buddies will sell all the supplies before they ditch it."

I must have looked at him blankly and only slowly appreciated the truth of what he said. Cook had impressed me as a devious, crooked little thug who would do anything to procure a woman or a bottle. Even a casual conversation with him lent credibility to the endless tales of his corrupt and even criminal conduct, and yet it seemed Robarge was right and Cook had adroitly prevented a murder.

I replied in wonder, "Gee, I guess you're right, Sarge. I don't care much for Lou, but he probably did save the colored guy's life. Do you think he really meant to, or was he just afraid to kill him in front of the whole town?"

Robarge shrugged and flashed his enigmatic smile, "Who knows, but it's better this way. Now I just hope none of these hotheads decide to teach the woman a lesson. Let's go over and see what they're up to."

When we reached the school the teacher was outside her apartment excitedly jabbering at some of the soldiers. The men were still in an ugly mood and shouted "nigger lover" and various obscenities at her. Robarge managed to quiet the men and then spoke to the teacher in French. She was startled at first but then composed herself enough to make an animated reply punctuated by a flurry of typical Gallic gestures. They conversed for several minutes while the surly crowd grumbled impatiently.

Then the sergeant turned to the men with his sardonic grin more pronounced than ever and said, "You know what the colored guy told her? He said he was an American Indian, how do you like that? Some line, eh? Big Chief, not Stepin Fetchit."

The men looked incredulous at first, but then a few started to laugh.

Almost immediately the crowd responded to the humor of the situation and the tension dissolved in hilarious guffaws. A crisis had become a burlesque. The woman did not understand the sudden change in attitude of the soldiers, but she was obviously relieved and took the opportunity to slip into her chamber.

After dinner that night Rutt Parker entered our room in the school and announced that Lt. Collins had assigned him to lead the advance party for our next move. He picked Robarge, Merrick, Caulkins, Henry and me to accompany him at dawn in three jeeps. The lieutenant would not disclose our destination, if he even knew it, but I was excited at the prospect of seeing new places and welcomed my assignment.

In the morning we gulped our breakfasts, grabbed some K rations and drove out of the village in a cold fog, a decided change from the clear weather we had enjoyed for several days. At the rendezvous point we joined a convoy of 28th Division vehicles, all with insignia and numbers carefully removed to comply with secrecy precautions. Daytime convoys were far better than the night variety, and an advance party was the best of all because we were not hindered by the slow movement of large equipment. Still, any convoy could be tedious, and this was no exception. The officers behaved like junior executives of a large company, officiously brandishing maps and orders, arguing about "my people and your people" and where they should go. I wondered what in the world could take them so much time when they huddled over their maps at nearly every junction.

At one such stop Robarge turned to me and asked, "How come you're not an officer like those guys, Holme? You're a college man and know a lot the rest of us don't. Hell, you're probably smarter than some of them."

I was surprised and a little annoyed by his question and more than a little irritated by his mocking tone. He was wearing his usual smile, blue eyes flashing, and eager to get my response it seemed.

I blurted out, "Look, Sarge, I'm just 19, I only had a little over a year of college, and I didn't learn anything that helps me here. They don't want guys like me as officers, you know I just get by as a private."

Robarge continued with what I could only construe as needling. "Oh, I don't know, you'd get along with those guys, you're like them. You know how college men are, they stick together, and they don't have much use for the rest of us. You know what I mean, don'tcha, Holme?"

I could feel myself flush at the baiting, and I replied angrily, "Listen, what's all this "Holme" stuff? You know my name, what are you trying to do? Are you saying I'm a smart ass or something? What have I done to make you sore?"

The sergeant blinked and the smile disappeared from this thin face. He looked at me soberly but without anger as he responded to my outburst.

"Naw, you're not a smart ass, I'm sorry if I hurt your feelings, but I was just kidding you. Holme's just a name people in my part of the country have for guys that know a hell of a lot but haven't been around much, sort of like they don't know the score. I was just riding you a little because you sure as hell do know a lot, but it's mostly book learning. I know some things too, but college men have always acted like they thought I was dumb. Dammit, maybe they're right, maybe I am dumb, I quit school after the eighth grade and went to work, but I've read a lot and tried to learn all I could. Oh hell, let's just forget I said anything, you probably don't know what I'm talking about anyway."

At this point I was even more perplexed than before. It was more difficult to respond to his explanation than to the needling, and it was obvious that he had very ambivalent feelings about me. I hoped I would not end up in his dog house because I had more formal education than he, and I was dismayed by the possibility that the sergeant's attitude would prevent us from being friends. Until that moment we had been developing a close and congenial relationship so far as I could tell, and I suddenly realized how much I valued his friendship now that it seemed to be at risk.

After a moment I answered, "Sarge, I wouldn't have known how far you went in school if you hadn't told me. I sure don't think you're dumb, and I feel the same way as you do about those smart ass officers. They may be big shots now, but most of them will never be anything after the war. They'll get into some kind of business and lord it over some people working for them while they suck around their bosses. I've seen those kind before, and I don't want to be anything like them."

The smile was back on his face and Robarge shot back, "What do you mean you're not going to be like them, what are you going to do with that college education if you're not going into business?"

"I'm going to be a doctor," I retorted.

The sardonic grin expanded into a warm smile as the sergeant said, "You're going to be an M.D.? Well, that's better, but do you think you can do it? It takes a hell of a long time, and it's damned hard work, I've heard."

"Oh, I'll do it," I replied. "You're right, it isn't easy, but I'm sure I'll make it."

"Well, I should've known you would do something like that," the sergeant added. "I've liked most of the doctors I've known, our doc back home is a hell of a good guy, he just sits down and talks to me like a friend, no airs or anything. If you're like him you'll be OK."

His enthusiastic approval of my plans tickled me and I laughed as I added, "I'm glad you think I'm doing the right thing."

Shouts and signals to start the engines interrupted our conversation, and soon the convoy was snaking over the hills of northern France. Apparently some knotty problem of route had been solved, for we drove more steadily with only infrequent brief stops until we entered Verdun. The city was badly damaged, much like LeHavre, and pathetic civilians picked their way through the debris. We stopped briefly in the rubble strewn city to eat our noon K rations, but ragged children appeared as if by magic and gazed wistfully at our humble meal. Robarge and I were so uncomfortable eating in front of the hungry urchins that we gave them the candy from our rations and finally the reserve boxes that we had squirreled away in case we found no chow line in the evening. I was glad when we left and headed north for the Belgian border.

The country became hillier, and the vehicles had more difficulty keeping their distances, bunching up at times and stretching out again very quickly. In the contracting part of this traffic accordion the entire convoy stopped suddenly, and we were jolted severely as Caulkin's jeep slammed into us. Nobody was hurt, my jeep was undamaged, but Caulkin's vehicle was leaking radiator fluid and had smashed headlights, grill and front bumper. Apparently he took his eyes off the road at the critical moment when the convoy halted. Parker was angry but not as furious as I had feared; like everyone else he was fond of DJ and could muster no more than some cross grumbles. After a conference with the convoy commander and an inspection of the jeep, the lieutenant told Henry to transfer to his jeep and directed Caulkin's to a repair depot in a nearby town.

The hills became steeper, and the landscape was more scenic as we drove into Belgium. Some stretches of road were cobblestones, which felt like washboards as we drove over them, and other portions were asphalt with gaping potholes.

After a couple of jarring bumps from the pockmarked road Robarge said sarcastically, "Jesus, Holme, don't you ever miss one of those damned holes? Can't you drive around at least one of them?"

I was stung by his derisive tone but decided to say nothing. I knew I was not a very good driver, and of course Robarge knew it too. I resented the "Holme" thing again but let it pass and concentrated on driving better. As the afternoon wore on the clouds thickened, and an early dusk descended. At the last stop someone had said that our destination was Spa, a name that meant nothing to me. As the last light of day was about to fade, we topped a hill and saw the old resort town spread before us. It looked attractive in the lengthening shadows, but our destination was an unused factory, not a hotel. After another discussion among the officers we were assigned spots in the musty old shop and laid our bedrolls on workbenches.

Our worst fears about dinner were realized; there was no food except what the men had brought with them. It looked like a hungry night for Robarge and me, but the sergeant was undaunted.

"We'll just find a bakery and get some bread," Robarge confided. "It'll be better than those damned rations anyway."

I thought he was either kidding or had gone crazy. Where could we hope to find any sort of food in this war ravaged land? I didn't want to incur any more of Robarge's sarcasm, and yet I wondered what my companion had in mind.

I asked timidly, "Where will we find bread, Sarge? I haven't seen anything that looked like a store."

"There are lots of them, you just can't read French and don't recognize a bakery when you see it. They're not like at home, big places with all the stuff in the window, but there are signs over lots of doors advertising bread and pastry. Just leave it to the old sarge and we'll have plenty to eat. I'll tell the lieutenant where we're going."

In a moment Robarge returned saying, "It's OK with the boss, so long as we bring some for him." As he climbed into the jeep he pointed the way and said, "Now drive back down the hill into town the way we came. Go slow and I'll tell you when to stop."

The streets were deserted and unlit as we cruised slowly past the shuttered buildings. Robarge scanned the dim shapes, squinting into the dark intently until he found what he sought.

"Stop here, it'll only be a minute or two, and I'll be back with the bread."

After the sergeant knocked on the door several times an upstairs window opened and a torrent of French poured forth in a tone that chilled my hope for a successful bread hunt. Robarge replied, and the party at the window gave a terse answer and closed the casement. I was sure that ended the encounter, but Robarge stood at the door, presently it opened, and he disappeared inside. After a few minutes the door opened again, and then I heard laughter and animated conversation punctuated by many "mercis" indicating that some sort of transaction had taken place. As Robarge climbed into the jeep I could dimly make out a man and a woman in the doorway waving amiably and bidding us farewell. The long loaf of bread Robarge handed me spoke for itself, and then I noticed that he was carrying his helmet.

"The bread looked and smelled great," he said, "And I thought we could use the rolls in my helmet too. Cigarettes and chocolate work wonders. I saved all the D bars I could lay my hands on, and I don't mind trading some of those damned Marvel cigarettes they send us either. Didn't I tell you old sarge would get some bread?"

"When the guy yelled out the window I thought he'd sic the dog on you. What did you do to soften him up?" I asked.

"I think it was my French," he exclaimed. "These Belgians speak a dialect more like my Canadian French. They couldn't get over an American speaking their language. They'd have given us just about anything, they even wanted us to spend the night there, but I knew the lieutenant wouldn't go for that, so I told 'em we couldn't."

When we neared the factory I could hardly wait to get inside and stuff myself with bread and rolls, but Robarge cautioned otherwise. "I'll sit here while you get the others, and then we'll eat out here so we don't end up feeding the whole damned convoy."

The five of us feasted on the baked goods, the best I had ever eaten. All my bread had come from a production line, and I had no idea how good home baked bread could be. We had hoped to save some for breakfast, but our hunger or greed won out, and we consumed every crumb before we turned in. The precaution of eating out of sight of the others was wise, for most of the men were grumbling about the rations as we prepared for sleep.

In the morning we begged K rations from a sergeant in headquarters company, who confided that he always carried extras "to get in the door and into mademoiselle's pants." Robarge and I were dispatched on a series of errands in and around Spa, which allowed us to cruise up and down the steep cobblestone streets of the quaint old town. It was undamaged by fighting and presented a beautiful landscape of hills, old houses, churches, and public buildings that looked as though it was lifted from a travel poster. I would have enjoyed a whole day of driving around this charming region, but by noon we had been resupplied with rations and gasoline and were on our way to the village where the troop was to be billeted. The day was clear and mild, and our route from one picturesque little village to another was a joy. The final leg of the trip led up a long grade on a narrow road between stone fences to a place called Fraiture.

After we stopped in the town square Robarge was in his glory, talking to everyone, dickering with the village leaders about quarters, and charming all of them in the bargain. It was quickly apparent that the friendly people of Fraiture were eager to help us in any way they could even before the sergeant reported the result of his conversations. The village consisted of a single street with a small square about midway along its length. A school occupied one side of the square, and a public building that seemed to serve all government functions stood on the opposite side.

The village fathers assigned the largest house in town to our use, a handsome structure in a grove of trees just beyond the village square. The owners vacated it with surprising grace, and the five of us were to stay there until the troop arrived, when the officers would have the house and the men would be billeted in the school. There was plenty of room in the square and around the house to accommodate our vehicles, so Fraiture seemed to be an ideal stopping place for the 28th Recon.

The interior of the house was spacious but old fashioned with massive furniture, ornate stoves, and an elaborate outhouse with an entrance directly from the house as well as from the yard. The place had electricity that actually worked, at least for the moment, but water had to be carried from a community hydrant. While Parker and Robarge inspected the school, Merrick, Henry and I carried gear into the house and opened a box of "Ten in One" rations that had been issued to us in Spa. This was a deluxe ration consisting of canned meat, vegetables, fruit, and bread along with butter, jam and coffee. It was supposed to feed 10 men for one day, hence the name, and was designed for use by mechanized units that were capable of carrying such luxuries. I became hungry just thinking of dinner, reveling in the knowledge that five of us had food meant for ten. By the time the lieutenant and Robarge returned, we had a fire blazing in the stove and had fetched 5 gallons of water from the hydrant. Robarge had learned that the regional health department had inspected the water supply and approved it for drinking, an important consideration after Hunk Wilson's experience.

Robarge was the unquestioned chef of the little group and produced a sumptuous repast from the superior ingredients. We ate the entire ration with relish and washed it down with water free of the noxious halogen taste. Afterwards we sat in the kitchen in a near stupor, warm, well fed, and somnolent, while Rutt Parker rambled on in a monologue about anything that crossed his mind. He was amusing as he vented his provincial Georgian views about the war, Europeans, and his postwar ambitions (a captain of industry or a successful politician). I dared not look at the others as the lieutenant expounded, but just relaxed and tried not to laugh as I savored this mellow interlude.

Our happy state was shattered when Parker looked out the window and exclaimed, "Well I'll be damned, it's dark as hell out there, and we don't have our security posted. These damned people may all be Nazis just waiting to cut our throats."

I dared not look at the others but kept my gaze on the floor as Robarge replied, "Do you really think we need to post a guard here, lieutenant? These are good people, and this town is probably safer than home."

Rutt's answer was predictable, "Robarge, you gotta learn that you can't trust any of these foreigners. Anyway, what if someone from division came up here and we didn't have our security posted? It'd be my ass, that's what. Since there's only five of us, I'll take a turn on guard, too. I'll take the first couple of hours, and you divide up the rest any way you want."

The night was uneventful, and the rest of the troop arrived the next afternoon. Our presence caused classes to be suspended in the school, and, once again, we quickly became Pied Pipers for the children. They followed us everywhere, looking at us in awe the way kids gaze at great athletic heroes, admiring and aping everything we did, eager to help with our chores, and grateful for even the slightest attention. When I was assigned to carry water for the mess, two little boys ran along behind the jeep and indicated that they wanted to fill the cans at the hydrant. The heavy containers were nearly too much for the youngsters, but they managed it with some grunting and straining and were ecstatic when I signaled them into the jeep for the ride back to the school. They stuck to me like glue, eager to help and bursting with pride at being companions of an American soldier. The same thing happened between other men and children of the town, and soon the adults overcame their reserve, tried to converse, and stood about admiring our equipment.

The school was a good billet, and we hoped to stay a while in this hospitable community. On our way into Fraiture we had spotted a barber shop in a nearby town, so some of us drove there for haircuts. The two women barbers had never had so many customers at one time nor a more profitable afternoon. We paid in cigarettes or soap, items more valuable than money, and the women were thrilled by their good fortune. Female barbers were a curiosity for most of the men, because at that time almost all barbers in the United States were men. Even a few crude attempts at seduction by several of the soldiers evoked nothing but blushes and giggles from the women, whose good humor and delight with their payments seemed endless.

On our return to Fraiture, Lt. Collins caught Robarge and led him into the town hall, apparently to serve as an interpreter for some negotiation. I was holding court with my following of kids when he returned.

"What's up?" I asked. "Did someone get us in trouble with the local law?"

"You won't believe this," Robarge replied, "But the women of the town invited everyone to stay in their homes, board and room, for as long as we are here. Can you beat that? The mother of one of those kids that hangs around you asked for us to stay at her place, dinner, sleep in a real bed, the works. How do you like that?"

I was flabbergasted, it seemed too good to be true. To be sure, this was not an invitation to a luxury home. The people of Fraiture lived in old fashioned houses without most of the amenities that Americans took for granted, but they were happily offering us the best of what they had. Who could ask for more?

"That's great, Sarge, whatever she serves will be better than what we get from our kitchen," I replied. "When do we go?"

"As soon as we find Henry and Gorlitz. The woman next door to where we're going is having the M8 crew," Robarge answered. "I hope all the guys in the troop behave themselves and don't try to rape their hostess or steal everything in sight."

Our family lived in a two story house on the town's only street. All the residences were situated close to the curb, and the barns were behind the buildings so that one did not pass the manure pile on entering the house as in Alsace. Our hostess appeared to be in her late thirties and greeted us in a most gracious manner even though Robarge was the only guest who spoke French. She said her husband was a prisoner in Germany, but her father-in-law, a widower in his sixties, lived with her and her two children. The nine year old boy was my constant companion, and a twelve year old girl was busy in the kitchen with the dinner. We knew that a good meal was in preparation by the aroma that permeated the house. We presented the woman with gifts of cigarettes, candy and soap, an act that seemed to overwhelm her. She spoke rapidly and darted into the kitchen, excusing herself on the grounds that she was afraid the little girl would let the dinner burn. The father-in-law, a shy little man who seemed bemused by our visit until now, smiled and told Robarge that this was the first time anyone had given her a gift since her husband had been seized three years earlier, and he was deeply touched by our generosity. Madame and her family exclaimed over and over about the gifts until we were a little embarrassed by their effusive thanks.

Then the daughter announced that dinner was ready, and we sat down at a long wooden table in the kitchen where madame served us fresh milk, oven hot bread, and home made butter as starters. The main course consisted of a seemingly endless supply of omelets, fried potatoes, and a sort of cole slaw. I ate until I thought I would burst, and then our hostess produced an apple pastry for dessert. It was so good I could not control my gluttony in spite of a mild belly ache. Robarge had managed to get some coffee from one of the cooks, and our Belgian friends were as excited by this addition as they had been by our earlier gifts. Madame brewed a beverage which was so superior to what our cooks served that I could hardly believe it came from the same ingredients. She said it was the first coffee they had tasted since the German invasion in 1940.

After dinner the children cleared the table and washed the dishes while the adults visited. The Belgians were amazed at how tall many Americans were, and they discretely marveled at how much we ate. I began to think we had eaten their food for the week in one evening, but the sergeant said they had plenty of eggs, bread, butter, milk and storable vegetables and fruits. The city people were in want because the farmers could not transport produce to market in sufficient quantity.

The Belgians were very interested in our ages, where we lived in America, and what we did before we entered service. Like many Europeans they knew people who had emigrated to America and hoped to encounter a soldier who knew their kinsman or friend.

Like a good mother, madame showed us to our rooms when she thought it was time to retire. Henry and I shared a tiny upstairs room at the front of the house. The roof was so low that I had to bend to avoid hitting my head, and the small bed was designed for two Belgians, not Americans, but it was a welcome change from sleeping on the floor in an increasingly rank sleeping bag. I had guard duty from 4 to 6 AM, but my predecessor knew where I was and could walk into the house and upstairs to awaken me. I doubt if any of the houses in the village had locks on their doors.

Throughout the next day, everyone talked about their visits and most were as enthusiastic as we in spite of the language barrier. Even some of the men who had not accepted invitations to a Belgian home now expressed interest in a visit. Robarge, Gorlitz, Henry and I were eager for another night with our adoptive family and spent much of the day scrounging for more cigarettes, candy and soap to present to madame. We were more than a little relieved that no misconduct had marred the almost idyllic atmosphere of Fraiture.

As we were enjoying a beautiful clear day and looking forward to another evening with our Belgian friends, we were summoned to assemble in the town square. Lt. Collins announced that we would eat an early dinner from the troop mess, pack our gear, and be ready to leave at dusk.

The people of the town were genuinely sorry to see us go and expressed great concern for our safety, although the little boys were madly excited by the prospect of our arsenal of weapons wreaking havoc among "le Boche". By the time of our departure the entire population of Fraiture lined the street and our slow drive out of town was warmed by their cheers and well wishes. Our brief stay in the tiny Belgian community had been a unique and heart warming experience for all of us. In succeeding days even the roughest of the troopers lapsed into wistful nostalgia at the mention of Fraiture.

Robarge generally rode with me rather than in the M8, and we talked of our stay in the village while we drove east toward Germany. We agreed that someday we would like to return to the village where the people had treated us so royally, but the rosy glow of our stay in Fraiture rapidly cooled in the chill winter night as we repeated much of the nonsense of our "secret" departure from Lapeoutroie. Blackout was enforced, and we crept along from one stop to another at a snail's pace. The only recognizable place was the ruined city of Aachen, our entrance to Germany and the site of mass destruction. When it seemed that rubble heaps were the totality of Aachen, I suddenly heard a clanging sound to our rear and turned to see a lighted conveyance approaching. I could not believe my eyes, but yes, it was a streetcar!

As it rumbled past Robarge grumbled, "I think I'll catch the next car and ride to the end of the line. How about that? The krauts have the streetcars running, or am I dreaming? A trolley was the last thing I expected to see tonight."

The streetcar incident then became even more bizarre as it seemed we were following the trolley through the city. Those of us in the middle of the convoy merely followed the vehicle ahead, but then the entire procession stopped when the tram turned into a circular track where another streetcar was parked, apparently ready to depart on a return trip. A few shadowy figures could be seen leaving or entering the cars, an incongruous sight in such a place.

Robarge muttered, "Why in hell are we stopped at the end of the trolley line? Whoever is leading this parade doesn't act like he knows what he is doing."

Before I could add my carping to the sergeant's, a jeep approached from the head of the convoy, and we heard the familiar voice of Lou Cook. "Turn around boys, it's the end of the line and I ain't got the fare."

We were lost and Cook was to blame. The only explanation he ever gave was that he "just got hypnotized by that goddamn trolley."

In contrast to Cook's jaunty good humor Robarge and I were grumbling and disgusted, irritated more by the cold, damp night than the delay. When we at last escaped the ruins of Aachen and the mysterious streetcars, we faced endless hours of tedious driving and a constant struggle to stay awake. My knees were cold and stiff, my feet were painful blocks, and I began to have hunger pangs. The night was dark as pitch without a glimmer of light from moon or stars; only the red lights on the rear of the M8 ahead of us stood out like evil eyes. Robarge drove some of the time, and it helped to wrap a blanket around my legs, but the feet seemed beyond relief. In spite of my fatigue and tendency to doze off, I could not get into a position that allowed me to get a real nap.

After a long silence Robarge said, "I wonder if we'll get some mail soon. I can't help wondering what's happening to Mary and the kid. Don't you get thinking about home even though you're not married?"

"Sure I do," I replied, "But I can see how it'd be worse for a guy with a family. It's nearly two months since we've heard anything from home. They keep saying it'll be any day, but I'll believe it when I get some letters."

"Sometimes I wonder if the damn army knows we're here, we haven't been paid since we got over here either, although I don't know what I'd do with the money," the sergeant continued.

Somehow the night passed and when dawn cast a somber gray light on the convoy, we were moving over low wooded hills on a road which may have once been paved but was now a ribbon of muddy ruts and potholes. It seemed as though we had traveled a great distance, but we were only ten or fifteen miles inside the German border. Slow speed, many stops, and a circuitous route made a short move into a long trip. K rations for breakfast did not improve our moods either.

We passed no villages but drove through a forest of fir trees. Numerous clumps of shattered trunks attested to the artillery fire that had raked the woodlands. At one point the forest was ravaged over scores of acres, the stumps poking up like ragged stakes, and the ground was covered by twisted and shattered boughs. At the center of this desolation we passed a road intersection marked by the usual crazy jumble of unit markers and one separate sign, "Heartbreak Crossroads". It was evident from the destruction all about that the battle for the junction had been a bitter contest where death and despair were memorialized in the name. The area had a brooding, melancholy air, as though death itself might emerge from the forest rubble or lie in wait among the trees beyond.

We now had to contend with truck convoys easing their way among huge mud holes in the road and further slowing our progress. As if we were not tired and cold enough, the ponderous vehicles threw dirty spray and great chunks of mud on us as they churned through the mire. When we finally left the main highway for a secondary road it was nearly noon. A few engineer troops were trying to repair the primitive byway which led into a dense pine forest. The dull day dimmed to twilight as we drove farther into the woods, and the dismal atmosphere was accentuated by light fog and myriad drops of water hanging from the pine needles. At last we came to a small clearing where a single house stood as a reminder that we were in a populated land and not a wilderness. Loaded jeeps of the 2nd Division Reconnaissance Troop were parked in front of the dwelling, and their crews stood around smoking and waiting for their lieutenant, who was talking to Collins.

Robarge called to one of the men, "Where are we? Have you guys been stationed here?"

The man nodded and replied, "Yea, and it's all yours now, Sarge. You're our relief, you get this fucking forest and God knows how many krauts in some damned big bunkers not far from here."

The familiar wry smile creased the sergeants thin face as he said, "Sounds like you boys are giving us a real prize. Where're you going?"

The man's companion, a sergeant, answered, "I don't know, but the rumor has it that we're going north of here for a big offensive to the Rhine. That's the trouble with the Second, we get all the shitty jobs."

Robarge and I looked at one another and smiled. We had yet to meet a man who didn't think he was in an elite outfit that was targeted for the most difficult and dangerous assignments. Before we could glean more information from the 2nd Recon men, they departed, leaving the 28th to man the dismal forest and whatever lay beyond.

Sgt. Hinkle ordered us to assemble in the clearing and gave us one of his terse briefings. "The mess crew will pass out rations, but you'll have hot chow tonight. Headquarters will be in this house, the platoons will be in the forest about a quarter of a mile from here. Cook and Samuels will assign space when you get there. Keep awake on guard; you're not in Belgium now."

What did he mean by "in the forest" I wondered. Did he mean we were to pitch tents? Nobody slept in pup tents over here, or so we all believed. Then my worst fears were realized as we turned off the road and came to a stop about 100 yards up a forest trail. Tire tracks showed where vehicles had parked, but there was no sign of a building anywhere. We stood mute and incredulous, staring at the dripping pines as though shelter was hidden somewhere among the trees if we just looked hard enough.

Robarge broke the stunned silence, "It's a hell of a change from

Fraiture, but if we all pitch in the old sarge'll show you how to live in the woods. Too bad Hunk isn't here, the big goof was always bragging about chopping down trees."

With this the sergeant unfastened the ax from the armored car and started inspecting trees, slashing those that satisfied him. All the while he directed the rest of us to gather boughs, clear an area he had marked, or to fell the designated trees. Grumbling at first but with mounting enthusiasm we worked to build a rude cabin. Taking their cue from us the other sections began their own construction projects, and the forest rang with the sounds of axes and the shouts of the hard working men. After a couple of hours of diligent labor we had a shanty about 6 feet high, 7 feet across and 10 feet long with enough boughs on the top and sides to break the wind. The final touch was to stretch the tarpaulin from the armored car over the top, an effective protection against rain and snow. With this the shelter seemed adequate, and I felt better about our new assignment.

Robarge looked over the hut and grunted his satisfaction and then announced, "It'll be pretty good once we find a stove and dry it out."

After the bread incident in Spa I was willing to believe that he would indeed find a stove in this unlikely place.

6

THE MONSCHAU FOREST

The dark interior of our shanty smelled like old Christmas trees, and the cold dampness seemed to envelope me in its clammy embrace. Still, the shack was better than no shelter at all, for it protected us from wind, fog, and a chilly mixture of snow and rain that seemed endemic to the Monschau Forest, and our bodies warmed the interior a little.

Sgt. Hinkle had promised hot food, and the mess produced it, although we had to stand around in the clearing at headquarters while we ate our rations. During breakfast on our first morning in the forest Dave Morton and George Lane invited me into their quarters in the solitary house. The building was old and decrepit, but each armorer had a couch to sleep on in a small room that was cluttered with weapons and tools. While we were talking one of the "old boys" poked his smirking face in the door.

"Davey, I hope to hell you didn't forget your fuckin' prayers today," he sneered. "Better look out or God'll get pissed off at you and Georgie."

Dave said nothing but looked at the floor in silence, perhaps praying for the man's blasphemous soul. George flushed and scowled at the taunter but said nothing, while I was too surprised to do anything until the fellow left the house chortling with his buddies.

"Dave, do you take that kind of stuff from those bums?" I asked. "You ought to punch that guy in the nose. What's he have against you?

Who does he think he is?"

Morton replied quietly, "Oh, it doesn't bother me. You know everyone has always razzed me because I'm a Christian, but they don't mean any harm. If I ignore them, they'll stop."

"You've been ignoring them since we joined this outfit. How long will it take for them to lay off? You could teach that guy a lesson, and then they would all stop bothering you."

Before Dave could reply Henry poked his head in, "Leon, we're ready to go. Sarge says to hurry up."

As we drove back to the shack I couldn't get the episode out of my mind. Dave was a fundamentalist Christian who never used profane or obscene language and gave thanks with a prayer before each meal. In basic training his piety had been the cause of some kidding, but it was generally good natured. After a time even the gentle ribbing stopped as his comrades recognized that Morton was a sincere man who practiced his religion but was no less of a man for his beliefs. I liked him and enjoyed his company even when his extreme rectitude was occasionally irritating. I suspected that the "old boys" around headquarters would have found some reason to harass Morton and Lane even if Dave's religious practices had not struck them as humorous. I was grateful that I was not in headquarters platoon and subject to abuse from the dregs of the 28th Recon, and yet it was ironic that a combat platoon seemed preferable to a safer spot as an armorer.

We were tinkering with the shack and cleaning weapons when a jeep pulled up near our camp. I was glad to see Caulkins climb out, although I didn't recognize him at first under a coating of road mud.

"Man, I had a great time in Vervier," he said. "The food was good, there were movies every night, and they had dances with lots of girls. I even had a room with a bed and a shower that worked. Those old boys at the rear have a picnic."

Samuels was nearby and overheard Caulkins' enthusiastic report of life in rear areas. "Did you get some of that good Belgian pussy?" he asked with a leer on his face.

"You know that's against my religion, Sam," Caulkins replied, "But it's enough to tempt a man. Those girls were really friendly"

"Next time you go to a place like that," Samuels interrupted, "I'll go with you to make sure you get screwed, blued and tattooed. You just need someone to show you the ropes, and I'm the man for that. It don't seem right for you to take that damned jeep back to Vervier when you wasted a chance for some fun."

DJ laughed off this assertion. "If you'd been there when I had the accident, I would have been glad to let you take it back, if the lieutenant didn't mind." Then, turning to our shack, "It's a lot different from where I've been the last few days, but I guess it's better than nothing. What are we doing here, guarding the trees?"

"It's the same old game, nobody tells us anything," Robarge answered. "We had a good deal for a couple of days in Belgium, but I guess we're part of some plan to shove the krauts across the Rhine, but nobody knows for sure. After we find a stove the shack'll be all right. It's pretty damp and cold now."

Caulkins looked at Robarge with the same surprise that I had felt at mention of a stove, but he said nothing. Before we could continue the conversation a jeep pulled up and a noncom announced that we were to report immediately to headquarters in proper uniform for inspection by the division commander.

I had shaved that morning as well as I could with cold water and a dull razor blade, but it was impossible to do much for the rest of my appearance. My coat was stained and torn in several places, my trousers were baggy and caked with mud, and even my helmet was scratched, but I couldn't believe that the general expected fastidious troops in the midst of the soggy forest. I knew that my carbine was clean if one of his aides decided to inspect arms, which seemed a more practical consideration. Two months earlier we would have scurried about in anxious anticipation of a visit by a major general, but now we were more curious than awed by the event.

We assembled on one side of the dilapidated troop headquarters in as regular a formation as the uneven ground and scrubby brush would permit. Soon a trio of jeeps chugged out of the forest murk. The first and third vehicles carried four MP's each, who were armed with submachine guns, while the second was a remarkably clean jeep with a red quadrangular plate attached to the front bumper on which the two silver stars of a major general were emblazoned. It was driven by an MP, and a second guard sat in the back seat. The general sat in the front passenger's seat, partly hidden by the windshield which was up to protect him from mud and wind, while his aide, my erstwhile passenger, Capt. White, sat next to the MP on the rear seat. The vehicles stopped and the guards took positions to protect their commander from whatever perils might lurk in the area. General Cota stepped out of his jeep and picked his way across the muddy and uneven ground to where Lt. Collins stood at attention. He was a heavy set man of medium height with a prominent aquiline nose, distinct jowls, and an impassive expression. During the entire visit Cota neither scowled nor smiled.

After exchanging a few words with Collins the general exclaimed in a husky voice, "At ease, men, and gather around me. I just want to have a little chat with you and welcome you to the 28th Division."

Cota then launched into a speech that recounted the history and renown of the 28th, expressed his pleasure that we had joined him in this glorious unit, told us how much he liked to exchange salutes with men of his command wherever he met them, and reminded us of the fate of cowards, such as the man who had been executed at Ste. Marie.

I was standing next to Robarge, and we exchanged knowing glances at some of the general's more fatuous statements. He concluded his oration with some words about our health.

"I don't want men of the 28th to be victims of so-called trench foot, that's just the result of poor discipline and hygiene. Change your socks regularly, and your feet will be fine. Dry the wet socks under your shirts, and you'll always have a change. I'm glad the division is out here in the woods, it's a lot healthier than sleeping in those filthy houses and barns where we were. Just think of this like a camping trip. You'll be healthier and stronger for it and better able to crush the enemy."

"Some shit!" Robarge whispered as the commander concluded his discourse.

Collins ordered us to stand at attention and again saluted the general as the latter turned and walked to his jeep. The MP's, apparently satisfied that no danger threatened the great man, resumed their positions in the jeeps, and the little procession vanished in the fog. Capt. White had followed the general by a couple of steps throughout his visit. No words were exchanged, but I had the impression that he was poised to supply his chief with any information that Cota lacked. At the same time he was noting every detail of what occurred so that he could advise the general about any shortcomings of the organization.

While we drove back to the shack Robarge grumbled constantly about the general's speech. "I bet old Cota isn't sleeping out in the woods. How could the old bugger stand there and tell us how healthy it is to be out in the damned forest? Did you notice, he didn't miss a chance to mention the guy they shot either. One thing, I'll be sure to salute his highness where the Germans can see it, if I get the chance."

I smiled to myself because the sergeant's resentment was real and his displeasure open without the coating of smiling sarcasm which often cloaked his true feelings.

"I'd like to know how many socks the general was drying under his shirt," I said. "Maybe that's why he looks fat, too many wet socks. I'll remember what he said every time I take my boots off and feel how numb my feet are. I wish the old sucker would get us some decent shoe packs instead of telling us all that shit we just heard," I continued, my momentary amusement at Robarge changed to bitterness as I thought of my worsening foot problems.

As I moved about my feet didn't bother me except for a slight clumsiness, but each night they seemed to be more numb and tingled more as I pulled off my boots. That night I noticed peculiar sharp jabs of pain as I unavoidably rubbed the flesh while removing my boots. I only owned four pairs of socks, so I wore two at a time and tried unsuccessfully to dry the others. I looked to see if my feet were discolored or peeling, but so far as I could tell by flashlight, they looked all right. I decided I was in the early stages of trench foot and resolved to try harder to care for my underpinnings, although I couldn't think of much else to do. Even dry socks got damp as soon as I pulled on my boots because the latter were never completely dry. Therefore, I decided to wear the enormous, awkward, overshoes over the boots when I had to walk in mud or water. This was a great nuisance because I could not use the galoshes while driving; they were so large and unwieldy that I could not tell which pedal I was stepping on, and in fact I often hit both the accelerator and the brake simultaneously. Still, I determined to put on and take off the overshoes as often as necessary, if I had the luxury of that much time. I was even more incensed when I noted that most of the men in the troop had waterproof shoepacks and were free of foot problems, but none wore size 13AA.

It wasn't just my footwear, I was angry about the rest of my clothing, too. An obviously shoddy coat that was falling to pieces, inadequate gloves, and a too small beanie that didn't protect my ears and neck were constant irritants. It seemed to me that the government could have at least made sure that men fighting a winter campaign had proper clothing. I had brooded over this for several weeks, but that evening I gave voice to my frustrations. I was embarrassed after my bitter outburst in what sounded like whining, but to my surprise the other members of the section were very sympathetic.

Hilton said, "Damn if you're not right, Leon. I hadn't thought of it before, but you do look worse than the rest of us. I bet that lazy bastard of a supply sergeant could get you some clothes if he wanted to."

"I'll get you some stuff," Robarge interjected. "Those headquarters bastards don't want to get off their fat asses to do anything, but I'll keep after them. You're damned right you need some shoepacks and a jacket."

The next morning Robarge and I found the supply sergeant, a short, stocky, fellow in his early thirties with a perpetually worried countenance and the air of a man struggling against overwhelming odds to accomplish an impossible task. Unlike others at headquarters he was not overtly hostile, but I could tell by his sideways glance at me that he didn't relish another request for supplies he did not have immediately at hand.

"Sarge," I began, "How about those shoepacks that I talked to you about? You said you'd order them, when do you think they'll come? I'm having trouble with my feet and my coat is falling to pieces so I need a new winter jacket too."

With feigned regret and concern he shook his head and replied, "Damn, soldier, I can see what you mean, but everything's in a hell of a mess. I'm doing the best I can. With all this moving around we're lucky to get anything at all. You just gotta be a little patient. You need something too, Robarge?"

"Jesus Christ, look at Ostrander," the sergeant shot back. "He can't wait until some rear echelon bastard gets off his fat ass and sends some clothes and shoepacks. Hell, the only way to get that stuff is to bother the sons of bitches until they send what you want just to get rid of you."

"You boys don't need to get so hot about this, you don't know how hard it is to supply this troop," he whined. "Everybody wants something, and I can only do so much."

Robarge fixed him with his sardonic smile and drawled, "I don't want to have to go to Hinkle about this, but, by God, I'll do whatever I have to do to take care of my men."

Even though Hinkle had a long association with most of the "old boys" he had developed a friendship with Robarge and would certainly heed any complaints that our section sergeant expressed against the likes of the supply sergeant. This was well known and accounted for the sulky, resentful glance the man directed toward Robarge.

"I'll see what I can do, now leave me alone, I'm busy," the man grumbled.

I enjoyed Robarge's pressure tactics but wondered how much effect they would have after we were out of sight. My sergeant, on the other hand, seemed confident that my problems were practically solved, and I fervently hoped that he was right.

Soon after we returned to our shack a jeep pulled up and Merrick and Lt. Parker got out. Rutt bellowed, "Sam, Nelson, Robarge, get your men out here."

Even before everyone was present he exclaimed excitedly, "Men, third platoon's got a mission. We move in 30 minutes, so pack up your gear, don't leave anything 'cause we won't be back. Robarge, get that tarpaulin off that shack."

From his almost breathless excitement I guessed we might soon see those big German bunkers that the men of the 2nd Recon had described. It didn't take long to load, and we were ready to depart much sooner than Parker was ready to lead us. He had gone to troop headquarters for final orders and did not return for nearly an hour. At last we moved out, churning through the slop and getting our usual mud bath as we drove through the mist shrouded forest. After a few minutes we reached a junction with a slightly better highway where the spot was marked by shell craters and splintered trees, a miniature "Heartbreak Cross Roads."

We turned right and crawled along toward ever louder, sporadic, small arms fire. Occasional artillery reports came from implacements in the forest. When we emerged from the trees we entered a village of a few half timbered houses with variable amounts of damage and an equal number of rubble heaps that had once been houses. An askew road sign said Harperscheid, so we at least knew the name of the place.

A regimental infantry command post occupied the largest house, but Parker and Samuels quickly scouted the others and picked a reasonably intact structure for third platoon. In spite of General Cota's praise of life in the woods as a health aid, I looked forward to a roof and a dry room for the night.

We looked around the village and inspected the house while Parker conferred with the regimental command and huddled with his sergeants. I did not see a single civilian and could only surmise that they had fled before the Americans arrived. The gunfire was desultory as one would expect on a static or "quiet" sector of the front. Still, a man could get killed in such a place, particularly if he got careless.

I was idly roaming through the house when Caulkins found me and said that Robarge wanted us all outside. As I came out the door I saw him standing next to our armored car talking to the rest of the section, his face sober and drawn without a trace of his usual smile.

"I've been telling the rest about our mission for tonight," he said. "They want a reconnaissance patrol to go into Schleiden and grab a couple of prisoners. That's the next town, and it's held by the krauts. It'll be a twelve man patrol, so there will be four guys from another section along with us. Some infantry captain will brief us this afternoon, and we leave at 2000 or 8 o'clock the way I tell time. Tape everything that makes a noise, and rub dirt on anything that shines, although it looks as though we're pretty well covered with dirt anyway. Any questions?"

The seven faces around Robarge were now as grim as his. It sounded like tough duty, particularly when we didn't know the lay of the land.

"Sarge, how far is Schleiden?" Caulkins asked.

"I've told you all I know. This captain is supposed to give us all the details at 1600 in the CP over there," Robarge replied. "I don't even have a map of the place, but Lt. Parker says we'll get maps this afternoon. The only good news is that we'll get hot chow at regimental headquarters before we go."

"Do they let us have whatever we want like in the movies when a guy is going to the electric chair?" Indy asked.

This attempt at humor drew only weak smiles as we milled around saying little and engrossed in our thoughts. Perhaps the vagueness and uncertainty about the patrol bothered me more than a dangerous but well defined assignment would have. The affair had the same purposeless quality as the mission in Alsace that cost Panos his life. I was certainly no glory hound, but I didn't think I was a coward either, and yet if I was going to take risks I hoped it was for a good reason. I had to admit to myself that whatever we were asked to do was better than the infantry's task of attacking the enemy across open fields, but that was still no reason to court danger needlessly. While these thoughts filled my mind, I walked aimlessly around the parked vehicles and stopped in the lee of an armored car where a wan sun provided a little warmth if one was sheltered from the wind. I was roused from my melancholy reverie by the unmistakable voice of Rutt Parker.

"Damn it, Robarge, I don't want to send my men down there, but the order came from division to the 112th, I saw it with my own eyes: reconnaissance of Schleiden by 12 man patrol from recon troop, capture two prisoners, if possible. What the hell can I say? If you don't want to lead it I'll send Nelson, but I'll need some of your men."

"Jesus Christ, lieutenant, you know I'm not trying to get out of it for myself. I'll lead the damned patrol, but it's a hell of a thing to bring men up here who've never seen the place and don't know where the hell they're going and expect them to carry out a successful mission or even get back without a lot of casualties. I'm just asking you to tell the colonel what I'm telling you, that it doesn't make any sense as far as getting whatever it is they want. You and I have a responsibility for these kids, and I don't want to see any of them hurt for no reason."

"Look, Robarge, I don't want any of my men killed either, but this is a damned war. I won't ask any favors, but I think you're right about our ability to conduct a successful reconnaissance; hell, I don't even know where the fuckin' town is myself. I'll talk to the colonel, but I wouldn't get my hopes up."

I hadn't meant to eavesdrop, but the concerns of Robarge and Parker increased my anxiety about the patrol. I doubted that Parker would be able to persuade the colonel or his staff that we were a poor choice for the mission. They were infantrymen and accustomed to sending scores of men on more hazardous assignments than this. It seemed unlikely that they would substitute some of their own troops when we could be used and indeed were billed as reconnaissance men. I went into the house where some of the men had lit a fire in a large stove in the center of what looked like a parlor. I took off my ragged coat and sat down on the floor to enjoy the precious warmth radiating from the heater. I must have dozed off because the next thing I knew Gorlitz was shaking me.

"Wake up, Leon, we're moving out. Have you seen Henry and Caulkins?"

I blinked and stretched and tried to get my bearings as I climbed to my feet. "What did you say, Chet?"

"I said we're moving out in a couple of minutes and I'm looking for DJ and Bud. You seen 'em?"

"I haven't seen anyone, I fell to sleep. Where are we going, on that patrol?"

"Nah, Sarge says that's called off or they're sending someone else. We're going to another town. Hurry up, we gotta get going before it gets too dark to see," Gorlitz urged.

It was nearly dark when I stepped outside and saw Robarge standing by my jeep with his usual half smile.

"Now I know who snored so loud and kept me awake back in the woods. You always snore like that, Holme, or do you save it for an audience?"

"I guess you'll always know if I'm sleeping on guard, Sarge. No noise, no sleep. Hey, what about that patrol, what's up now?" I asked.

"The lieutenant was about to go to the CP to tell the colonel he didn't think we would make a good patrol because we had just gotten here when some captain found him and said they'd decided to send a reinforced infantry platoon instead. They want to make sure they grab some prisoners and find out where all the guns are. That lets us off the hook, but now we're assigned to an observation post in some little place that looks across a valley into Schleiden. We gotta go soon; we can't use lights, the road's under fire from the krauts. If it gets too dark we can't see where we're going. Sounds like a nice place, but it's probably better than that damned patrol."

By this time Gorlitz had returned with Caulkins and Henry, and our section moved out. Robarge rode with me in the lead jeep, followed by the armored car and then the other jeep. We groped our way along the road until we came to a dirt lane to the left where we turned and slowly moved up a grade. As we got to the top I was struck by how bare the hill was even in the failing light. I couldn't see a tree or even a bush and thought this must be the place where the Germans can pick off anyone entering the village. About 300 yards past the crest of the hill we entered a hamlet of perhaps 20 houses, most of them badly damaged by shells or bombs. It was nearly dark now as Robarge halted the little column and set out on foot with Caulkins to find quarters for the section. When he signaled we crept forward to a U shaped house on the left side of the street. The far arm of the U was badly damaged with a collapsed roof and only parts of the walls standing. The near arm was more or less intact and the space between the wings was ideal for parking vehicles.

Reardon backed the M8 into the area between the wings of the house, and then Henry and I parked the jeeps so that we had quick access to the vehicles and yet they were sheltered from view and to some extent from fire. The small arms rattle that we had heard in Harperscheid was much closer in the hamlet but less frequent now that night had fallen. When we entered the intact portion of the house we found a room about 10 x 12 feet with a reasonably clean floor and a stove. A door opened from the room to the outside next to the armored car so that it was easy to communicate with the radio operator on duty. We had two boxes of Ten in One rations and scavenged a supply of firewood from the damaged portion of the house, so we were well quartered compared to our shack in the woods.

The quiet of the village seemed more ominous than reassuring. A battalion aid station was housed on the opposite side of the street, but few soldiers moved about, and those who did stayed close to the buildings and seemed wary of unseen perils. Even if we did nothing our assignment would be taxing; Weiner and Hilton had to alternate on the radio at all times, eliminating them from most other duties and leaving the sergeant and five other men to handle guard duty and all other missions. Our first orders were not long in coming.

Indy gave us the message that we were to send two observers forward where they could spot artillery flashes. One man was to maintain constant surveillance while the other was to report the locations of the German guns to our radio operators who would then relay the information to troop and division. No time limit was mentioned so it sounded like a busy night. It was left to us to select a vantage point for this reconnaissance, no small task considering that none of us had seen the place in daylight. We had a general idea of where the German lines lay, but we needed a better appreciation of the topography of the area and the situation of the enemy if we were to locate his artillery. Wandering around in the dark posed other hazards, the possibility of being shot by other Americans or a German patrol or triggering an antipersonnel mine. These devices were commonplace where the front was static for a long period of time and the enemy had opportunities to infiltrate with relative safety. We were very much aware of these dangers but said nothing when Robarge assigned Caulkins and me to the first shift as observers.

"I don't know where we should go, probably in a house if we can find one with the upstairs still standing," Robarge mused as we started up the street. "I'll go with you so I'll know where you are. We'll relieve you in a couple of hours."

We kept to the edge of the street as we walked through the village, but no firing broke the silence of the night, and we met nobody until we reached the end of the hamlet where the street made a sharp right turn and disappeared in the dark. Three houses stood on the left side of the road, the nearest a large two story structure that seemed intact. Even in the darkness we could see that the other two dwellings were nearly destroyed. As we approached the first house a man slipped out the door and relieved a sentry hidden in the shadows. Robarge gave the password and the guard gave the countersign when we were very close to the building.

"Who's in there, soldier?" the sergeant asked.

"F Company headquarters and some artillery spotters," the man replied.

"Do they need some company?"

"Who are you?"

"Recon troop, looking for a place to spot German artillery."

"Well, I wouldn't bother the captain, but the headquarters is all on the first floor. You can probably do your job upstairs where the artillery guys are."

We entered a hallway and clattered over pieces of plaster on the floor. Doors on our left and ahead led to rooms from which a faint light shone under the crack and the drone of voices could be heard, the F Company headquarters. To our right a stair rose into a dark void, presumably to our second floor destination, and we quickly climbed into the darkness. The room we entered at the top of the stairs was not illuminated by even a hooded lamp, but as my eyes adjusted to the place I could make out a large chamber with dormer windows on the rear of the building. Two men were gazing into elaborate scopes while a third sat on a chair or stool facing a dark object.

"Either of you see anything over there, or are we going to spot the damned half track by the rockets?" the seated man asked.

The speaker paused and then said, "That you, Ernie? Who's with you?"

"We're from recon," Robarge replied. "We have orders to spot kraut artillery and this looked like the best place, but I guess you're doing that already."

"Jesus, that's just like the dumb shits at division; how the hell many reports do they need? It's probably because infantry doesn't trust artillery to do the job, so they send you guys, and I bet they didn't even tell you what they're looking for," the man added.

The two spotters chuckled and one said, "Unless you got scopes like these you can't tell anything worth a shit; with these we can get a good read on the range and the angle. If we're quick our 105's will drop a load of grief on the damned krauts."

"You fellows are welcome to stay, and you'll surprise hell out of your old man when you send back the dope we'll give you," the seated man added.

"We appreciate that," Robarge replied. "I'm leaving my two men here, we'll have someone here all night. Let us know if we are in the way, or if we can help."

It was quiet for a few minutes after the sergeant left, the spotters continuing their silent vigil and the third man fiddling with the dials of a radio, which I now discerned in the dark. Our mission seemed even more ridiculous when I realized what an expert team was already collecting the information that we were assigned to gather. Then I heard someone else coming up the stairs.

"I broughtchas some coffee, Morgan. Hey, you'se got company," said the new arrival, a dim figure carrying a container.

"Damned division sent these guys from recon to spot artillery, Ernie," Morgan replied. "We'll both look, if that's what it takes to keep the assholes happy."

"Pretty quiet tonight. I like it better when it ain't so quiet. Last time it was like this them krauts grabbed them signal guys right outside here. They ain't so like to send patrols in here when the Mimis 're flyin'."

"What are Mimis?" DJ asked.

"How long you boys been over here?" Morgan asked.

"About a month and a half."

"You been in combat?"

"We got shot at near Colmar."

"Well, the krauts were trying to get across the Rhine down there. Here they're defending home, they know if we get through into Germany they're done. They use anything and everything up here. Screamin' Mimis are rockets; they put a rack with about a dozen launchers on a half truck and fire them all at once. You see the big flash, and you better get your ass to cover because you'll hear a God awful shrieking noise as those babies come in. They're big suckers and land in a pattern so they can wipe out a building with one salvo. There's a launcher over there behind the kraut lines. He fires from different places but usually only gets off one or two salvos before we make it too hot for him, but we haven't caught him yet. They don't like clear nights 'cause the air force picks 'em off, but they don't have to worry, it's never clear up here."

"Do the Germans have other artillery over there, too?" I asked.

"Yeah, they got the usual stuff, but we know where their guns are in the big concrete bunkers; one shot from one of those babies and we can put shells right in the gunport, so they go more for big mortars and the rockets, stuff they can move around. The mortars are the worst, you never hear them coming in, and we don't know when they fire them either. They usually follow up on the rockets with a mortar barrage to catch anyone running around outside. We just go down in the cellar when we see the Mimis and wait until the Jerries finish their fireworks," Morgan explained.

"What time does the shooting usually start?" Caulkins asked.

"It's never the same, but they like to cut loose about this time, hope to catch some GI going out to take a piss before he goes to sleep, I guess."

"Here they come," shouted the spotters as they headed for the stairs.

DJ and I clomped down the steps after the artillery men and Ernie, but before we could get to the cellar the piercing sound of the rockets rent the silence followed almost instantly by a cluster of nearly simultaneous explosions that shook the house. As we felt our way to a corner of the cellar we could hear the men above in the F Company headquarters cursing and moving about.

"You say they drop mortars on us after the rockets?" I asked.

"Usually, but they may come back with another bunch of Mimis. The krauts are tricky."

"How long do we stay here?"

"I'll tell you when to go up. Generally, if nothing more comes in 5 minutes they're not serious about it and we go up. We have been wrong, so don't blame me if we get more presents from Jerry."

When we climbed back to the second floor, Caulkins and I stood at the window not used by the artillery spotters and peered into the darkness. I saw nothing, but presently one spotter detected a light and announced a position to Morgan. He called us to look through his scope, and with some imagination, I thought I saw a vague movement, but I was not sure enough to have reported it on my own authority. DJ was more certain, so I assumed that the Germans were doing something. We had just retreated to our window and I was in the midst of a great yawn when multiple shafts of light flashed from the ground where we had seen movement. Everyone dashed pell mell down the stairs, but again the eerily shrieking missiles landed before we could reach the cellar, but at least we were not on the second floor where we heard a great explosion and the clatter of pieces falling off the building. We sat in the post salvo quiet for at least ten minutes, waiting to see if the enemy would send his other mail, before we returned to the second floor. Part of the roof had been blown away at one end of the house, and debris was scattered everywhere. Miraculously, the scopes and radio were undamaged, so the artillery men resumed their vigil. While still in the cellar, we heard our artillery firing, and the spotting crew were hopeful that our barrage had caught the German rocket launchers.

Soon afterward we heard conversation below and then someone climbing the stairs. Two figures emerged from the stairwell, groped in the dark for objects to guide them, and then we recognized Henry and Gorlitz, who had come to relieve us. As we were telling them about our adventures as observers, Ernie returned.

"The damned krauts ambushed a big patrol down near Schleiden tonight. I was just talking to a sergeant who was there, and he said two new guys fucked up. They'd captured a couple a' krauts and sent 'em back with these guys, but they got scared and decided to shoot the Jerries. Hell, they didn't even do that right, they only wounded 'em, so the noise of the shots and the yellin' of the wounded krauts gave the whole patrol away, and the Germans caught 'em with machine guns and mortars. Lotsa casualties 'n' the old man is mad as hell 'cause they didn't even find out anything except the krauts are still there and full of fight."

The four of us from recon said nothing, but I'm sure we had the same thoughts. It could have been us who were caught in the ambush and shot by the Germans. Since we didn't know the area, we probably would have muddled into an even greater fiasco than the infantry platoon.

Caulkins and I climbed down the stairs and warily sidled along the village's one street until we came to our house. I looked forward to a couple hours of sleep before I had to stand guard just before dawn. As we entered the house we could see the glow of a cigarette in the darkness of the room we used for all purposes, and Robarge materialized behind the bobbing ember.

"You guys want some coffee? It's not very good, but it's hot."

"What're you doing up, Sarge?" I asked.

"Oh, I just woke up and decided to get a cup of coffee. Anything going on up there?"

We whispered the tale of the rockets and the fate of the infantry patrol while we drank the coffee. Robarge responded with a few grunts and soon we settled down for some much needed sleep before something else happened.

In the morning we were ordered to reconnoiter the area and report the positions of all troops, both friendly and enemy. This vaguely defined mission was puzzling; it was inconceivable that division did not know all about this sector where the front had been static for at least ten days. Robarge shrugged and told Caulkins and me to find the most forward infantry and determine from there where the Germans were situated and plot it on the map.

In the light of the overcast day the hamlet was even less appealing than by night. Over half of the houses were so shattered as to be useless, and none had escaped damage from shells and rockets. The place was situated on top of a rounded hill and surrounded by rocky meadows, and beyond this bald elevation the fir forests stretched into the distance. Sporadic bursts of small arms fire to the east of the village pointed the way to the forward positions of the infantry. I felt a sense of relief when we cleared the hamlet, because it was such an inviting target for mortar fire. My mood changed to euphoria, an irrational and inexplicable surge of excitement, as we crossed a meadow toward a line of trees where the land dropped down as it approached a valley. It wasn't far to the woods, a mixture of firs and deciduous trees, that provided cover for men of E Company, 112th Infantry. They, or their 2nd Division predecessors, had built a rude log dugout for a command post, and as we approached a sergeant emerged from the structure and looked at us quizzically.

"Who are you boys, and what are you doing here?" he asked gruffly.

"We're from the recon troop," DJ replied, "And we have orders to come up here and find out where everyone is and report back to division. Can you tell us where the front line is?"

"You gotta be kidding. Who the hell would send you on a wild goose chase like that? If those dumb bastards don't know where we are and the damned krauts without sending the recon, we're shit outa luck."

"Sarge, we don't want to be up here any more than you want us here, but we got orders. We're just doing what we're told," I countered.

"Well, you're almost there. About fifty yards and that's the end. The platoons have dug in some there, but it's too rocky for real fox holes. Don't show yourselves, the krauts have machine guns zeroed in on this hill, and keep low, be ready to hit the ground. They drop mortar fire in here regularly. We have a few casualties every day. Oh, and be careful where you step — whole damned area's full of mines, blow your foot clean off if it doesn't kill you."

Caulkins and I nodded silently and then started picking our way among the trees and over rocks as cautiously as we could until we spotted some soldiers in a shallow excavation. Instinctively we bent over in negotiating the last few yards before we crawled into the depression among the infantrymen.

"You guys the new replacements?" the man nearest to me asked.

"No, we're from the recon troop, and we were sent here to find out where our lines and the Germans are," DJ replied.

A man on the other side of Caulkins snorted, "Well, we're here, and if you go any farther it's all krauts. What the hell kind of mission is that? They gotta know all that back there. We were hoping for some replacements, but I knew you were something else with those carbines."

The first man said, "If you ease forward a little and carefully spread some of those branches you can look down into Schleiden. The town is blown to hell and gone, but the krauts are still in the ruins. If you look carefully you'll see where the big concrete bunkers are in the hillside behind the town. Don't move anything too fast, or we'll get a stream of tracers; lotsa machine guns over there."

We took turns looking into the valley where a small river twisted among the remains of the town. Water filled craters of various sizes dotted the entire area, and the place was bisected by a road, but the bridges over the stream had been destroyed. At first I couldn't make out the bunkers behind the town, so clever was the camouflage, but after staring at the hillside for a minute or two I saw the concrete intermingled with the native stone and finally I spotted several apertures which were gunports.

While we had been peering at Schleiden a soldier had crawled over toward us, and he introduced himself when we slid back down into the depression.

"Name's Tony Hobson; I hear you guys are from recon. Hell, I used to be in recon myself, sort of, but in the infantry. Bet your outfit's short of men, and a guy like me would be a big help, I know all about recon. If your CO is looking for a good man, tell him about me. OK? Just tell him about me, will ya?"

Hobson was a man in his late twenties, a little more tidy and better groomed than most of his fellows, or for that matter, any of our section. The two E Company men we had been talking to had turned their backs and were conspicuously ignoring the job seeker. Caulkins and I exchanged glances, and I deferred a reply to DJ.

"Glad to meet you, Tony. Yeah, we need more men, and we'll tell our captain about you when we see him, but he's in the hospital, so it'll be a while. Wha. . . . . "

Kaboom, kaboom, kaboom.

Instantly every man was squeezed as flat as he could squirm into the shallow holes, where we could feel the vibrations of the exploding shells. All the while we were serenaded by the angry whine of shell fragments in the air and showers of twigs, bark and small limbs from the trees that had born the brunt of the mortar barrage.

"Anybody hurt, any casualties?" a sergeant called.

Various noncoms reported from the scattered holes that their men were unharmed, and it appeared that the shelling had caused no casualties. The men we had talked to rolled over and muttered about the mortars and krauts, and when no more shells fell the infantrymen resumed their cautious movements and activities. Caulkins and I decided that we had completed our silly mission and crawled out of the depression and picked our way over the rough ground in stooped posture until we were back in the meadow. As we strode across the brown prairie of dormant grass toward the hamlet we saw a column of smoke and then realized that it came from the house where we had observed the rockets the night before. The place was ablaze and would join it's neighbors as a burned out hulk in a village that was gradually being reduced to total ruin.

A man approached from the village, and when he got closer we could see that he was a captain.

When we met he asked gruffly, "Who are you men?"

"Privates Ostrander and Caulkins, sir," DJ replied. "We're from the recon troop and were ordered to determine and report the position of all troops near Schleiden."

"You what? Who told you to come up here? Don't you know you could get killed or get other men killed wandering around in an area like this?"

"We have orders from division headquarters, sir. We were just doing what we were told," I added.

"Don't you know the krauts can see you on this slope? They're liable to drop a few rounds on us just because we're standing here. Now you get back and make your report, but don't come into my company area again unless you have a real job of work to do. You understand?"

We mumbled, "Yes, sir," and were glad to get away from the irate officer. We hurried past the blazing building that had been our observation post during the previous night and eagerly made for the half ruined house which had become our section's lair, a place that seemed more hospitable to me by the minute.

We entered the dark room and sat down on the floor amid our comrades in what seemed the most secure retreat in the scarred village. Heavy wooden shutters protected us against flying debris and shell fragments, but the thin shafts of light that shone through the cracks cast the chamber in permanent twilight even at mid-day. We poured over a map with the aid of flashlights and determined the present positions of our infantry and the Germans on the Schleiden front, while Robarge looked on and asked questions about our reconnaissance. His sardonic grin and sarcastic comments spilled forth when we told of our encounter with the angry captain.

"Jesus Christ," he exclaimed, "He sounds like the most sensible officer you've met over here. If he couldn't see any sense to what you were doing up there, it's probably all a crock of shit. Well, shit or not, let's give the bastards what they asked for."

With that the sergeant took the positions we had plotted to Hilton in the armored car for transmission to the troop and then to division. This completed our mission, so we were temporarily out of work. Although I had little sleep the night before, I was more restless than sleepy and ready to do something besides sit and wait for the next foolish assignment.

Robarge must have sensed my mood as he turned and asked, "Holme, let's find a stove. I don't know where we'll go next, but it might be another forest. There's got to be a good stove in one of these houses."

Ignoring the "Holme", which had become more a term of familiarity and even affection than of derision, I smiled and agreed.

"Lead on, Sarge, I'm all for having a stove in reserve."

We started with a cautious search of the ruined parts of the house we occupied, taking care to avoid anything that could possibly be a detonating device. Every day men were killed or wounded by cleverly disguised booby traps, and some of these gadgets were planted in houses. The back wall of our residence was completely gone, and the ceiling sagged ominously, so the rear of the house was of no use as a shelter. Our predecessors, German, American, or both, had obviously concluded that it was an ideal latrine, a place where a man could defecate sheltered from the elements and partially protected from shell fire. Piles of human excrement were neatly spaced about the room, but the focal point and the trigger for our sudden uncontrollable laughter was in the center of the room, surely the largest turd I had ever seen.

"Jesus Christ, Holme, whoever laid that one must have felt good afterwards," Robarge chuckled.

"Are you sure it's human?" I countered. "If it's man made the guy who did it probably has blood on the seat of his pants."

"It's a good thing it's cold enough to freeze all this shit or we'd smell it in where we are," Robarge added. "It's not a bad idea to use this area as a latrine; I don't want to be squatting next to the house or in an open field when those mortars or rockets are coming in."

We moved across the rubble strewn street and picked through the remains of the house that once stood there. The sergeant threw aside a large section of plaster and lathe and let out a triumphant shout as though he had been handed his discharge papers.

"Give me a hand with this, Holme," he exclaimed. "It's just what we need, a real little beauty, and it'll fit right on the front of the jeep."

The object of his admiration was a shiny black stove, about 18 inches square and 3 1/2 feet high. It was primarily a space heater, but the top was hinged so that one pan could be heated. It was beautifully made and must have been a joy to its owners, but they were gone, their house was destroyed, so the heat would now warm some American recon men.

We lifted the stove out of the rubble and carried it to my jeep, where we suspended it on the front bumper, two legs hooked behind the bar. We then looped some cord under the lid and secured it so that it could not bounce off.

"Sarge, you weren't kidding about the stove," Indy said admiringly. "If we're stuck in another forest, that baby'll do the trick. It looks better than the one we're using in the house."

"I wonder how old Rutt will like that on the front of the 'quarter ton'," Hilton said sarcastically.

"If that pissant doesn't like it he can shove it," Henry sputtered. "Rutt and Samuels and their buddies in the headquarters section are probably just loafing around Harperscheid and complaining 'cause they can't find any women."

We all laughed at Bud's feisty contempt for our leaders, but there seemed to be some truth to what he said. They seemed in no hurry to visit us and find out what we were doing.

By this time all members of the section had inspected the latrine room and had marveled at the enormous turd in the center of the floor. This aberration provoked so much mirth that the conversation degenerated into anecdotes about excrement. Everyone had experienced the "GI's" from time to time, and we could appreciate the crude humor of each story.

"You know," said Robarge after a few minutes of such talk, "I just wish I could get my hands on the guy who shit all over the floor at Ste. Marie and left it for his buddies to walk in. I had the runs myself, and I tore down the hall and into the can. I remember I wondered why there was mud on the floor when it was cold enough to freeze the balls off a brass monkey and was sore as hell 'cause I got it all over my feet while I was sitting on the pot. But then I get back to my sack and start to pull my feet up to get in and got a good whiff of what I had on my feet, not mud but shit. So here I am, four o'clock in the morning, washing my goddam feet so I can get back to bed. I vowed that someday I'm gonna catch the bastard who did that, so help me."

I couldn't control myself and started to laugh convulsively until the conversation stopped and I found myself the center of attention. Whether it was lack of sleep, a need to confess my sin, or just the vulgar humor of the way Robarge told the story, I will never know, but I was sure that my secret was out.

"Holme, don't tell me you're the one who shit all over that house. It was you wasn't it?" the sergeant asked.

I couldn't see his face, but from his tone I surmised that confession was in order.

"Yeah, Sarge, but I didn't mean to leave it," I replied. "I was so sick that night I just had to lie down and get warm before I cleaned it up. I fell back to sleep and the next thing I knew everyone was cussing a blue streak, and I didn't have the guts to admit it. I tried to help clean it up, but it was too late."

The others started to laugh and the giddiness became infectious; we couldn't stop. The whole episode had become a giant bathroom joke sending wave after wave of laughter through the group.

"Well, Holme, all I can say is next time stand still and keep it all in one place." Robarge advised in a voice cracking with mirth. "And if you can't clean it up, at least leave a lantern."

"What are you guys doing?" Hilton asked as he stepped into the room from his post in the armored car. "You're laughing so hard I could hear you outside. Somebody goosing everyone else in the dark?"

"We're just shooting the shit —" Gorlitz replied as he let out another guffaw.

"Well, we may have a lot more shit," Hilton continued. "They just called from troop and said the coordinates for those German positions were screwed up and nobody checked them until they'd started moving division and corps reserves. They say we had the krauts 10 miles behind our lines."

"Do you still have the coordinates I gave you, Hilton?" Robarge asked.

"Yeah, I think I stuck 'em in my pocket, just a minute, yeah, here they are."

"Let's check 'em against the map."

We carefully plotted the positions and got the same result as before.

"Call the troop and find out what coordinates they sent up to division," the sergeant said.

"OK, Sarge. Shall I tell 'em we didn't make the mistake here?"

"Not yet, just ask 'em what they sent. Somebody got the numbers backwards, but we don't know where it happened, and I don't want to take the blame if we didn't do it," Robarge said.

"They haven't thought of any more good missions for us tonight," Caulkins observed.

"Don't count on it, it's early yet," the perennially skeptical Henry countered.

"You guys getting hungry?" Robarge asked. "If you can find some fat and potatoes, I'll make some French fries to go with the Ten and Ones. There's probably some around the kitchen in the wrecked part of the house."

As Henry and Caulkins left to search for ingredients for our feast, Hilton returned with a wry smile on his phlegmatic face.

"Sarge, they had the coordinates reversed at troop, but they swear that's the way they received 'em. They said I made the mistake, they'll never admit that they might have screwed up. I know I sent 'em just as they are on that paper."

"Division doesn't care, they'll just blame Recon and let Collins find someone to be the goat. Call Lt. Parker and tell him what happened; I bet we'll never hear another thing about it," Robarge said.

Caulkins and Henry returned triumphant with a can of ersatz lard and a helmet full of potatoes.

"Caulkins, keep your helmet on," Robarge cautioned. "We can get fire here any time, no sense taking any unnecessary chances."

As if to emphasize his words a close succession of explosions resounded at the other end of the village. Soon a second and closer volley, and then another and another until a series of shell bursts shook the house and seemed to be right outside the door. We could feel the earth shake, hear the dirt and shell fragments flying through the air, and then smell the pungent odor of the explosive. Automatically we all flattened against the floor until the shelling ceased. Robarge was the first up to check on Hilton and to tend to his cooking.

The barrage had not harmed Hilton or the vehicles, and we soon forgot our fear as we relished the meal. So far we seemed to be forgotten by division intelligence, so we looked forward to sleep interrupted only by guard duty. I don't know how long I had slept before I awoke to a conversation between Indy and Robarge.

"I'm not kidding, Sarge, it's Dave and George, they want the serial numbers of all our guns, all of 'em."

"Why do they need them tonight? We can't climb around in the dark with flashlights looking for numbers, the krauts 'll blow us all to hell," Robarge complained. "Tell 'em we'll do it in the morning."

"What's all this about numbers?" I asked.

"Your friends, Dave and George, say they need the serial numbers of all our guns right now," Robarge replied. "If it was anyone else I'd say it was a joke, but that pair mean it. What a crock of shit!"

By this time everyone was awake and incredulous at this ridiculous request. Indeed, it was an order, not a request. According to the radio operator at troop headquarters an immediate inventory of arms had been ordered by some potentate at division headquarters, and George and Dave were just following orders. Somehow the silliness would not go away, and we were not experienced enough to ignore a foolish order, so finally Robarge and I took a flashlight and field jacket to hide the light and went out to the vehicles. Reading numbers off the machine guns, mortar, and 37mm gun was not easy even then, but we succeeded without drawing fire from friend or foe and retreated into the house where the others had recorded the numbers from our carbines, rifles, and submachine guns.

"Don't get the numbers mixed up or some asshole will have a fit," Robarge said to Indy as he passed the list to the radio operator in the M8.

It was nearly 3:30 AM when we flopped down and slept again, a rest that was terminated by a wake up call from the Germans in the form of a 7 o'clock mortar barrage.

After eating breakfast and cleaning up as best we could, we waited uneasily for our next orders. So far all our missions and duties seemed superfluous, but not without risk. We hesitated to go out of doors for fear of mortar attack, so we sat in the dark room and talked of trivia. The morning passed quietly until about noon, when we were told to prepare to leave the village as soon as a section of second platoon arrived to relieve us.

We loaded our bedrolls and waited for our relief. I was glad to leave a place where we seemed to have no duty except to serve as targets for the Germans.

The second platoon section was under the command of Jim Thompson, a friend from basic training, who climbed out of his M8 smiling broadly.

"You all look like you got yoah tails between yoah legs and can hardly wait to haul butt outta heah," he exclaimed in his thick Mississippi accent. "This little old place looks pretty quiet to me, a few mortars get you boys all nervous and scared?"

"Just following orders," Robarge replied. "You see how you like it up here, but be careful. It's not as quiet as it seems."

"Well, you all just relax and enjoy a little rest an' let the old second take ovah. We'll let you know what happens up heah," Thompson added.

We drove away amid more childish chiding by our replacements, but several of the men looked sober almost to the point of grimness. I expected my Mississippi friend to change his tune after a few days in the hamlet. I held my breath as we rolled over the exposed part of the hill in broad daylight and full view of the Germans. At Harperscheid we waited outside while Robarge went into Rutt Parker's quarters, but he soon emerged with a broad grin on his face.

"I told you that stove would come in handy," he crowed. "We're going back to the forest; our shack should be OK with some heat."

I never expected the rude shelter in the dripping forest to be appealing, but it was almost like going home. We unloaded the stove and set it at one end of the shelter with the pipe sticking out of the roof at a crazy angle, but with a priming of gasoline a blaze was soon crackling in the shiny little beauty, and we soaked up the delicious warmth.

We had only been there a short time when we heard whoops of joy from outside. On emerging from our cozy nest we joined in the celebration, for there was the troop mailman with nearly a jeep full of letters for us. Fergie, the mail carrier, was one "old boy" who was invariably pleasant to everyone, and his personality coupled with his job made him the most popular man in the troop. He had even tied the letters in bundles, so the mail was distributed quickly. When I counted them I found I had received 53 letters, a fact almost beyond my comprehension until I realized that I had been without mail for two months. I started to read a letter where I stood, but the comfort of the shack beckoned, even though I needed a flashlight to decipher the small writing on many of the letters. Relatives were encouraged to send "V Mail" letters to servicemen overseas, a small, thin tissue paper like missive that took up less room on overseas carriers, but the tendency of the writer was always to inscribe the message in tiny script that was hard to read except in good light.

I read all the mail from my parents first and then letters from other relatives and friends. I tried to keep them in temporal order so that ongoing tales made sense, but the postmarks were not completely reliable. I was relieved that all my family were well, but I was surprised that nobody had received a letter from me since I left the States. The contents of the letters could best be characterized as reports of the humdrum lives of uninteresting people, but I could almost hear my parents utter the trite phrases, and in my mind I had a vivid and almost painful image of home. It is impossible to explain how much I appreciated each little serving of that safe, secure, loving, comfortable and monotonous life back in Michigan.

As I reached the bottom of the pile of mail I opened a letter from a friend of my mother, a woman about her age, whom I had known all my life. As I unfolded the page a five dollar bill fell out, and I'll never forget kind Mrs. Hock's generous message: "I'm enclosing a little money because I know there's no place on earth where an American $5 bill won't get you at least a good dinner." I looked up at the walls of our shack and burst into uncontrollable gales of laughter.

"What the hell's the matter with you, Holme?" Robarge asked.

I read the message in the letter and held the bill aloft to the delight of my comrades.

"Well, now that you showed us yours, I got one too from my wife," the sergeant said. "Shall we go out and have a big steak dinner tonight and leave these guys with the Spam?"

"You can write back to that lady and tell her you've found the one place where five bucks or five hundred won't buy you shit," Hilton added dryly.

In our hilarity over the money we had not noticed that one of our members was weeping.

Caulkins suddenly stopped laughing and asked, "What's wrong, Jack, you got some bad news, something wrong at home?"

Jack Reardon tried to hide his tears but failed to check a sob as he blurted out, "It's my pig, he died."

"Your pig! Why I thought maybe something was wrong with your folks or some other kin. You shouldn't cry over a pig," Caulkins exclaimed.

In a combination of grief and anger Reardon shouted, "I wouldn't expect any of you to understand. I raised him and showed him, he wasn't just any pig, he was like a friend. Oh hell, what's the use of talking to you city boys, you don't know what I'm even saying."

With that he bolted out of the shack to mourn his pig alone. He was right, the rest of us were from cities and didn't appreciate the relationship between a show animal and the boy who raised him.

The next day we were hunkered in the shack to avoid a steady fall of wet snow mixed with rain at times, a thoroughly disagreeable form of precipitation that chilled one to the bone. Our monotony was broken when Lt. Parker poked his head into our lair.

"I'll be goddamned if this isn't a cozy shack you all have here. I got some business that'll make one of you happy, I reckon. The TO calls for a corporal in each section, and we have permission from division to appoint corporals where appropriate. I leave it to you, Robarge, whoever you want. He doesn't have to be from your section, but I expect you'll want one of your own men."

Robarge looked uncomfortable, and I thought how characteristic of Rutt to burst in with such a proposal and make the sergeant select someone in front of all the others instead of talking to him privately and perhaps discussing the merits of several men.

After a brief pause Robarge said, "I don't need to go outside the section, lieutenant. It's between Caulkins and Ostrander, they're both good men."

"Well, you can't have two corporals, so you gotta choose one or the other. You want some time, or can you tell me now?"

"Make it Caulkins," Robarge muttered, but then he added gratuitously, "Hell, Ostrander should be at least a general."

"Caulkins it is, and if they come looking for another general I'll give 'em Ostrander's name," Parker said.

DJ and I were good friends, and I was pleased that he had made corporal, but I had to admit that I was disappointed. If someone had told me a year earlier that I would be dejected because I was not promoted to corporal, I would have laughed. Then everything about the army seemed inconsequential, an experience one lived through and then returned to civilian life for really important pursuits. That sort of rationalization no longer made sense, for like it or not, I was now a soldier and had my pride in what I was doing. The army and the war were the only realities for me now, and academic progress and civilian profession were far away abstractions. I was bothered too by Robarge's crack that I should be at least a general. I guessed he still considered me a strange duck, a smart aleck kid who was a repository of a lot of useless knowledge, but not steady enough for a leadership position. I suppressed my disappointment and congratulated DJ, but I was glum for the rest of the day.

Perhaps my dejection made me more aware of other problems, but when I pulled my boots off that night my feet hurt more than ever and the tingling little jabs of pain continued even after I crawled into my sleeping bag. The pain occurred over a peculiar sock-like area of numbness on my feet, a feeling as though I had a thick covering over them that prevented me from fully appreciating the sensation of touch. I was still trying to dry my socks and follow all the rules of foot care, but the sensory symptoms seemed to worsen in spite of my efforts. At least the feet had not started to change color or temperature, so I refused to even consider sick call. A few other men had similar symptoms, all of them individuals who were still wearing inadequate footgear.

The next day was unusual because it wasn't raining or snowing when we got up. At breakfast we were told to be ready for a trip back to Eupen, Belgium at 10 AM for showers. It was March 1, so I had gone over six weeks without really bathing. We left the armored cars and crowded into jeeps for the trip which took about two hours over dryer roads than usual.

The shower operation was an ingenious affair of the quartermaster corp consisting of a series of tents like a circus sideshow. Duckwalks and vast amounts of hose and flexible pipe adorned the interior of the tents. We entered a small anteroom tent, where we stripped and gave our clothes to a big laughing Negro T4, who held them at arms length as he stuffed them into bags and carried on a monologue: "Mm, mmn, you boys be really ripe, I ain't smelled clothes this bad fo' a long time, mah oh mah!"

Now completely naked, we walked past a rack where we picked up small bars of soap and then into a tent about 20x30 feet where one could barely see across the enclosure through the magnificent, comforting, cleansing clouds of steam, the result of about 20 shower heads spraying incredible streams of warm water over a like number of dirty hides. We lathered up quickly and reveled in the luxury of a warm rinse, and before we knew it the joy of the hot shower was over. Nobody hurried us, and yet the men were unselfish and did not linger beyond the time necessary for a thorough wash. In the next tent we received towels, and after drying proceeded to the last stop where two Negro soldiers handed out clean garb with the same jaunty humor as the man who collected the dirty clothes. I was surprised and delighted that I actually got garments that fit, and thus clean and refitted we reclaimed our boots and outerwear before returning to the jeeps. Next to mail call the shower was my greatest joy of the week, but the only sour note was that my dilapidated coat seemed even worse now that the rest of my clothing was either new or clean and repaired.

This period in the forest was a time of ups and downs. After the exhilaration of the shower we learned that Capt. Doyle had died. I had known him better than most of the men in the platoon, and he seemed to be a good man, conscientious, brave, and concerned with the welfare of his men. The course of events had been so rapid that the fighting at the Rhine-Rhone Canal where he received his fatal wounds, already seemed long ago. The sense of remoteness cushioned feelings about his death, although the news saddened me at the time.

The next day we were ordered to return to the hamlet above Schleiden to relieve the second platoon. Nothing had changed there except for more shell craters and greater damage to the remaining houses. Thompson and his section were a serious and subdued crew now that they had experienced several days of life on this "quiet" front. They left with none of the bravado of their arrival but a few days before.

We settled back into the half ruined house as though we had never left, and our first mission was not long in coming. We were ordered to confirm reports of German troop movements into new positions near the twisting little river in Schleiden. Robarge told Caulkins and me to go up where we could see the valley and try to see whether the krauts were actually doing anything. He also cautioned us not to take any unnecessary risks on what sounded like another harebrained assignment.

We trudged through the hamlet and across the field where we had met the irate captain without seeing a soul. It was all so quiet that one would think the area was deserted for the moment. No GI's stirred, no artillery fired, and even the crackle of small arms fire was stilled. As we cautiously picked our way through the trees to the shallow declevities that sheltered the infantrymen we became aware of their conversations and soon spotted half a dozen men taking their ease on the rocky ground. I didn't recognize any of the men from our earlier visits and was relieved that Tony Hobson wasn't anywhere to be seen with his obsequious palaver about a job in recon.

"We're from the recon troop," Caulkins said to the two men closest to us. "We have orders to let division know if the Germans are moving into new positions along the river in Schleiden. Have you guys seen anything down there?"

"The krauts are all over down there, have been as long as we've been here," one of the men replied. "I don't look down there unless I'm told to. If I can see them, maybe they can see me, and that can be trouble."

"Then you don't think they're doing anything different lately?" DJ asked.

"To tell the truth, I don't know. Like I say, I only look when someone tells me to. So long as the bastards aren't coming up here, I'll leave 'em alone. We hear that all we have to do is keep 'em hemmed in here and they'll have to surrender or retreat pretty soon because the front is moving toward the Rhine north and south of here."

"Seems pretty quiet up here right now," I commented.

"Don't let it fool you," the other man replied. "They've been firing more, this is just a lull. Some think it's because they're going to pull out soon and can't haul all the ammunition, so they'll use it up. Thing about the krauts is that they don't just waste it, they try to make sure it'll do some damage."

"Looks like we better slide down where we were the last time and start looking down into the town, if we're going to find out what we came for," DJ said.

We crawled to the spots where we could see the town and took up our vigil. The ground was damp, the air raw and cold, and we dared not move for fear of drawing fire. It was a miserable way to spend the day, and soon we were both shivering sporadically. Nothing moved below and one might have thought that the valley was deserted, but just when boredom and discomfort seemed to reach their ultimate level of vexation, I spotted a movement. Yes, it was real, and two gray clad figures walked from one cover to another along the rubble strewn banks of the little river. Then two more men appeared, and finally we spotted at least ten Wehrmacht men on their way to some unknown destination. We watched them disappear from view to our right, lost behind the rock that formed part of our cover. I was intent on finding out where they were going, and, forgetting all else, I crept around the large outcropping and found myself behind a low ridge. I scrambled up and was rewarded with a wide, sweeping view of the valley. I saw the squad of Germans entering the ruins of a large house next to the river. The roof and part of the second floor were gone, but the first level looked solid. The place must have been a splendid residence before the town became the target for shells and bombs, for the grounds were at least 100 yards square, and the shattered stumps of several large trees were remnants of handsome landscaping.

Brrrrp, brrrrp ——

I dropped to the ground as though I had been shot, and indeed I would never come closer. In my absentminded peering at the Germans in the valley, I had exposed myself and drawn vicious machine gun fire. The slugs passed so close to my helmet that it felt as though a hammer was pounding on the steel at an incredibly rapid rate. I lay on the ground with my heart pounding and a cold sweat chilling my body.

"Hey, recon, you all right? Didja get a shot at him?" one of the infantrymen called.

"No, no shot, I just got down, I didn't even see where it came from, but I'm OK," I replied in a shaky voice.

"You boys better get back up here and into a hole. They'll drop some mortar fire on us now sure as shit," the man added.

"You sure you're OK, Leon?" DJ asked as we crawled up and then slid into the shallow trench.

"Yeah, I'm all right, but I sure did a dumb thing. At least I saw where the krauts went, it's a big house by the river. We should be able to locate it on the map because it's by a big curve."

"We better get back and send the report ——"

Karumph, karumph, karumph ——

The mortar shelling had begun, so we flattened ourselves against the ground, hoping the enemy would not get lucky and land a round in the trench. It went on longer than usual and was more intense, so maybe the GI was right who said they were using up the ammunition they couldn't take with them. Finally it ended, and Caulkins and I scrambled out of the hollow and hurried back to the hamlet. I was surprised that my knees were still shaking, and I had an unpleasant tight sensation in my stomach. I was embarrassed and angry that my close call bothered me so much, and I had to admit to more apprehension while crossing the open field than on earlier trips.

When we reached the rest of the section I was glad to slip into the house and sit down in a corner by the stove. Apparently our report was useful, because Henry and Gorlitz, our replacements on the observation point, reported that a barrage from our artillery leveled the house where we had seen the German patrol enter. I just wished they could have said that a certain kraut machine gunner had been nailed, but perhaps I should have been grateful that he wasn't a better shot.

The shelling was more frequent and intense than on our previous stay in the hamlet. The Germans seemed to favor dusk and dawn for their fireworks, but they mixed it up enough so nobody went outside unless it was necessary. Even the partially sheltered latrine room was no place to be in a barrage, and I recall an hour of agony waiting for the shelling to cease while my buddies amused themselves at my discomfort.

"You can't shit in here, Holme," Robarge insisted with his most irritating sarcasm. "Ste. Marie was enough, we're your friends and you can't dump another load of shit on us. It's either take your chances with the mortars or hold it."

I hadn't even suggested that I would go in the room where we ate and slept, but his banter seemed to amuse everyone as I waited and fumed. When it finally seemed to be over I dashed for the room with the monster turd and all the other fecal monuments. As I squatted another salvo of shells suddenly crashed down not too far away. I finished my business in some sort of record time, aided by the strong peristalsis that followed the first concussion, and raced back to the more secure shelter of the sleeping room. I was greeted by gales of laughter as I fumbled to fasten my trousers and raged about the German fire.

The next morning was relatively bright with only a high overcast to block the sun. After the morning barrage all was quiet, and the temptation was strong to go outside to get away from the dark, depressing room where we spent so much time. DJ and I heated water in a battered pan and quickly shaved using the rear view mirrors of the jeeps. Our clothes were so grimy that it was hard to believe that we had showers and clean garments a few days earlier. Just as we finished our clean up a jeep chugged up the street and stopped in front of our lair. Lt. Parker and Merrick stepped out, and Rutt looked around with an amused expression on his homely face.

"So this is where you men are fucking off. You all living in that house?" he chortled.

"Yes, sir," Caulkins replied. "Sarge is inside. We had best all go in, the Germans shell us every now and then."

"Looks peaceful enough to me," Rutt countered. "Come on, Merrick, let's go inside and see what these boys have in that wreck of a house."

As Parker entered the house he exclaimed loudly, "I'll be goddamned, Robarge, if your men aren't living like a bunch of hogs, and this fuckin' place looks and smells just like a pig pen. You oughta get these men out and exercising on a day like this, first time it hasn't rained or snowed in a week. This whole section needs to clean up, too. Jesus, you men get out of my sight and you act like a bunch of hobos."

"Jesus Christ, lieutenant," Robarge remonstrated, "this isn't a playground up here. The Germans shell the town three or four times a day, people get shot here all the time, that's why we're not out walking around."

"That's no reason to be filthy," Rutt continued. "God damn, look at Caulkins, first time I've ever seen a man too lazy to wash his whole face when he shaves. The only part that's clean is where he had the shaving soap. I swear, you all have got so lazy that if you was dogs you wouldn't lift your legs to pee."

Part of Parker's talk was his brand of humor and part reflected his ignorance of what was going on in the hamlet. He didn't protest against holding the conversation indoors, apparently impressed by the destruction that was testimony to the shelling. I sensed that his visit was for the purpose of reporting that he was in personal contact with his men. By the time he had left he had chided each of us on some deficiency and expressed again the opinion that we exaggerated the shelling.

After he left Indy muttered, "Why the hell can't the krauts send us some rounds when we need them?"

The rest of the day passed without further incident except for heavy shelling on several occasions. The wan morning light faded into the more usual damp overcast of the Schnee Eiffel, but we were not ordered to undertake any more missions.

Before dawn we were awakened by the heaviest barrage yet. The house was struck in several places, but fortunately our refuge room was spared and the building did not catch fire. When we emerged at first light I was surprised to see an M4 tank parked next to the house and two others nestled up to the remains of other buildings in a vain attempt at concealment. The crews were lounging near their vehicles but looked about uneasily.

"I don't know what the hell the old man was thinking about when he sent us up here," a young lieutenant complained. "There's not a damn thing we can do here except be a clay pigeon for the krauts."

"Just got a message, lieutenant," shouted a man who popped up out of the turret. "We're to go back to Harperscheid and wait for further orders."

"Hell of a time to tell us, just hope they don't have an 88 zeroed in on that bare assed hill we have to cross," the lieutenant replied.

The tankers lost no time in beating a retreat, but their nonsensical mission made me feel better. At least we were not the only troops who were ordered to do things that seemed useless and even foolish. I just hoped that no more tempting targets parked next to our quarters.

The day passed much as the last except that we were low on rations. Robarge fretted that we should have been resupplied and wondered if they planned to rotate us out of the hamlet again. Finally he asked Indy to radio for instructions. The cryptic answer was that no orders had been received, but if we sent a jeep to Harperscheid we could get more rations as well as some other supplies.

"You guys mind waiting until after dark for dinner?" Robarge asked. "I don't want to get shot driving out of here in daylight."

We posted a guard inside the walls of a wrecked room adjacent to our lair, and the rest of us sprawled on the floor, fueled the fire, and talked or slept. After dark Robarge took a jeep and insisted on going to Harperscheid by himself. We were getting very hungry when he returned, but the old negotiator had done his job. We had two boxes of Ten in One rations, copies of the "Stars and Stripes", and a heavy winter hip length jacket that he handed to me.

"You and Gorlitz are the only ones big enough to wear this and he's got one, so it's yours, Holme," he said. "That little bastard of a supply sergeant must have really been worried that I'd get him in trouble or he wouldn't have bothered to get this and send it up here."

I thanked the sergeant and eagerly tried on the jacket. It was perfect, and I lost no time disposing of the ragged remains of the old coat.

"You know, Sarge, " I said, "if you can just get me some shoepacks now, I'll be all set."

"You're just like all this damn labor," the sergeant retorted with his wry grin, "Management gives you something, and all you can think about is more."

Again that night I marveled at how Robarge kept going. He was always awake when I went on guard or returned, always said he had just awakened and was having a smoke, and always said he got plenty of rest and wasn't tired. I never saw him nod off like the rest of us when we sat down in a warm place after a meal. It was uncanny and a little frightening; I wondered how long a man could shoulder all the responsibility that our sergeant assumed for himself. Although he never said it, I knew that he was determined to get all of the young kids in his section home safely, and yet to perform his military duties properly. No wonder he didn't sleep, for no matter what he did, the dangers were great enough that any or all of us could be killed momentarily. It was too heavy a burden, and I worried that Robarge would be worn down by it. I had heard of "Old Sarge" cases, where an excessively conscientious noncom cracked mentally when some of his men were killed in spite of his efforts to protect them.

Before dawn the next day I heard the rattle of small arms fire in the hamlet. Soon after I heard Henry, our sentry, say something to an unknown person outside, and then Robarge was at the door before I could pull my boots on. I was just stumbling to my feet when the sergeant returned and ordered everyone up.

"German patrol spotted in the town. Everyone up. About a dozen of 'em, killed a couple of infantry guys not far from here. Ostrander, you and Henry cover the front, Caulkins and Gorlitz the rear, Indy, you stay on the radio, Hilton, get up in the turret and man the .50 caliber and you help him Reardon. Keep your eyes peeled, but be sure it's a kraut before you fire."

We took our posts in the shadows, peering into the dark to catch sight of gray clad raiders. Time dragged at a maddeningly slow pace, all was quiet, and yet one never knew whether the Germans had departed or not. I thought the patrol might still be near because the early morning barrage had not started, perhaps delayed to avoid killing some of their own men. As a faint gray light began to edge in from the east, everything in the street took on different shapes. I was almost sure that a German soldier was kneeling next to the ruins across the street, waiting to shoot the first American to pass and unaware that he was an easy target for me, and yet I was not sure enough to shoot this evil specter.

"Bud, is that a kraut across the street?" I asked.

"Where? I don't see anyone."

"Right there below that window frame that sticks up. Don't you see what I mean?"

"Well, now that you pointed it out, could be, but I just don't know."

Thus we pondered the shadowy shape. Finally after a quarter of an hour the light had increased enough so we could see that the "German" was nothing more than a piece of siding leaning against the front wall of the house. By that time the alert was surely over, and as if to confirm the departure of the patrol, the enemy gave us a particularly heavy mortar barrage. I thought it would never end as I lay flat on the floor, feeling the house shudder with the closer explosions and hearing heavy pieces of plaster and lathe cracking from the concussions. At last it was over and we warily resumed our usual morning activities.

Division wanted more information about Schleiden, so Caulkins and Henry took a trip to the view point, with many cautions about unnecessary exposure. We had five bombardments that day and night, and I wondered how long our luck could hold before a direct hit caused some casualties among our section. I had thought static positions were safer after our experiences in Alsace, but sitting looking at one another while waiting for the next barrage was no bargain either. The wind came up during the day and a wet snow blew through the bleak ruins of the hamlet. Nobody said much that night as we endured yet another heavy "good night" shelling.

At dawn we cautiously opened the door and looked around. The weather was still terrible, but no mortar shells had fallen since the heavy barrage of the night before.

Just then Hilton poked his head out of the M8 and shouted, "The krauts have left Schleiden. We're to go to Harperscheid right away."

7

THE PURSUIT

Harperscheid was churning with activity when we added our armored car and two jeeps to the jam of military traffic on the town's main street. Order gradually emerged from chaos when vehicles from recon, a tank company, engineers and trucks of infantry formed a column to exploit the German withdrawal from Schleiden. Recon led the force except for a couple of trucks of engineers to clear impediments and assess the ability of the remaining bridges to bear the weight of heavy vehicles. Bridging equipment followed farther back in anticipation of the need to span small streams where the bridges had been destroyed or were too weak to support heavy loads.

Lt. Parker in Samuels' section led the recon platoon followed by Nelson's section and then ours. Our only instructions were to be extremely careful to avoid mines in Schleiden, because early probes of the town indicated that the Germans had wired everything imaginable during the long period they had held the place before their retreat. We were not to enter any building or pick up objects that excited our curiosity or seemed desirable as souvenirs. Even the bodies of fallen soldiers might be booby trapped to kill anyone who moved the corpse in search of loot. Beyond these warnings we had no idea what our goals were after we passed beyond the wreckage of Schleiden.

Rutt Parker strode about like a banty rooster, reveling in his role as recon commander in a joint task force with infantry, armor and engineers. I could see his chest swell as he discussed the mission with a lieutenant colonel, a major, and two captains. He seemed oblivious to the icy mist that chilled me to the bone and cast objects more than 100 yards away into ghostly shadows. Patches of dirty snow spotted the mud of the little town, and drops of water formed on the branches and needles of the trees that ringed the place. The effect was an eerie, otherworldly atmosphere, something foreign to any of my previous experiences.

"Jesus, Holme, I wish we had the stove we left back in the woods," Robarge growled as we walked around the jeep, stomping our feet and beating our arms against our bodies in an effort to dispel the clammy chill. "We may be stuck in this damned forest and might not find another one, at least not like the one we had."

"Maybe we'll get out of the forest and into some towns once we're past Schleiden," I suggested. "Germany can't be all woods. I wonder what we're waiting for?"

"What's your hurry? Let the krauts get as far ahead as they want, less chance they'll be waiting for us somewhere up there. The lieutenant said they pulled out because the outfits on either side of us broke through and they were about to be cut off. I guess they're all trying to get across the Rhine now. How're you at swimming?"

"No good in March. Do you think they'll keep on fighting even after we get to the Rhine?"

"I don't know. You're the expert on all that stuff. I remember we heard all along at Riley that we'd just be occupation troops, the war was nearly over, or we'd go to the Pacific. That was all a crock of shit, so don't count on this being over until they all surrender. Hell, they're even talking about the krauts fighting on in the mountains and woods after we capture the rest of the country, so who knows what's going to happen."

"Well, so far we haven't even seen any Germans except the Wehrmacht, but we're not very far into the country either," I replied. "I don't know what they mean by not fraternizing with them, I mean, I don't want to be buddy-buddy with the bastards, but we'll have to talk to them, at least enough to get information or tell 'em what to do. Are we supposed to pretend they don't exist?"

"I think they mean you're not to shack up with them or sit around drinking beer with 'em. I bet that won't last long. Once you turn a bunch of Americans loose in this country they'll be talking to everyone and his brother," Robarge opined.

"Well, it looks like we're ready to go," I interjected as the engines of the lead vehicle started and Samuels signaled for us to follow.

We moved slowly down a grade where the road curved around a hillside covered with dense forest until we emerged near the little river we had seen from the observation post. The land near the stream was apparently used for farming, but the fields were pockmarked by craters from artillery shells and bombs. The river was larger than it appeared from a distance, a roiling, dark brown, rush of water surging high against its muddy banks, swollen almost to flood stage by snow melt and rain. We crossed the torrent on a Bailey bridge which the engineers had just completed. This necessary preliminary to our passage explained our wait in Harperscheid and presaged more delays to our pursuit of the retreating Germans. The heavily damaged road wound along the base of the hills on the east side of the river, from where one could better appreciate the massive fortifications dug into the rocky slope and buttressed by concrete bastions. Suddenly the column stopped just as we were about to enter Schleiden, and our jeep came to rest next to a large gate which was designed much like a railroad crossing gate except it was constructed of heavy gauge steel rather than wood and light iron straps. Apparently the gate was used to control traffic entering or leaving Schleiden, for it could be locked into place by a heavy latch. This guardian of the town was open, suggesting that it was not part of the military defense of Schleiden, but the idea of a town gate in the 20th century intrigued me.

"Sarge, I wonder why they have that big gate at the entrance to the town," I said idly.

"Beats the hell out of me. Maybe Hitler knew we'd come for him some day," Robarge replied with a wry grin.

Still fascinated by the gate I walked over to it, felt the heavy bar and stanchion, and let my eyes wander down to a handle protruding from the gatepost. This mighty control seemed to be made for the hand of a giant, and without thinking I reached out, grasped the great handle, and pulled with all my strength. It squeaked out a couple of inches revealing a shaft the size of a railroad rail extending into the gatepost.

"Jesus Christ, Holme, what did you expect, gum?" Robarge exploded. "This whole damned place is full of mines, we're not supposed to touch anything, so you have to pull a damned lever that could have been connected to all the TNT in town."

"I'm sorry, Sarge, I didn't think," I muttered ruefully.

"Well, for a smart guy you sure pick some damned poor times not to think. We're lucky the krauts don't know enough about Americans to realize that some guy would have to pull that thing."

Our conversation was interrupted by a dull boom from the other end of town. We looked at one another and Robarge shrugged.

"I suppose some guy pulled the wrong handle up there. Hell, I wouldn't even pick up money off the ground in this damned place," he added.

Soon we got the word that two engineers had been killed while bridging a small stream at the other end of the town. They had started to move a piece of debris and detonated a mine which had not been detected by their sensing devices. In spite of this incident the work progressed rapidly and we soon passed through the shattered remains of the town and then out of the valley. As we reached the top of the gentle grade we were again enveloped by the evergreen forest, a somber cloak of dark green split only by the narrow road that disappeared into the veil of gray mist. Our slow progress allowed full appreciation of the carnage wrought by our air force on the retreating Germans. Shattered vehicles and the bodies of horses and gray clad soldiers were strewn along the road at frequent intervals. Most of the wreckage was on the shoulder or in the ditch where the Germans had been caught while seeking refuge from strafing aircraft.

We stopped at the first crossroad, where Lt. Parker conferred with his sergeants. When Robarge returned he said we were to proceed while Samuel's section scouted to the right and Nelson's to the left. A squat little man with a mine detector had tagged along after the sergeant and stood waiting while he talked to the section.

"This is Louie," Robarge said, pointing to the diminutive soldier. "He's an engineer, and he'll sit on the hood of our jeep and watch for signs of mines. When he signals, you stop, Holme, and he'll check with the detector before we drive ahead. That means we go damned slow, and Reardon, you and Henry stay awake and don't run into us when we stop."

We crept forward with Louie perched on the hood so that I could only see part of the road. I hoped that he was paying attention, but somehow I felt more uneasy than I would have if the responsibility for spotting suspicious areas in the road had rested with me. In fairness, Louie signaled frequently and dutifully hopped off the hood and swept the mine detector over questionable spots. He would conclude each search with a grin and shout "No damned mines" as he climbed back onto the hood.

Less than half a mile past the intersection we encountered the gruesome remains of a larger German convoy than those we had passed before. The men and horses had not been dead very long, and one of the ditched vehicles was a half track with a rack of rocket launchers.

"No more screamin' Mimis from him," Robarge observed, and then, "Hey, Louie, what're you doing?"

"I'm jus' gettin' some loot," Louie replied. "Jesus Christ, da kwauts got some nice stuff."

The little man was waving his detector over the bodies and then began a feverish search of the corpses. Robarge's face was a mixture of disgust and rage as Louie retrieved a couple of watches and was eagerly going for more.

"Louis, you little bastard, get your ass on this jeep and let's get going. We're not here to steal from dead krauts," the sergeant roared.

"Don't get mad, Sarge. If we don't get this stuff da wear echelon guys'll get it all," Louie explained. "Oh shit, you know what? I jus' noticed, I di'n't have da damned detector turned on, lucky we di'n't hit a fuckin' mine. Got her on now, so weady to go."

Robarge looked at me with an expression of incredulity, and for once he was speechless. Finally he snarled, "If you're really sure that damned thing is turned on, we'll start."

Louie nodded, and we crept forward into even denser fog. Only the eerie shapes of the fir trees loomed out of the murk on either side of the road; we seemed to be moving through a ghostly world of our own that was isolated from all the rest of creation.

More to break the unearthly spell of our surroundings than to make sensible conversation I commented idly, "I wonder how long until we catch up to the krauts?"

"At the rate we're going we'll never catch 'em, and that's fine with me," Robarge replied. "What's your hurry to catch them anyway? I just wish they'd wise up and quit."

Before I could answer that I was not anxious to overtake the Germans, the M8's siren sounded briefly, and we stopped to see what was wrong. Indy yelled, "We're to wait here for the other sections, Sarge. OK if we eat?"

"Might as well, it's better than trying to eat while we're moving and everyone is looking for krauts and mines. It's one thirty and I'm hungry enough to even eat the damned K rations," the sergeant grumbled.

The cold, tasteless glop seemed fit for the mood of the dark forest. We munched silently while peering into the fog, uneasy about whatever perils lay concealed beneath its cover. I could barely control a tendency to shiver now that I was not concentrating on driving and Louie's signals. When the other sections arrived we resumed our advance until we came to the next crossroads. A tiny hamlet was situated on the far side of a clearing to the left of the highway, but to the right the road disappeared into the foggy forest without a hint of any human presence. Parker sent Nelson's section to the left to reconnoiter the hamlet and the forest beyond and ordered us to scout the road to the right for at least half a mile or until we contacted other troops. Louie rejoined Samuel's section on the main road, so we had to watch for mines on our own, a chore I was glad to assume after a morning with the tongue tied little engineer.

We had only gone about a quarter of a mile when Robarge exclaimed, "Hold it, Holme. There's someone up there at the edge of the woods. I'm sure I saw a couple of men duck down as they spotted us."

Turning to the armored car he added, "Hilton, cover us with the .50 caliber. Ostrander and I are going to walk up ahead and see who those guys are."

The figures seemed to have vanished into the mist and trees as we trudged along the road, and my shivering increased at the thought of a possible German machine gunner about to cut us down.

"Who are you?" Robarge shouted. "We're Americans, 28th Recon. Come out if you're Americans."

Cautiously two and then half a dozen men emerged from the woods and I was relieved to see that they were GI's. Neither group relaxed their vigilance, however, until we were only 50 feet apart and more confident of each other's identity. Germans had impersonated Americans often enough to make us wary of anyone in disputed territory.

"69th Division infantry," the nearest man announced. "You never know where the lines are when the krauts take off like that. Glad to see you boys and not some damned Jerries. I figured you had to be Americans with the armored car and jeeps, but you can't be too careful."

The speaker seemed to be the leader of the little group of soldiers, but he was very young, probably no more than 20 or 21. Neither he nor any of the others wore signs of rank, and I was surprised when one man addressed the leader as "lieutenant." I didn't blame him for shunning his bars in combat; the Germans took special pains to pick off officers and noncoms and thus gain advantage over leaderless foes.

We parted from the infantrymen after reporting the contact and receiving orders to rejoin the advance on the main road. As we settled into a slow crawl through the gloomy and seemingly endless forest my shivers got worse in spite of the distraction of driving and my conscious efforts to control the embarrassing shakes.

"You getting sick, Holme?" Robarge asked.

"No, I'm just cold, I guess. I don't know why I'm shaking," I muttered.

"At the next stop I'll drive for a while, and you wrap up in a blanket."

I didn't argue when Robarge insisted on switching places and soon felt better with a blanket around me. Only my feet continued to pain, a pair of numb, prickly, burning stumps, or so it seemed from the sensations I could feel. They had been wet all day because of our constant movements in and out of the jeep, and for the same reason I could not use overshoes. While I gained a modicum of comfort in the blanket, I noticed that Robarge was shaking sporadically too. In a way I was relieved to know that I was not the only shivering weak sister. I insisted on driving at the next stop so that he could warm up in the blanket too.

"You know, Holme, it must be nerves or something. We've been in a lot colder places, but there's something about this damned forest that gives me the creeps," the sergeant confessed.

I nodded agreement. "I hope we find some place to crawl into for the night. I'd hate to sleep out in this stuff."

It was already getting dark when we entered a clearing where a village once stood. Only rubble and a few irregular sections of walls miraculously still upright marked the site of the hamlet. There was no sign of civilians, no domestic animals or anything else to signify that the place had once been a living community. We stopped amid the debris and waited for the order to advance. After what seemed a very long time but was probably no more than 20 minutes the vehicles ahead started their engines and the procession crept ahead until we seemed to be on the edge of a swamp. Robarge got out and conferred with Lt. Parker and several officers from the infantry who were following us in trucks.

When he stalked back in several minutes his face was a picture of cynical disgust. "They want us to drive through that, Holme. One jeep made it, they say it's not too bad, but I don't like it. Well, the lieutenant says go, so I guess we go."

With a surfeit of advice from officers and noncoms, to say nothing of Robarge, I put the jeep into low gear and four wheel drive and ground forward into the bog, where the water was above the hubcaps. The little vehicle chugged ahead, and I thought we would make it, when suddenly the front dropped and we stalled with the water to the top of the hood. Robarge cursed, and the chorus on the bank emitted a cacophony of orders, oaths, and obscenities, but regardless of the noise, the jeep was going nowhere without help.

After more confusion on the bank, Parker shouted, "Robarge, you and Ostrander stay there, a tank is coming to pull the vehicles across. He'll drag you outta that damned mudhole."

"He needn't worry," Robarge muttered. "I'm not going to try to swim to shore."

"I'm sorry, Sarge, I thought we had it, but I must have hit a hole," I said contritely.

"You're good at finding all the holes in the road, but I didn't know you could spot them under water too. Hell, it isn't your fault, the first guy was lucky, nobody can tell where there might be drop offs in this damned swamp. We're probably lucky it's not over our heads."

Further conversation was impossible as an M4 tank lumbered into the quagmire and maneuvered around in front of us. One of the crew dropped a large hook at the end of a steel cable into the water and another fearless soul attached it to the front bumper.

"Now we'll find out how strong that bumper is; it'll probably come flying out and the jeep'll stay here," Robarge fretted. "I sure as hell would hate to be the poor bastard who stands in the water to hook us up. Jesus, I thought they'd snap it on the rear and pull us back, then hook it to the frame and haul us across. I hope that damned cable doesn't break, it could snap around hard enough to take our heads off."

Under the stimulus of the sergeant's concerns my shakes started again only to be forgotten when the jeep shuddered and then moved forward and out of the bog behind the roaring tank. To our astonishment the little workhorse started and seemed none the worse for its immersion in the muddy water. Gradually all the vehicles were dragged across the swamp, and the column reformed to move a short distance beyond the crossing. It was now completely dark, and mine detection was impossible without the use of lights, which would make us targets for any stray German aircraft or a patrol sent to cover the retreat. Parker ordered us to pull onto the shoulder and stop, but to my surprise several six-bys of infantry drove past and parked in front of us on the shoulder. I wondered if this meant that we would stop here for the night because the trucks had always stayed well back in the convoy during our daylong advance. I decided that the infantry were now drawn up to aid in the night security of the force.

The officers met in a low building about 50 feet from the road, where I supposed they would decide whether to continue the advance in the dark regardless of risk or to wait for dawn. The armored car was parked no more than six feet behind my jeep, but there was little conversation while we waited for a decision from our commanders. The night was very dark without a hint of moon or stars, but soon a breeze began to blow, and a few wet snowflakes landed on my face as I sat numbly at the wheel of the still jeep. The same fatigue that immobilized me apparently affected the other men in the force as well. It was unnaturally quiet for such a large number of soldiers, a forbidding sort of silence. Robarge had gone to the door of the shed so that he could be one of the first to know the decision. He was still propelled by the same nervous energy that seemed to allow him to function with so little rest. Nearly every other man in the force sat huddled where he could, resting from the long and wearing day and trying to renew his strength for whatever the night and morning might bring, but the sergeant moved about constantly and fussed about the uncertainties of our situation.

I had dozed off into a fitful sleep when Robarge shook me. While I was gathering my wits about me he awoke the others and quietly told us to start the engines. "We lead, so pull up onto the road and past those six-bys. They'll move up enough so you can get past them.

I edged the jeep forward as the truck ahead moved on the shoulder to give me room. Suddenly a tremendous explosion and a blinding flash of flame rent the night before my startled eyes. I slammed on the brakes and screamed at Reardon to stop the armored car. I had an awful vision of the M8 shoving me forward into the inferno of fire and heat that was already consuming the truck. The armored car stopped a foot behind the jeep as flames shot forty feet in the air from the stricken six-by. Dark figures struggled to escape the flames and some were afire as they leaped from the rear of the truck. Other infantrymen quickly extinguished the flames of the human torches once they were clear of the vehicle. I sat transfixed, gazing at the horror unleashed on one truck load of infantry when their six-by struck a mine. It seemed as though I was hypnotized by the sudden noise and light in what had been a world of silent darkness.

The spell was broken when I heard Lt. Parker's voice, "Where's Ostrander, are your men all right, Robarge? What happened?"

"Our men are OK, lieutenant," the sergeant shouted. "Ostrander was behind a six-by that hit a mine, but he wasn't hurt. I gotta help these men," as he moved toward the blazing truck.

He returned almost immediately when he realized that the other infantrymen had come to the aid of their comrades and carried the wounded into the shed. The officers reconvened their meeting while the rest of us waited and stared at the burning truck. Ammunition in the six-by exploded intermittently, but no additional injuries were incurred. After the uproar that accompanied the explosion the scene reverted to silence except for crackles, snaps, and hisses from the rapidly dwindling flames. I tried to put the horror and shock of the blast out of my mind, but it seemed I could not think of anything else as I sat woodenly with my eyes fixed on the truck. I don't know how much time had passed when I heard Robarge again.

"Holme, are you all right? You better wrap up in that blanket and get some sleep, we're not moving out until dawn. It's probably better to sleep in the jeep than on the ground. There's not even enough room for the officers in that shed, and there's nowhere else to sleep around here."

"Where are you going to sleep?" I asked.

"I got a spot picked out on the back deck of the armored car that nobody else seems to want, and I can keep an eye on things from up there," he replied.

I suspected he would do more watching than sleeping, but I was too tired to think about what anyone else did and quickly fell into a restless sleep. I had repetitive wild dreams of the truck exploding and flaming men leaping about. I must have talked or mumbled all night, because the armored car crew said I was pretty noisy, but I remember that whenever I awoke I felt wet snow flakes on my face and heard other men moaning or talking in their sleep.

I was glad to move about at the first light of dawn to dispel the stiffness and aches that seemed to encase my body. I felt better as I flexed my arms and legs and beat my arms against my body to restore the circulation. Even the K ration breakfast was welcome, although I had hardly finished the stuff when we were ordered to move out. Even in the daylight I felt a clammy fear as Robarge and one of the engineers signaled me to drive forward and up onto the pavement.

We drove through a countryside of rocky, barren fields and tiny hamlets where we saw numerous German civilians for the first time. They gazed at us impassively, neither friendly nor overtly hostile. Almost every house had a white sheet or other makeshift surrender flag hanging from a window. Civilians seemed to be unanimously in favor of surrender.

"What happened to the GI's in the truck?" I asked.

Robarge grimaced as he replied, "The kid sitting over the gas tank got a load of hot metal up his ass and was sprayed by burning gas, he died almost as soon as they got him into the shed. A couple of others were in bad shape; they sent 'em back to the rear. The rest were just a little singed and scared as hell, so they're still with the rest of the infantry."

We said no more about it and concentrated on the road and countryside. There were many hastily strewn mines on the highway, so progress was slow, but our spirits revived when we approached a sizable town bedecked with so many white banners that we started to laugh.

"Maybe this is the day the kraut women air their bedding," Robarge chuckled. "At least it's not raining or snowing, so they won't have to sleep in wet beds tonight."

The sergeant was right, the weather had improved. The fog was entirely gone and the flurries had ended, but it was still chilly and overcast, although far less depressing than the conditions of the day before. According to a road sign the town was Blankenheim, the first inhabited place of any size we had encountered in Germany. The column stopped in the center of the town while the officers huddled, a lull that gave me an opportunity to appreciate what a picturesque place it was. We were parked in front of a large building on the central square that looked like a medieval castle, and narrow cobblestone streets led away between half timbered houses that looked as I had always imagined Germany should. A few bold civilians sidled past and looked sideways at the invaders of their land, but the fraternization ban was not tested during this first encounter between soldiers and civilians. Each side scanned the other with curiosity, but there was no attempt at conversation. During the wait we ate our noon K rations and sauntered around the vehicles, but everyone remained alert for a sudden hostile act. Pickets were posted at key points and the column was prepared for any sort of attack.

When Parker returned he summoned his sergeants and began explaining our next missions while tracing lines on his map that was spread on the hood of a jeep. Robarge and Nelson carefully checked their maps against the lieutenant's, and when they were satisfied that they understood the assignment returned to their sections.

"They want us to go as far as we can this way," Robarge said as he spread his map and pointed to a squiggly line leading from Blankenheim to a series of lesser places. "A tank section and a couple of squads of infantry will follow, but we're to reconnoiter as far as we can and not wait for them. They think the krauts have left or are ready to surrender up there, but nobody knows for sure. I guess I don't have to tell anyone to look out for mines; a couple of engineers will go with us to check out suspicious places on the road."

The mine experts rode in the jeep with Robarge and me, where they perched atop the box of mortar shells we carried in the back seat. If we happened to hit a mine there would not have been pieces big enough to identify us, so I was determined to drive with extreme caution. In casual conversation the pair seemed much more capable and sensible than Louie, so I felt somewhat more secure than I had the day before.

Our first task was to find the road from Blankenheim to the villages that were our target. All roads looked alike, and there were no signs pointing the way to such insignificant places, so we had not the slightest idea which of several byways meandering from the town would lead us to our destination. Finally we pulled up near a man walking on the sidewalk, and I called to him. He responded promptly and greeted us with a barrage of German that was much too rapid for me to understand. He seemed friendly, a smiling, gray haired fellow about 60 in a worn dark brown suit and an even more decrepit tan topcoat. I explained our problem as well as I could in my halting German and showed him where we wanted to go on the map. He thought for a moment while studying the map and then carefully and slowly told us exactly how to get on the right road. I thanked him, and he responded to my "danke schön" with a dignified "bitte schön". Robarge offered him a cigarette, and he responded with a broad grin and an emphatic "danke schön".

We drove away from Blankenheim on a paved road that was dotted with water filled pot holes. We had no way of knowing what might be hidden in the puddles, so I drove slowly and cautiously around all potential hazards. Enough unconcealed mines were scattered along the road and its shoulders to convince us that the danger was real, and the engineers examined all suspicious spots that we could not bypass. Some of the mines were wooden box types, a design meant to thwart the metal detector type mine locating equipment. These devices were in containers that resembled Kraft cheese boxes, but because of their oblong shape they were more difficult to conceal quickly in a pot hole than the round metal "teller" or dish mines. Still, the presence of the wooden mines added to my anxiety, and I could tell that the engineers were as uneasy as Robarge and I. We managed to drive around or straddle all the mines and suspicious spots we encountered, a fortunate circumstance because moving such devices could be as dangerous as driving over them. Many were set to explode when lifted as well as with compression, a simple adjustment for even a novice explosives man.

While the drivers were paying strict attention to the road everyone else was on the alert for any sign of ambush, but the countryside was peaceful and deserted for the most part. We stopped twice at tiny hamlets to check our position, but the civilians remained inside their dwellings. The next place was at the junction with another road, where we were to turn left and cross a small stream that we had been following for several miles. After passing over a bridge we were to ascend a gentle grade on the opposite side of the valley where a village was visible just below the crest of the rise. This hamlet and another just out of sight beyond the hill top were our destinations, so that our mission would be complete after we reconnoitered these places.

The community at the road intersection seemed to be slightly more important than the first two hamlets and boasted a few more houses, a store, and some sort of small official looking building. We halted a few yards short of the bridge while the engineers inspected it for mines and structural strength. While we waited, a stocky man of about 50 came out of the official looking building and presented himself to us. He recognized rank and addressed his rapid stream of German to the sergeant. He seemed baffled by Robarge's enigmatic smile and his casual motion for the man to direct his remarks to me.

I told him to speak more slowly, and then I got the drift of what he had to say. He was the burgomaster of the village and insisted that he was no Nazi, a claim that was very questionable in view of his official position. Still, at the moment we had little interest in whether individuals were party members or not so long as they were cooperative.

One of the engineers interrupted to say, "Sarge, I don't know about that bridge. We get a lot of metal on the detector, it seems like too much for just bridge bolts, but I don't know. Do you think this guy can tell us if it's mined?"

"Let's try him. Holme, ask his honor if the damned bridge is mined."

I put the question to the burgomaster. He paused momentarily and then asserted emphatically that the bridge was free of mines. However, there was a furtive, deceitful air about the burgomaster that was more than just the unattractive appearance of his fat, unshaven face.

"I don't believe him," Robarge countered when I told him what the man had said. "Tell the old sucker we'll shoot him if the bridge is mined; see what he says to that."

I relayed the sergeant's threat, whereupon the man became visibly upset and began to protest that he was only a civilian and did not know about such military matters. He explained further what a good family man he was, a simple peasant, and then he equivocated by saying that the bridge was not mined as far as he knew, a different story from his first assertion.

"Now he says it's not mined as far as he knows, Sarge. I bet there's not much that goes on around here that he doesn't know."

"Tell the son of a bitch to get on the hood of your jeep and ride across the bridge with us."

The visibly frightened burgomaster reluctantly climbed onto the jeep and settled himself, but when I started the engine he shouted, "Nein, nein, minen, verstehen sie? Minen!"

I understood all too well. The memory of the night and all its horror coupled with my fatigue and emotional tension must have combined to provoke me to sudden rage. I sprang from the jeep, grabbed the German by his coat collar, hurled him off the hood, and had my carbine cocked and the safety released and was bringing it around to shoot the deceitful man when Robarge caught my arm.

"Easy, Holme, we can't do that. I feel the same way, I'd just as soon see him splattered on the pavement too, but we can't do that."

"Aw, Sarge, you shoulda let him shoot the bastard," Indy yelled from the armored car. "That old sucker woulda stood there and laughed while we were blown to hell and gone."

The two engineers added their passionate endorsements to Indy's plea for execution, but after we cooled down all agreed that Robarge was right.

The burgomaster, meanwhile, stood with his mouth agape, trembling like a leaf and probably wondering if his death had been canceled or merely postponed.

"What do you want to do with him?" I snarled.

"Have him stand right next to the bridge while we work on it. If there's some trick gadget maybe he'll know about it. If she blows, he goes too!"

The engineers removed the first two planks of the bridge under the fearful eye of the burgomaster, their unwilling overseer.

"Jesus Christ, look at this," one engineer exclaimed. "The damned krauts wired two 88 shells under here, why there's enough TNT there to blow a tank up into the air."

I held my breath while the engineers skillfully deactivated the device and deposited the shells in a nearby field. When they had completed the job, the burgomaster stumbled away toward his office, a pale and shaken man. We crossed the bridge and found the road to the top of the ridge far better than our previous route. There were no mines or suspicious areas as we approached the first village. There were about 15 houses in the hamlet, and the road turned sharply to the left in front of a house with a large stack of hay in the front yard. The streets were empty, the only signs of habitation were the white "flags" hanging from the windows. With our weapons at the ready we moved through the hamlet and quickly covered the last half mile to the larger village at the summit. There the street was full of Wehrmacht men standing abjectly in groups behind their neatly stacked arms and helmets. The white banners completed the picture of surrender for at least 200 German soldiers. A smaller number of black uniformed Volksturm troops, the home guard, wandered about looking confused and even more dejected than the Wehrmacht men. The Volksturm consisted mostly of older men and teenage boys, but a few military age men with disabilities also found their way into this sorry militia.

The leader of the German troops, a captain who bore a striking resemblance to Robarge, nodded his agreement when I told him that the main body of our force would arrive soon to accept his surrender. I emphasized the overwhelming strength of our units to discourage any inclination the Germans might have to reconsider their surrender and slaughter our puny 10 man force. From their demeanor, however, we were quite sure that this Wehrmacht group had their fill of war and probably could not be enticed into further combat whatever the odds.

Having completed our reconnaissance we returned to the previous village where Robarge had spotted an attractive house where we could rest while awaiting further orders. We also thought we would feel more comfortable without several hundred German soldiers surrounding us. We had parked the vehicles and were walking toward the door of the house when two shots rang out, and bullets ricocheted off the armored car.

"Goddamit, just when I thought we were safe," Robarge exclaimed. "Where in hell did those come from?"

"The hay stack, Sarge," Caulkins snapped while crouching behind the M8.

"We could give it a blast with the .50 caliber, but those slugs would go right through that house and maybe kill the people inside," the sergeant said. "I bet it's a couple of crazy kids. Those shots were more like a .22 than a regular army rifle."

"They can kill you, too," Caulkins replied.

"Yeah, I'm not as worried about the Germans in that house as I am about getting shot," I added. "We ought to just blast them."

"We'll be OK in the house," Robarge insisted. "Indy, find out how close the tanks are. Those guys will come out when the tanks show up, and nobody will get hurt."

"The tanks are close, Sarge. They'll be here in about 20 minutes," Indy announced from the armored car.

"OK, duck down and get inside the house, we'll wait for them," the sergeant ordered.

Inside we warmed ourselves by a gorgeous stove, and Robarge brewed some strong coffee. Our obligate hostess, a middle aged woman in black clothes, had retreated to her parlor as soon as we entered the kitchen, but she peeked around the door from time to time to see what sort of mischief the Americans were perpetrating. After he warmed up with a cup of coffee and relaxed with a smoke, Robarge's face lit up with a roguish smile.

"Let's give the lady a cup of real coffee, she probably hasn't had any in years. If she's enjoying a cup of coffee maybe she'll be less apt to toss a grenade in here."

The poor woman seemed almost to dissolve in her anxiety when I carried a mug of coffee to her and told her it was a gift from the sergeant. "Danke schön", she murmured as I handed it to her. Then I saw pictures of a middle aged man and a young man on the table. Both wore Wehrmacht uniforms and the frames were rimmed in black. As I stared she whispered, "Mein mann und mein sohn, tod gefallen in Russland."

She seemed the picture of grief and dejection, and she clearly expected the worst in spite of my attempts to reassure her. I felt a surge of pity for the pathetic woman and then began to realize how difficult it would be to maintain an objective attitude toward the Germans. Only a little while earlier I had wanted to shoot the treacherous burgomaster, but now I felt like crying for the sorrowing widow.

"How's our hostess like the coffee, Holme?"

"She seems to like it, but she's scared to death and about as sad as any person I've ever seen. She lost both her husband and her son in Russia."

"Yeah, I guess these people have had a tough ——"

The crack of an artillery shell followed quickly by another interrupted the sergeant's sentence. The straw stack and half the house behind it were gone as two tanks clanked into the hamlet.

"You guys don't fool around," Robarge called to the tank commander.

"Why didn't you guys blow the bastards outta there yourselves?" the tanker asked.

"We thought they were probably some kids and they'd surrender when the tanks showed up. We didn't want to harm the people in that house either, the sergeant explained.

"Whoever they were, they were as crazy as hell. They shot at us, so I say to hell with 'em," the man replied. "I'm not taking any chances on some lunatic Nazi killing me when the damned war's nearly over. Shoot first, I say."

We cautiously poked through the rubble where the 76mm shells had wrought havoc, and, as Robarge had suspected, found the bodies of two young boys in Volksturm uniforms. They had ancient sporting rifles and a small cache of grenades.

"God, this war is shitty," the sergeant muttered as we turned back toward the widow's house.

A few minutes later we were ordered back to Blankenheim. The return trip was almost as slow as our advance because the road was still mined, and we couldn't assume that hostile Germans had not planted a few more since we had passed earlier. When we reached the town we found troop headquarters in the large castle-like building on the central square. Second and third platoons were billeted in adjacent houses on a nearby side street. We were the last section to return from patrol, and to nobody's surprise the mess had not bothered to save any hot food for us. It was getting dark as we heated C rations in a crowded room of a dingy house. Then the world brightened as Fergie, the mailman, entered with letters for everyone. In addition to the welcome mail from home he was the first to tell us that the Americans had captured a bridge across the Rhine at Remagen. I felt overwhelmed by so much good news at one time, but then I got so sleepy that I couldn't stay awake to read more than a couple of my nearly fifty letters.

When I woke in the morning, I realized that I couldn't even remember the contents of the letters I had read, so I had the pleasant prospect of reading my mail, eating a hot breakfast, and cleaning up after several weeks of fairly continuous action. When I looked out the window my spirits soared even higher because I saw the sun shining on the quaint houses of the old town, and I hoped I would have some time to explore the place.

8

CIVILIANS

So far as we could tell from radio reports we were far behind the armored units dashing for the Rhine. Our duties in Blankenheim and the surrounding countryside were either unknown or seemed so ill-defined that I optimistically hoped for a period of rest and sightseeing. The town was dominated by the castle-like structure on the central square, which now housed troop headquarters, the kitchen, and part of supply. The motor pool was quartered in a nearby garage, which had a large parking area, so that the entire troop was in close contact, a mixed blessing as it turned out. The men in our section would have preferred an assignment away from the troop where we would have been free from many petty irritations. The "old boys" were still insulting when not hostile, and men such as Glowacki, Cook, Samuels and most of the officers were tiresome bores, but on the positive side we could get hot meals and regular mail when near headquarters.

The fraternization ban was a hindrance to enjoyment of the town for several reasons. It obviously impeded the pursuit of female company, but I was sure the rules would be circumvented in that case by one means or another. In addition it prevented inquiries about the town's history, architecture and usual activities, the tourist type of interests. While one could easily arrange a clandestine meeting with a woman, a soldier would be in immediate trouble if he engaged a citizen of the town in conversation about the buildings on the central square.

I had learned from Ike Herzberg, a German speaking sergeant in the second platoon, that the castle-like building was the city hall, but he had been unable to learn more about the place. I was sure it had a more glorious history than "rathaus" for such a small town. I regretted that I had no camera to photograph points of interest including the building on the square, even though the medieval air of the latter was marred by three garbage cans, a half track, and an armored car distributed before its majestic walls. Narrow streets flanked by a jumble of half timbered houses led from the square. Near the center of the town the first floor of each building was usually given over to some retail business such as bakery, clothier, dry goods, grocery and the like, while the upstairs appeared to be living quarters for the merchants and their families. As one walked farther toward the edge of town the houses were smaller and often included a barn or other out building. The larger residences seemed to house more than one family, but such details were uncertain without talking to the townspeople.

I saw no men of military age on the streets, and most of the pedestrians were women and children. A few middle aged or elderly men walked about and posed a problem because they wanted to talk, invariably prefacing their self introduction with cither "nicht Nazi" or "I have a cousin in Milwaukee" (or some other American city). I did not want to appear either rude or stupid, but neither did I want to run afoul of regulations, so I deflected these overtures with a nod and a smile while retreating from the garrulous codgers. The Germans always looked puzzled and often countered by additional protestations of their innocence of Nazi sympathies. By the time I had circled the town I had to chuckle to myself at the miracle of German war making might in the face of a citizenry that overwhelmingly opposed Hitler and his party.

When I mentioned that among a group of recon men Henry observed tartly, "Yeah, you're as likely to hear a kraut say he's a Nazi as you are to hear a boy admit that he farted in church. I can't understand the lingo, but I know every bastard I meet is trying to tell me he's not a Nazi."

"They're the biggest bunch of brown nosers I've ever seen," Hank Bryant added. "Ike and I were walking around, and he said some of them were trying to get in good by squealing on their neighbors. It's always the guy next door or up the street who's the Nazi."

"Well, all I gotta say is let's shoot all the men, rape all the women, plunder the town and carry the children off into bondage," Weiner exclaimed with a giddy cackle.

"I haven't seen any woman I'd care to rape or anything I want to steal," Robarge laughed.

"Aw, Sarge, you just want to spoil the fun," Indy replied. "What's a war without sacking a few towns? We haven't had a chance to kick up our heels since we've been over here. Hell, we deserve to plunder at least one little place like this!"

Everyone guffawed at Indy's deadpan presentation of his outrageous proposal, and the hilarity attracted Lou Cook to the cluster of troopers.

"God damn, boys, I do like to hear the troops afunnin' around, 'n' ol' Lou's got a little story that'll make you laugh some more even if it's on me. You all notice that lil' ol' blond headed gal with the big boobies an' a ass that moves like it's on a universal joint, the one that lives in the house we're in?"

A dozen heads nodded as one and a voice piped up, "Hell yes, Lou, we ain't blind!"

When the snickers died down Cook continued, "Well, let me tell you about her, 'n' I want your advice. Last night I liberated a little schnapps from some ol' boy up the street, got to feelin' mighty good, 'n' whadda you know, I bump into this lil ol' gal as she was ascootin' outa the house with some of her stuff. Hell, I'm just an ol' country boy, don't speak no German or nothin', but that don't make no difference to her, I reckon, 'cause she just takes me by the arm, gigglin' like a school girl all the while, 'n' before I know what's happenin' I'm in her bedroom in the house across the street, she has my pants down, 'n' is playin' with mah peter. The schnapps is havin' its way about then, 'n' ol' Lou ain't much of a Romeo, but that don't make no difference to ol' Gertrude, that's her name."

He paused and smiled slyly, savoring the rapt attention of his audience, before he continued.

"Well, one thing leads to another, and before I knew it Gertrude blew me three times. Now would you believe this, when ol' Lou got his strength back enough to leave, I kissed her goodnight. Now, I just want to ask you boys, does that make ol' Lou a cocksucker by proxie?"

The troopers hung on every word of Cook's story, but the ending caught them by surprise, so that for a moment not a word was uttered, and then a nervous titter moved through the crowd, gradually swelling into ribald snorts and belly laughs. Cook was as pleased as a peacock by the response to his tale and stood beaming at his audience.

Finally one man asked what others surely were thinking, "Is that really true, Lou?"

Feigning a hurt expression Cook replied, "Well God damn, brother, ol' Lou don't lie about his drinkin' or his fuckin', an' that's a fact. May the good Lord strike me dead on the spot if that ain't the truth, but I gotta admit, I'd ask the same as you if some ol' boy told me that story. One other thing, that lil ol' gal found out why they call me lucious Lou," and with that he left.

"Jesus Christ, Holme, we've got more characters in this outfit than in a movie," Robarge muttered in disgust.

"Do you believe that tale or is he just kidding everyone?" I asked.

"Who knows," Robarge replied. "With Cook you never know when he's telling the truth or lying. From what I've seen of that dame swinging her ass at everyone it wouldn't take much to get her into a bedroom."

Just then Caulkins, a mischievous grin lighting his face, joined the group of idlers. "We got new replacements, I just saw them over by headquarters. They're right from the States and we might even get one."

"What's so funny about that?" Robarge replied. "We're almost straight from the States ourselves."

"I think these old boys are more stateside than we were, but you'll have to see for yourselves."

"How many are there?" I asked.

"Two."

"Two! Is that all? Is this some kind of joke, DJ?"

"They look like bad jokes, but like I said, you gotta see for yourselves."

"What's so damned funny about these two guys?" Robarge asked, a tone of annoyance in his voice. "Hell, nobody looks like much after that trip from the repo depot."

"Well, there's one little scrawny boy, looks to be about 13 years old, his clothes are too big for him, and he can hardly carry his M1. The other's sort of a fat boy, looks to be older, had his coat buttoned up wrong and nearly fell on his face getting out of the six-by. These boys may be better than they look, but I doubt it."

"With our luck we'll get both of 'em," Robarge replied. "We need some help, make it easier on guard and missions, but we don't need someone we have to wet nurse."

Later at dinner I eagerly anticipated a look at the new men, but even when I hung around headquarters after the meal I saw no sign of the pair DJ had described. As I was about to leave Sgt. Hinkle walked out of the ornate entrance of the castle-headquarters.

"Sarge," I said, "I hear we have a couple of replacements."

Looking off toward the half-timbered houses across the square, now bathed in the mellow golden rays of the setting sun, Hinkle let a smile soften his weather beaten face and drawled, "Yeah, division sent us a couple of boys the 112th couldn't use. They're kinda wore out from the trip, so I told 'em to sack in."

"You mean the infantry didn't want them?" I asked with a note of incredulity in my voice.

"Well, I wouldn't exactly put it that way, but they didn't seem to fit in there," the first sergeant responded, a grin spreading over his rugged features.

"What'll they do here? Are they trained as cavalry?"

"No, but we'll see what they're good at. Might try 'em out in platoons, haven't decided yet."

I was dumbfounded by Hinkle's comments about the new duo, and after digesting the gist of what he had said I weakly bade the first sergeant good night and returned to our crowded billet.

My comrades were as shocked as I when I told them about my conversation with Hinkle.

"Oh Cob, I just hope we don't get them," Caulkins declared.

"Well, we'll get at least one," Robarge said. "Our section has been three men short for a long time, worse off than most of the others, but it won't help if we get some guy who's no good."

"Did Hinkle say what's wrong with these guys?" Gorlitz asked. "Maybe they're OK but have bad feet and can't march or something like that."

"I don't think it's their feet, it's the other end that's bad, they're sad sacks," Caulkins said emphatically.

"Hinkle didn't exactly say it, but from the way he looked he doesn't think they're worth a shit," I added. "He could hardly keep from laughing when he said they might try 'em in platoons."

Hilton looked at me and laughed, "Sarge really belongs in the M8, and then you can have one of these new guys for a buddy in your jeep, Leon."

Before I could express my distaste for this idea Samuels approached. "Hey, Robarge, the lieutenant wants to see you, we got a little job for your section," he chortled with a sly grin.

"I wonder what the son of a bitch wants us to do now," Reardon grumbled to me.

"Probably wants a Gertrude or two and some of that schnapps Cook was talking about," Indy chimed in as the sergeants left.

"Yeah, Rutt and Samuels spend most of their time shacked up while the rest of us do all the dirty work," Henry added.

"How do you know that?" I asked.

"I saw 'em last night while I was on guard. Cook wasn't the only guy prowlin' around. Yeah, and I was talking to Moore today, and he said those two piss ants spend most of their time looking for ass."

The conversation continued in this vein until Robarge returned, the members of the section expressing their dislike for Parker and Samuels with mounting indignation.

"Load up your gear, we're leaving at 10 o'clock," Robarge announced. "The lieutenant says we'll like this one, a check point in a town a few miles from here."

"What're we checking for?" Hilton asked.

"Escaping Nazis, I guess."

"Some shit," Indy exclaimed. "What're we supposed to do, ask 'em if they're friends of Hitler? And why tonight?"

The sergeant turned his enigmatic smile on Weiner and replied, "Jesus Christ, Indy, what the hell is eating you? It may be better than here. We'll have Ten in One rations, so we'll eat better for sure."

Amid more muttering the men slouched off to gather their belongings and prepare for departure. Although the mission was not billed as a combat reconnaissance, the location, strength, and attitude of the many remnants of the German army were uncertain enough to cause anxiety. We knew that a stealthy ambush in an unfamiliar place could easily overwhelm our section, and the possibility of hostilities seemed quite real. Action by guerrillas or irregular forces was considered a serious threat by the army command, a fact that added to our uncase.

"We'll lead, Holme," Robarge said as we climbed into the jeep. "We leave town past where we washed the vehicles this morning and then turn left at the first crossroad. The lieutenant says it should be easy to find."

"How would he know, has he been there?"

The sergeant replied with a touch of surprise in his voice, "What's everyone so touchy about?"

"Oh, we were just talking about Rutt and Samuels while you were in there. They don't do anything except cat around and send us to do all the work."

"You jealous of them or tired of work?"

"Well, I guess I would have liked a night's sleep before starting this stuff again," I answered sheepishly.

"We'll probably make out better on our own, so don't get so hot under the collar."

The night was light enough so that I could see the road easily and had no trouble avoiding the occasional wrecked vehicles and most of the pot holes where some zealous Nazi might have deposited a mine. As we neared our destination Robarge emphasized my role in our occupation of the town.

"We're to take over this place and stop everyone passing on the road. You're the only one who speaks German, so we'll have to depend on you to do the talking. The lieutenant told me there may be a cache of weapons in the town, and we're to make sure none of that gets into the wrong hands. It looks like we'll have enough to do to keep us busy."

As we entered the village I was struck by the deserted appearance of the place. When we stopped in front of the house Robarge had picked for our billet the utter stillness of the street seemed to engulf us. Not a glimmer of light shone from any window, and I seriously wondered if the residents had fled. When I confided my suspicions to the sergeant, he laughed.

"You're a city boy, these people are farmers, so they go to bed early and get up early. Why don't you just wake up the people in this place so we can go inside and get some sleep ourselves."

I must have betrayed my timidity about waking people in the middle of the night by my hesitant approach to the house.

"Don't worry about bothering them, Holme. Hell, they'll be glad it's not the Gestapo to throw their asses into jail. Go ahead and roust 'em out so I can go to bed."

I knocked on the door with authority, or so I thought, but nothing happened. I knocked again, still no response.

"Jesus Christ, Holme, you're not calling to pick up your girl to go to the movies. Make some noise, get 'em up."

I pounded hard with my fist and repeated the racket when my efforts produced no result. Cringing at the thought of the razzing I was sure to suffer if I couldn't even waken a kraut farmer, I shouted for them to open the door. Still no answer, except a few titters from my companions, so I stepped back, cupped my hands around my mouth, and yelled as loudly as I could for the occupants to open the door, adding an officious "mach snell" for good measure.

As I stood waiting for a reaction to my bellowing, the dead silence was broken by a Hoosier twang drifting from the armored car.

"You tell 'em horseshit, you've been on the road!"

Hilton's pithy remark produced a louder round of titters, but then to my relief a light shone in an upstairs window, the casement was slowly unlatched, and a woman looked down and sleepily asked what we wanted. My German must have become even worse than usual under the pressure of my friends' giggles and asides, for the woman acted as uncomprehending as if I had addressed her in Swahili. But at last she nodded, closed the window, and soon appeared at the front door, which she opened slowly, even grudgingly. She looked to be about 60, fat and phlegmatic, and her demeanor betrayed no emotional response to her midnight intruders. There was no hint of fear or loathing, but neither was there even the slightest indication of cordiality or even curiosity. Her main concern seemed to be to return to bed, which she did as soon as we had staked out an adequate portion of her house for our needs. Her aplomb in relinquishing her home to a band of enemy soldiers was truly extraordinary.

The house was built almost to the curb of the street, but there was a little yard to the side which was separated from the street by a wall. With care we were able to back the armored car and jeeps through a portal sized for farm wagons and close the heavy wooden gates so that our presence was not immediately obvious to a casual observer on the street. Robarge assigned Henry and me to the first stint of guard duty and told Indy and Hilton that they would be in the rotation because they did not have to maintain constant radio communication with the troop on this mission.

Bud and I walked slowly along the single street of the silent village, alert to any movement or sound, but the eerie stillness enveloped the place as if it were under a spell. Most of the houses were smaller than our billet, and many had a manure pile in the yard. Near the far end of the village a stone church with a tall steeple dominated a small square. As we approached the front steps we noticed the door ajar and four Wehrmacht helmets piled near the entrance, an incongruity in a house of worship. Cautiously we climbed the steps and slipped into the building where alter candles cast a dim glow over the interior of the place, which housed a vast arsenal of small arms, grenades, ammunition, and other military paraphernalia.

"Would you look at that!" Henry exclaimed.

"Well, I guess there is a supply of arms in this place," I replied in awe. "I just hope we don't meet the owners."

"There's enough here to supply a battalion," Bud continued. "I wonder why they piled it all in here?"

I shrugged and shook my head as we began to walk around the sanctuary, all the while aware of a growing uneasiness about the eerie place. The utter stillness of the church and the ominous glint of the flickering light reflected off the weapons fueled my apprehension even more.

"You know, this is a spooky place," I half whispered. "I don't want to fool with any of this stuff, it could be mined, and there could even be armed krauts around here waiting to clean us out."

"Yeah, we better go back and tell Robarge about it."

To my surprise the sergeant was asleep when we returned, a sure sign that he considered the village a safe post. Still, he sat up wide awake with the first nudge and listened intently to our account of the arms cache.

"Let's go look at it, I gotta see this for myself," he said.

Robarge emitted a low whistle of wonder when we entered the church with its congregation of weapons.

"Either they've all quit and collected this stuff for us, or they left it for someone to use against us. Whichever it is, nobody should touch anything, don't pull any levers or lift anything, Holme. The biggest charge could be in the cellar," the sergeant cautioned with a grin in my direction.

The stillness of the town seemed almost palpable as we spent the rest of our stint on guard trying to dispel the chill of the early spring night by brisk walking, swinging our arms, and occasionally stamping our feet, all to little avail. At last our shift was over and Henry went in to rouse Gorlitz and I found Weiner snoring peacefully.

"Hey, Indy, time to go on guard," I whispered while gently shaking his shoulder.

No response.

I tried again more vigorously.

"Go 'way, I'm not gettin' up."

"You gotta get up, you're on guard, come on Indy."

"Leave me be, I'm sleepin' dammit!"

At first I had been amused, but now I was getting irritated. I wanted to get some sleep myself, and I was in no mood for Weiner's selfishness.

"Come on, Indy, no more shit, you get out of there right now!"

"Damn you, leave me alone. Who the hell do you think you are telling me what to do? Just because you're always sucking around Robarge doesn't make you my boss!" and with that he jerked the sleeping bag around himself and gave every indication of going back to sleep.

Now I was really angry and growled, "I don't care what you think, get your ass out of that sack, you're on guard and I'm tired of fooling with you."

My change of tone sank in and he climbed out slowly without another word to me, although he was mumbling to himself as he stumbled to the door.

"Gorlitz will tell you all you need to know," I added.

If I had not been so tired Hilton's ridicule of my efforts to awaken the old woman and the brush with Weiner would have bothered me, but I was asleep as soon as I got into the sack and was aware of nothing until Caulkins shook me in the morning.

By day the village was more appealing, a cluster of solid farm houses closely bordering the road for a couple of hundred yards. As I stepped outside, the door of the house across the street opened and a little boy about three years old was gently propelled from within by his mother. The agile youngster hopped up on the cement curbing around the family manure pile, deftly dropped his little pants, and squatted to add his mite to the dung heap. I chuckled as I watched the little fellow perform his business with no hint of self consciousness or embarrassment. The entire procedure was obviously a regular part of his daily routine.

"I'd like to see a kid try that back home in San Angelo," DJ declared as he too smiled at the child's innocent performance. "That might shake up the old neighborhood."

"You mean you still have manure piles in San Angelo?" I joked.

"Cob yes, don't you know that it's still the wild west out in Texas," Caulkins bantered back.

While not exactly a hive of activity, the village showed other signs of life in the light of day. Women fed chickens, a few children scurried about, and an occasional old man gawked at us from a distance.

"Holme, tell the old lady we'll trade her some canned meat for eggs and potatoes," Robarge said. "I'll fry up some bacon, eggs and potatoes for breakfast."

The woman readily agreed to the trade, but still no sign of emotion crossed her impassive features."

Caulkins echoed my feelings when he said, "That old gal gives me the creeps. I wish she'd either smile or get mad, but I can't tell what she's thinking right now."

"She probably doesn't know what to think of us," Reardon interjected. "Hell, how would your mother feel if a bunch of German soldiers moved into her house and then wanted to trade some lousy rations for eggs?"

We all laughed and nodded in acknowledgment of his point. It always seemed that Americans expected foreigners to greet them with smiles and even enthusiasm regardless of the circumstances. We laughed even more when Hilton added his wisdom.

"Geez, I'd pity any soldiers that tried that in my mom's house."

We finally decided that the old frau was all right considering her situation and dug into the sumptuous breakfast.

"Hey, Sarge, where's the toast and jam?" Weiner asked with a grin and a twinkle in his eye.

"There's jam in the rations, I just forgot to get it out, but you chowhounds 'll have to get along using those cement crackers for toast."

"Speaking of crackers," Henry said, "It's nice to be away from Rutt and his pal, Sam."

There was universal agreement on that point, and an air of comity seemed to have replaced the fractiousness of the night before.

Just then Gorlitz came in from the yard and announced in disgust, "We better not stay here too long or we'll have to shit in the street like that kid across the way. The crap is piled so high in the outhouse that you have to shove it aside with a stick to take a dump, and the stink is something awful."

"The honey dumper must have been drafted," Henry chuckled.

Other than monitoring nonexistent foot traffic on the road and guarding the arms cache we had no specific duties. We took turns patrolling the little town like policemen on a beat, a more enjoyable task by day than at night. While I was on my first tour of the village a trio of exuberant young men approached shouting something that sounded like "viva America". It was obvious that they were not Germans, so they had to be displaced persons. One, a short swarthy man in his twenties, identified himself as an Italian, and, in better German than I could muster, said that his companions were Poles. It seemed that the trio had been employed in farm work, apparently well treated, and the Italian even confided that he had "kept some German women happy while their men were away in the army." The two Poles were less proficient in German but stood by smiling amiably while their friend rambled on about the town. I recalled that Robarge understood a little Italian from his in-laws and Gorlitz claimed to speak some Polish, so I sent the men to our billet while I finished my rounds.

When I returned the three displaced men were seated in the kitchen talking incessantly to my largely uncomprehending comrades. After a short time I understood that the Italian was giving his version of the political views of all the Germans in the village, and after further convoluted conversation I convinced him to save his intelligence for the military government men who would ultimately rule the area. He seemed surprised, indeed dismayed, that we were not going to punish all Nazis that he could identify for us, but then he shrugged and asked if his American friends would like a fine Italian meal. When I assured him that the men in that room relished all good food he was overjoyed. With pride bordering on vanity he boasted that he would cook us the finest pasta we had ever eaten if we would allow him to use "our old woman", her kitchen, and his woman to prepare the feast. When I explained the proposition to the others they were all enthused about the scheme, although Caulkins and Henry were skeptical about the man's claim to great culinary talent.

"Tell him he can have all the women in town to help," Robarge added with a laugh. "This should be a lot of fun, and we may even get a good meal."

I wondered how the old woman would react to this new imposition, but she didn't bat an eye as she set to work under Antonio's direction. "His woman" was much younger, a giggling blond whom he summoned via one of the Poles, a floozy if I ever saw one, but a willing servant of her Italian lover. The men enjoyed every minute of this show and sat in rapt attention as the pasta was rolled and other ingredients were requisitioned from hiding places known only to their owners and Antonio. Nobody wanted to leave the show for patrol; not only were we learning how spaghetti was made but the interplay between the cooks was hilarious. Antonio could even charm a little smile from the taciturn old frau, but the latter could not conceal her contempt for the blond doxie, who in turn would look at the old woman with brazen insolence and then titter something to the Italian. Antonio would respond with a kiss or a pat on her rump unless he had both hands in the pasta, in which case he merely rolled his eyes lasciviously and grinned. I finally decided that I better take another turn on patrol before I offended the chef by laughing at his farce.

The village remained tranquil without a run on the armory in the church, a parade of Nazi fugitives, or any other activity more threatening than the country folk tending their livestock. No travelers or vehicles of any kind passed by, and no orders came to dislodge us from this peaceful haven.

By late afternoon the feast was ready and Antonio seemed about to burst with pride as he set before us mountains of spaghetti, fresh bread, butter, cream, tomato sauce and canned fruit. It was indeed a memorable repast, one that ranked with the meal in Fraiture for sheer delight to both palate and stomach. It was the kind of dinner one spends time with. There was nowhere else to go or any other amusement, so even the "stuff and run" men became "munch and savor" types as we ate our way through a staggering amount of food. Antonio had gone to great pains to make sure that his American friends would not leave the table hungry, but even he was amazed by the capacity of the trenchermen in that room. The floozy giggled at our gluttony, but the old frau mostly ignored the whole affair once the work was done. The cooks and the two Poles had eaten with us but gave up long before the hungry troopers were finished.

As we finally pushed back from the table and looked for places to recline and allow our over distended stomachs to deal with their contents we heard vehicles outside. Henry, the sentry at the time, entered with Brock and several of his second platoon men. The new arrivals took in our quarters and noted that we had just finished eating something other than GI rations.

"Damn, if I'd known you boys was eatin' we'd of got here sooner. And Robarge, you didn't even save any for your ol' buddies," Brock chided. As one of Cook's section sergeants he often sounded as though he were trying to out-cook the original.

"Nobody told us you were coming," Robarge replied, "but maybe Antonio and his helpers can whip you up something."

It turned out that Brock's section was to relieve us, and we were to return to Blankenheim. As we prepared to leave the good feeling of the day seemed to fade at the thought of returning to the drab, crowded house, dull food, and eternal wrangling of some members of the troops. Recognizing our reluctance to leave Brock broke into a broad grin.

"Hey, this must be good duty if you boys are so pissed about leaving. What is it, the wine or the women or both? It sure ain't the song," he quipped, laughing uproariously at his own little joke.

With a roguish grin Robarge replied enigmatically, "It's not the women, it's that woman," pointing to the old frau. "She's more than you ever dreamed of."

As we drove away I chuckled aloud at the expressions on the faces of the second platoon troopers in response to Robarge's remark.

"That'll give 'em something to think about," the sergeant added behind a smile more impish than ironic.

"They probably took you seriously," I replied. "Brock is just the guy to get funny with the old lady, and then what'll happen?"

"Don't worry, she can look out for herself, but I'd love to see it."

When we entered our billet in Blankenheim, a familiar voice could be heard from the room beyond.

"You fuckin' babies are lucky, why hell, you might even get outa' Europe in one piece, but you'll sure as hell get it in the Pacific. You smart assed kids 'll grow up or die over there, and I'll bet they got plans for you already," Glowacki declared. "If your old ladies don't get their gold stars you'll see the Golden Gate in '48, if you're still able to see anything at all."

"What're you goin' to be doin' all this time, Ed?" Moore asked. "What makes you think you won't be right there with us?"

"I've done my time and I'll be back in Worcester, Mass., hackin' for Butch Reiman, or maybe even runnin' one of his joints. Yeah, and I'll be shackin' up with Nora while you babies are invading Japan. Hell, I'll feel so sorry for you I might even send you somethin'."

"Whatcha goin' to send, Eddie," Joe Colleto asked, "A picture of some clapped up old broad you're tryin' to fuck?"

"Aw, shut up you little guinea. What the hell do you know about women except some nigger whore in Roxbury?"

Robarge and I looked at each other and no word was necessary to express our mutual disgust for the incessant babble and prattle of the crowded billet. It was as if we had never left, the same old arguments and quibbling, and soon everyone in the section seemed to have been affected by the atmosphere of the place. Petty grumbling and bickering replaced the good natured banter of the time in the little village. The next 24 hours constituted one of those tedious, boring, meaningless periods that make up so much of service time. In such an environment, pastimes such as baiting Glowacki or fantasizing improbable sexual or drinking escapades seemed to be the principal social activity. Just when it seemed it had gone on a week rather than a day and after a dinner that tasted like cardboard, Lt. Parker screeched for Robarge. From the diabolical grin on the lieutenant's homely mug I guessed it was not good news.

"Robarge, we have to give everyone training in night exercises while we're in this rear area, so your section is to leave at 2100 tonight to relieve Brock."

"Jesus Christ, lieutenant," Robarge remonstrated in tones and words now familiar to all of us, "Why do we have night exercises now? That's all we've done since we've been over here. Why don't we just drive over and relieve Brock now?"

"Dammit, you know that and I know that, but when they say night exercises at division I do what I'm told and so do you. If the general says shit we all squat, you know that. And anyway, you'll have a new man in your section, Onderdonk. He's one of the replacements. It'll be good for him to go on a night patrol, give him a little experience for when we go into combat again."

For a moment Robarge said nothing, but his face told all. The half smile was gone, and I could almost hear his mind turning as he groped for some excuse to refuse the replacement.

"But lieutenant, do you think it's a good idea to add a new man right now? I mean, this is a smooth running section and a new guy might not fit in."

"Oh hell, Robarge, he'll fit in just like all the rest. He's coming over from headquarters and you all can get acquainted."

It was hopeless to argue, we were three men short, but the glum faces told the tale. We might have our differences, but, like a family, we were not about to admit just anyone to the clan.

Onderdonk seemed pleasant enough, a chubby, blond haired fellow of medium height who seemed genuinely happy to join our section. He said he was 26, unmarried, and glad to be in a recon outfit rather than the infantry because his feet killed him if he walked too far. He added that he was from Baltimore, where he had worked in an aircraft factory until he lost his deferment and was drafted. I had about decided that he might be all right when the most painful blow fell.

"Onderdonk, you ride with Ostrander in the mortar jeep," Robarge ordered. "He'll tell you all about what we do. You'll learn a lot in a day or so, so don't worry if you don't understand everything right away. We have a training mission tonight, so that should be easy."

I knew that Robarge was supposed to ride in the M8 and any new man would probably take his place as my companion in the jeep, but I had become very fond of the sergeant and would miss our conversations that did so much to alleviate the boredom that characterized so much of our time. The new man said little as we prepared for the mission, busying himself with a clumsy effort to compact his belongings into a bedroll and musette bag. When I saw that he still had a duffle bag as well as his pack I realized that he was attempting the impossible. We had plenty of space in the jeep, so I told him to toss his stuff in the back seat and sort it out later.

"Much obliged," he said. "I guess I got more crap than you guys. Just tell me what you want me to do."

"Well, there's not much for you to do," I replied. "If you see anything unusual, let me know. We'll drive under total blackout tonight, so I'll have to look out for wrecks on the road, but we've been to this place before, so it shouldn't be much of a job to get there."

Once we were underway Onderdonk became a chatterbox, asking endless questions about me and other members of the section, often of a most personal nature, and in turn telling me more than I could ever want to know about himself.

"So you ain't been over here long yourself," he said. "Hell, you and the other fellows except the sergeant are just young kids, so it's a good thing I come along, it helps to have someone who's a little older and knows the score."

"Well, we may be young, but we've had a lot of experience since we've been over here, and Robarge has enough for all of us," I replied.

"Yeah, that sergeant acts like he knows it all. Is he any good or is he just a blowhard?"

"He's the best and he's no blowhard," I replied testily.

"Hey, I just noticed, you must be driving on the wrong side of the road, there's lots of room on this side, ain't you afraid you'll hit someone coming from the other way?"

At first I thought he was kidding. I was hugging the left side because I could see the edge better from the driver's seat while keeping an eye on the tiny red tail lights of the armored car creeping along in front of us. I decided to go along with Onderdonk's little joke about traffic from the other direction.

"Who are you expecting from the other way?"

"Hell, I don't know, maybe some farmer coming home late or someone going to town. Let me tell you, I almost got killed up by Gaithersburg one night just like this, fellow driving on the wong side of the road with his lights off just like you."

By now I did not care whether Onderdonk was persisting with a stupid joke or was really so dense that he expected traffic on this road. In either case, I was fed up and my irritation must have showed.

"Well, this is Germany, a combat zone, not Maryland, and if anyone comes from that direction I'll give you my next month's pay."

For a minute or two he was quiet but then resumed his cautions. "I didn't wanta make you sore, but I'd sure as hell feel better if you'd drive more to the right, there's lots of room over here, I can see it."

Just then a wrecked German command car loomed ahead, half on the shoulder and half on the road. I made a quick move to the right and missed it, but this stimulated my passenger to even more complaining.

"I don't wanta say I toldja so, but you damn near hit that car. If you'd a been more to the right you wouldn't of had no trouble. Hey, I notice you wear glasses, you probably don't see so good so you can't help it if you don't drive good at night."

"Look," I replied, "I see perfectly well, I've been driving in blackouts long enough to know what I'm doing, so you just relax and we'll be there soon."

"Well, I ain't tryin' to give you a hard time, but you said yourself to tell you if I seen anything funny, so I did. You know, I got $25 at Martin once for a suggestion, I mean I'm the kinda guy that keeps his eyes open and ain't afraid to speak up. You know what I mean?"

By now I knew all too well what he meant, and I shuddered to think of this blatherskate talking my ears off for the duration.

"What did you suggest that got you $25?" I asked, hoping to interest him in something besides my driving.

"Aw it wasn't anything big like a new design of a part or anything, it was about collecting the scrap. Anyway, they tried it for a while, but the foreman didn't like it, so they went back to the old way. That pot licker probably didn't like it because it was my idea, we didn't get along so good. Hell, I might still be there if he hadn't told the big shots they didn't need me, and before you know it I'm 1A and gettin' my physical."

"What was your job?"

"Like I toldja, I picked up scrap. It was a helluva job with everything moving so fast, I could hardly keep up with it most of the time."

We were entering the village, much to my relief, for I hoped to rid myself of Onderdonk for a while or at least share him with the others. To my dismay Robarge assigned Onderdonk and me to the first shift of guard duty after we relieved Brock's section at the check point.

We had not completed one circuit of the town when Onderdonk inquired, "Where's a fellow get a bite to eat around here?"

By now I was not surprised by anything my new partner said and replied gruffly, "The only thing to eat is a ration if you can find one in a jeep or the armored car."

"What kind of ration you mean?"

"C or K are the only ones, what difference does it make?"

"I ate some of them C rations on the way here, and they ain't so good."

When we reached our billet I rummaged through the jeep but found no rations and then turned to the M8 where Weiner was fiddling with the radio.

"Hey, Indy," I called, "Any rations in there? Onderdonk's hungry."

Indy cackled gleefully, "Oh yeah, do I have a ration for him! Onderdonk ol' buddy, I wouldn't give this to just anyone 'cause it's my favorite, corned pork loaf with carrots and apple flakes. Man, how I love those apple flakes. But since you're new and hungry and all, I'm goin' to give you this ration, my last one, to show you I'm a good buddy."

I could hardly stifle my laughter at Indy's extravagant buildup of a ration we all hated. A sharper man would have recognized the spoof, but the gullible newcomer eagerly seized the ration and attacked it with gusto.

"You eat while we patrol," I said officiously. "We're supposed to be on guard, not eating."

Onderdonk had quickly polished off the meat and biscuits from the ration and was sucking on the hard candy when I finally asked, "How did you like it?"

"Well, I didn't like it as much as Indy, but I guess it was OK. I really hoped I could get a banana, that's what I like best at night."

I was nonplused by this statement. It was apparent that Onderdonk was in Germany physically but back home mentally. I decided to let him ramble on for the rest of our stint and tried to ignore his preposterous assertions. When our time was up I shuddered to think that he might spread his bedroll next to mine and continue his prattle into the night, but fortunately fatigue silenced even Onderdonk.

In the morning we feasted on bacon and eggs, the latter supplied by the old frau, who was amazingly friendly and refused anything in return. She smiled warmly at us like a kindly grandmother, apparently glad to awake and find us as her freeloading tenants again. Onderdonk was the last to come to breakfast but made up for his tardy start with a disgusting attack on his food that awed the rest of us, who were not exactly models of table etiquette either. While he had his face practically in the plate Indy asked the question I was waiting for.

"How'd you like that corned pork loaf last night, Onderdonk, especially those carrots and apple flakes?"

Without even a pause in his eating the oaf replied through a full mouth, "Ish OK, not ash good ash I shought id be, guesh I wanted bananash."

"You wanted what?"

With a less full mouth, "Bananas. I like bananas at night. The other was OK, but I'd rather have bananas, and today I'm goin' out and find a fruit stand and swipe a bunch."

"Onderdonk, would you do something for me?" Robarge asked with a straight face. "When you swipe those bananas, would you get some for me?"

Oblivious to the mirth his ridiculous assertion had generated the dolt assured the sergeant that he would bring back enough for the section. With this generous pledge he smiled broadly and departed on his quest.

I was immediately bombarded with questions.

"Is he putting on an act?"

"Is he as dumb as he lets on?"

"What did he do last night?"

"I thought he was kidding too, at first," I replied, "but just let me tell you about last night."

As I recounted my experiences with Onderdonk the room fairly rocked with laughter, and I wondered how we would be able to keep straight faces when the simpleton returned. While he seemed like a harmless nincompoop, we agreed that he was not a man we would want as a member of the section in a dangerous situation.

When the new man did not return in an hour Robarge said, "Holme, you better look for Onderdonk. He may have gotten lost or into some kind of trouble, but I'll be damned if I know how in this little burg."

I had only walked a short distance when I spotted him talking to a pair of displaced persons. The latter gestured enthusiastically and all three palaverers grinned from ear to ear. When I drew near I heard Onderdonk's flat voice.

"I'm from Baltimore, you understand Baltimore?" Heads nodded. "I'm looking for a fruit stand, you know, oranges, apples, all that stuff, you understand?" More nods. "Where can I find a fruit stand?" Still more nods.

The displaced duo, men in their twenties, obviously understood not one word of his ridiculous babble, but responded by animated nods of agreement to every unintelligible statement.

"Hey, Ostrander, I can talk to these people, they're friendly and we understand each other."

"What did they say to you just now?" I asked.

"Well, I don't understand them too good, but they know everything I say."

"How do you know?"

" 'Cause they nod their heads, see, like that."

"Tell 'em they eat shit."

"Hey, they're nice guys, I don't wanta make 'em sore."

"Well, I'll do it then. Hey, you guys eat shit, you understand?"

The pair's broad smiles and affirmative nods did not faze Onderdonk one bit. "That wasn't very friendly, but they like us so much it don't make no difference."

"You better save the talk for later. Sarge wondered where you were. He's waiting for his bananas," I said sarcastically.

Poor Onderdonk finally began to realize that he was a laughing stock, but this did not stifle his constant babble or seemingly irresistible tendency to commit faux pas. He was so dense that he had no comprehension of why the men laughed at him, but to his credit he maintained a good natured equanimity during his stay in the section.

The displaced persons to whom Onderdonk had been talking were not residents of the village but part of a trickle of non-Germans who took to the roads soon after the Americans arrived. In a short time this movement would swell to a flood of humanity and create problems we could not yet imagine. We were completely unqualified to uncover Nazis or collaborators among the scores of thousands of refugees who soon emerged from every community in Germany.

When I returned to the house I was surprised by the old frau, who approached me with a broad smile and an offer to cook us "a real German chicken dinner that would be better than Italian food." I accepted the unexpected proposal enthusiastically and watched our hostess set to work on the feast. I decided that she preferred us to the other section and hoped to keep on our good side by catering to our gluttony.

"I could stay here a month," Gorlitz declared. "People can keep right on cooking us dinners, we don't have to listen to Rutt or the rest of them in the platoon, and the work is a snap."

"Yeah, but it's a pretty dull place except for eating and sleeping," I reminded him. "You know what we need? If we had a ball and bat we could have some fun when we weren't on patrol."

"And if we had a movie theater we could see some shows," Hilton laughed.

"Or if we had wings we could fly," Caulkins added.

"You've been around Onderdonk too much. Next thing you'll want ice skates and a rink," Robarge chimed in.

I realized that I had picked the wrong time to mention my idea, but I was too stubborn to quit.

"I'm not kidding, let's look for a ball, just about any sturdy ball will do, I know we won't find a real softball over here. And then we could use an old table leg or anything round for a bat and have some games."

The others thought about it for a minute and then gradually gave the idea grudging approval and agreed it would be a lot of fun to play some scrub or regular softball if we could find enough players. From this we verged into a conversation about the upcoming major league baseball season. I don't know how long we bandied that about, but it was probably over an hour. Our learned analysis of the diamond was interrupted when we heard a jeep stop in front of the house and Sgt. Samuel's swaggered into the room.

"I thought I'd best drive over and make sure you boys are up to handling this check point," he said. "You all seemed so eager to get back here I figured you must have a nice little deal going. Hey, what's that smell?"

"It's our chicken dinner," Robarge replied. "That old lady likes us so much that she's cooking us a big meal."

"Where'd she get the chickens?" Samuels asked.

"From the house across the road, where the chickens are running around the yard," Caulkins explained.

"Yeah, they've got enough chickens to feed the troop," Samuels agreed with a smirk. "You know, these krauts are pretty well off, maybe too well off."

Somehow Samuels seemed out of place in our section, a man of different temperament and interests. His awkward efforts to join in the conversation embarrassed and irked him until his irritation boiled over and he stood up abruptly, knocking his chair over in the process.

"Guess you boys know I'm the best damned shot in this outfit."

We sat dumbfounded by his declaration, a claim made defiantly as though he expected one of us to dispute the assertion.

"Well, I heard you're a great shot," Robarge answered cautiously, "And I'd like to watch you on the range sometime."

"Range my ass," Samuels retorted. "I feel like a little shooting right now, and I don't mean shooting the shit in this damned house. I'll bet anyone here a month's pay that I'll shoot the heads off all those damned chickens over there without missing once."

We were speechless at this proposal, and I wondered if he was drunk. Nobody said a word, not even Onderdonk, as we waited to see what Robarge would do.

"Don't you think that's a little hard on those people?" Robarge replied evenly. "Why don't we find a field where you can shoot crows or whatever they have over here?"

"Goddamnit, I don't feel like walking out to some field to shoot varmints, I feel like shooting the heads off those fuckin' chickens 'n' I haven't heard anyone make a bet. It's no fun without a bet, what's the matter, afraid to bet against me?" Samuels continued irritably.

"Nobody's going to bet against you, Sam, everyone knows what a great shot you are," Caulkins answered in a soothing tone.

The evil smirk again spread across Samuels' face as he declared, "I guess I should've known better than to expect to get a bet from any of you mama's boys, but I'm still going to show you some real shooting."

With that he stalked out of the house and positioned himself next to his jeep where he had a clear shot of about 75 feet to where 18 or 20 chickens were prancing slowly around the yard, cackling and pecking at the ground.

"The trick is to blow their heads clean off so the chicken drops and doesn't spook the others. Hell, they're so dumb they don't even notice they're being shot until every last one is dead."

After laying an extra magazine on the hood of the jeep Samuels lifted the carbine to his shoulder and started firing. I watched in fascination as he quickly decapitated half a dozen hens while the others continued their prancing and cackling as though nothing had happened. At the first shots the woman of the house had opened the door as if to protest, but she quickly withdrew at sight of the wild gunman.

"Now I ask you, is that shooting or is that shooting?" Samuels gloated.

"Damned good shooting, best I've ever seen. You've convinced me, I'll take your word for the rest," Robarge said hopefully.

"Well, I don't want any of you boys to think I was just lucky. I said all of them and I mean every last one of them cacklers."

With this he slipped a full magazine into the carbine and quickly dispatched the rest of the chickens. Then, grinning maliciously, he turned to Robarge.

"If that old bitch in the house runs out of chickens, I sure as hell know where she can get more. It's about time to eat isn't it?"

Relieved that Samuels' crazy show was over but ashamed to have been part of it, I entered the house where the old woman was grumbling to herself, her face once more an impassive mask. The senseless shooting of her neighbor's chickens had erased the earlier smiles, and she treated us as coldly as if we were bandits. The meal was good, but nobody said much while we ate, a somber mood having replaced the earlier frivolity.

Pushing back from the table when he had finished eating Samuels announced, "Well, you boys had a cozy place here, but you have orders to go back to Blankenheim tonight. We're all going to move soon, and military government or some such rear echelon bastards will take over here."

We returned to Blankenheim in silence, and even Onderdonk said little, apparently pondering his platoon sergeant's idea of fun. When we drove up to the billet I was delighted to see Hunk Wilson standing before the house, apparently recovered from his gut rot. I decided that even if we were stuck with Onderdonk, Hunk and I would set the tone and the sad sack could accommodate to our tastes. I had barely gotten in the house when Lt. Parker approached and bawled in his usual raucous voice.

"Ostrander, you be ready to leave early tomorrow with the advance party, they need someone to talk German, so I'm sending you."

I was pleased at that assignment and could hardly wait for morning when I would see new country and have the first look at our new area of operations.

9

AN UNCERTAIN FUTURE

The advance party consisted of a Lt. Baker, a Sgt. Carey from second platoon and me. The lieutenant and the sergeant seemed to be good friends and carried on an intermittent conversation while I sat in the back seat of the jeep and admired the scenery. The weather had changed from warm sun to cloudy, windy and cool, but the route passed through a countryside of hills, vineyards, quaint villages, and an occasional old castle looming above a valley. All too quickly we arrived at a town named Mendig where the lieutenant conferred with a group of officers in a newly established regimental headquarters. Our billet was about a mile away near a crossroads hamlet called Niedermendig in a tranquil setting of rolling fields and scattered woods. The billet was a very large house from which the inhabitants were carrying personal belongings as we approached, thus relieving me of the job as interpreter.

The house was roomy and well equipped with a large barn and yard which would be ideal for the motor pool. Apparently others had used it for similar purposes because a German half track and a military motorcycle were parked in the yard next to a civilian automobile with four flat tires. I expected these vehicles would exert an irresistible attraction for some of my friends.

The rest of the troop arrived the following day amid rumors that this comfortable billet would be our permanent base for occupation duty. Several bridges now spanned the Rhine, and the news was full of stories of allied advances beyond this last line of defense for Germany's heartland. No wonder most thought our role in the European war was at an end.

Onderdonk had been reassigned to headquarters with the return of Hunk Wilson and the arrival of about 25 replacements. At first I thought we had fared badly again when I met one of the new men, a weather beaten little old fellow named Horace Conger. He looked older than my father, with gray hair, deeply lined face, and ears that protruded from his head like open car doors. He quickly let us know that he was 45 years old, proprietor of a service station in Hays, Kansas, a veteran of the First World War, the proud father of six children, and "as good as any other goddamned soldier and better than most."

The other new man for our section was John Spada, a 33 year old veteran of the Ardennes battle, who returned to duty from the hospital. John waved off any glory that might be attached to his wound with the simple declaration, "Hell, I broke my ankle running away from the Germans, and you don't get any medals for that."

With these additions our section reached full strength for the first time. Conger, who immediately became "Pa", a title he relished, took over as driver of the machine gun jeep with Caulkins in charge and Henry and Gorlitz as crew. Hunk resumed his job as driver of the mortar jeep with Spada and me as mortar gunners, a skill almost totally foreign to both of us.

We had barely unloaded and staked out our quarters in the big house when Lt. Parker summoned his sergeants with one of his characteristic bellows, and we knew we would soon be off on some kind of mission. When Robarge returned he told us that the entire platoon had been ordered to a nearby village to establish a check point.

After dinner we drove the short distance through fertile fields dotted with prosperous looking villages and enough low hills and woodlands to complete the picturesque scene. Our destination was a tidy little burg with several large houses among the more modest dwellings of the farmers. We stopped in front of the most impressive looking residence, a large two story house surrounded by an attractive stone and brick wall. Through the open gate I could see a drive leading back about 50 yards to a substantial barn, a structure in keeping with the well-to-do appearance of the place.

"Ostrander," Parker yelled, "you come with Sam and me so we can tell these damned krauts to shag their asses outta that house."

We walked up the drive and then onto a path to the main entrance to the house. Almost before Samuels knocked, the door opened a crack and a young woman asked what we wanted. As I laboriously explained that we needed the house for the night I caught sight of two small children peeking at us with wide eyes from the other side of the room. One was a girl about 5 and the other a little boy no older than 3. The woman began to cry when she understood our request and spoke so rapidly that I could not understand her. As I patiently tried to slow her down Parker exploded.

"Jesus Christ, Ostrander, don't argue with the bitch, just tell her to get her ass outta the house. Why does it always take you so long to tell these damned people what to do?"

"She's trying to tell us something and I don't understand her; I'm trying to slow her down."

"Oh hell, I don't care what she's saying, so long as she knows what you're saying. Tell her to get outta there quick."

I then caught what she was trying to explain. The children had been sick, she had no place to go, and she just wanted to use one room in the house while we occupied the rest. When I explained this to Parker he erupted again.

"Can't she sleep at neighbors? Hell, she can sleep in the barn, I don't care, but not in the damned house. Get her out now, and that's a direct order, dammit."

He made me feel like a Nazi sympathizer with his grumbling while I conveyed the message. The woman accepted the harsh edict with resignation, and, still crying, turned to gather up clothing and blankets for the family's exile to the barn. When I asked why she couldn't stay with neighbors she explained that the children were quarantined because of their illnesses and could not mix with other youngsters.

Parker and Samuels stomped into the house even before the family had left, ranting about the woman's slowness and weeping. In the parlor I spotted a large framed picture of a man in an SS officer's uniform, and I asked if it was her husband. She nodded and hurried the children out the door as though the photo might condemn them to an even worse fate.

"Is she married to that SS bastard in the picture, Ostrander?" Samuels asked.

"Yeah, that's what she says."

From the next room I heard Rutt bellow, "Hey, Sam, I've found my bed, look at this."

When we entered a large bedroom off the parlor I saw Parker sprawled fully clothed, boots and all, on a very large bed, at least the size of a double bed in America, an almost unheard of luxury in Europe. An elaborate spread covered the mattress and formed a ludicrous background for the stocky lieutenant lying recumbent among its flowers and leaves. He grinned mischievously as some humorous notion flashed through his mind.

"God damn, this is better than a furlough. All I need is a woman, and I'm set for the night," he declared. Then looking at me he added, "Ostrander, you seemed to feel sorry for that damned woman, so I'll do somethin' nice for her. You tell her she and the kids can sleep in the house, only she'll have to sleep with me. God damn it, Sam, won't that be somethin', to fuck an SS man's frau!"

Both Parker and Samuels were now grinning like errant schoolboys, and my face must have revealed my disgust for Rutt's proposal. I seemed to stand there dumbly for an eternity before I could stammer a reply.

"You're kidding, aren't you lieutenant?"

"Kidding my ass. You get out to that barn and tell her what I said. Tell her she'll have chocolate 'n' cigarettes 'n' lots of cock."

I walked out of the door in a daze and slowly made my way to the barn while the others were parking and unloading the vehicles.

"It looks OK, Holme," Robarge called. "I couldn't have done better myself."

"Yeah, it's all right, maybe a little crowded, so save me a spot," I replied.

When I entered the barn I blinked and tried to adjust to the dark before I spotted the woman and her children in the hay. She had wrapped the little boy in quilts and he was already asleep, but the little girl huddled among several blankets and cried. As I approached she looked at me in abject terror.

"What do you want?" the woman asked suspiciously.

I was ashamed to have any part in Parker's sordid scheme, but I wasn't bold enough to refuse to be his messenger. I must have betrayed my discomfiture by my hang dog demeanor, for the woman became even more wary and repeated her question.

In a cowardly effort to shed complicity in Rutt's game I prefaced my remarks by telling her unctuously that the lieutenant was a bad man and then told her his proposal. Before I could finish she stiffened and angrily spat out, "Nein!" Relieved by her unequivocal reply I beat a hasty retreat. Parker was disappointed but not surprised that the woman had rejected his proposal, but her refusal seemed to make him even more irritable than usual.

"Damn it, I better not hear of anyone helping that Nazi bitch; she had her chance, and now she can sleep in the barn. You hear that, Ostrander?"

By now everyone knew of Rutt's scheme. Some thought it hilariously funny, while others were as disgusted as I. Our assignment was nothing more than guard duty on a deserted road, a task hardly requiring a cavalry platoon of 34 men with 3 armored cars, six jeeps and an imposing array of weapons. Even when I climbed into my bedroll I could not get the image of the woman and her sick children out of my mind. I told myself that she was a German, wife of an SS officer, probably hated Americans and would kill us if given the chance, but no rationalization justified Parker's behavior.

Early in the morning we were ordered back to Niedermendig and I was glad to leave. I did not see the family as we left but assumed that they were still in the barn waiting our departure. This stop also marked the beginning of another kind of shameful conduct by some members of the platoon. I was amazed to see men looting the house before we left, carrying off a radio, silver and other household items including a handsome pair of women's boots that surely would not fit the thief. It seemed as though some had taken seriously Indy's little joke about pillage and rape.

The next few days was a period of patrols, boredom, and uncertainty. We were abruptly sent to check points and just as suddenly recalled. There seemed to be no focus or goals to our activity as the war seemed to have passed far to the east of us. Rumors flew; we were to be occupation troops, the 28th was about to be shipped directly to the Pacific, all cavalry would be massed as a super mechanized force to race through Germany, capture Berlin, and end the war, and even less believable scenarios. Still, a few memorable events from this period come to mind.

The weather was generally sunny and mild giving our patrols the atmosphere of a peaceful sightseeing tour of the country. One of our first missions was a reconnaissance of the north bank of the Moselle River to its junction with the Rhine. As we approached the confluence of the two rivers Coblenz could be seen on the south bank of the Moselle. We had been warned that some die hard German units still held out in Coblenz and on the east bank of the Rhine in this area. The deserted streets lined by shell damaged buildings along our route gave mute testimony that here at least we were once again in contested territory. Pa Conger had already given notice that he was a feisty little gamecock, perhaps more venturesome than wise, and he sounded off loudly when we stopped in one of the battered villages to check our position.

"By God, I don't think there's any damned Germans in that town, and I'd sure as hell like to see it," he declared.

"Well, you're lucky, Pa. They say all the bridges are blown, so that'll save you from getting your ass shot off," Robarge replied.

"How the hell would those rear echelon bastards know what's going on up here?" Pa snorted.

"There are airplanes, you old coot," Reardon countered in exasperation.

"Well, I ain't seen none except them big bombers way the hell up in the sky. I've lived long enough so I don't believe all the shit they tell me like you young fellows."

"Keep on looking for trouble, and you won't live much longer," Hilton added.

"Oh hell, I think you boys are just gun shy from what happened before I got here. Seems to me the damned war's as good as over."

"Break it up, you guys, time to move on," Robarge interjected. "Pa, you just take it easy, be glad if we don't get shot at and don't take any damned fool chances."

I could tell from his tone that the sergeant had now added Pa Conger to the flock of youngsters that he intended to lead home safely, if not for the old man's sake at least for the benefit of his wife and kids back in Kansas. We had gone no more than a quarter of a mile when a bridge across the Moselle came into view, and to my amazement it appeared intact. As we crawled along the road I could hardly take my eyes off the span and wondered if our advance would be met by a barrage of fire from the Germans in Coblenz. By the time we reached the approach to the bridge I was tensed in expectation of hostile fire, but suddenly I forgot the Germans as the lead jeep turned right and started onto the bridge toward the city. I wondered if Caulkins had lost his mind or if Pa had made the move on his own and without warning to the corporal. Almost immediately geysers of earth erupted around us and the ground shuddered from the violent explosions of heavy mortar shells. Hunk wheeled our jeep around and sped for cover in the lee of a cluster of buildings where we hopped out and flattened ourselves in the gutter to wait out the barrage. We were followed in seconds by the other jeep and the armored car, whose crews followed our unheroic example and hit the dust.

"What the hell did you guys think you were doing on that bridge?" Robarge yelled. "You know better than that, Caulkins."

"It was my fault, Sarge," Pa interjected contritely. "Hell, I coulda sworn there wasn't a German in the place, so I just thought we should go over and take a look at it."

"Didn't I tell you to be careful?" the sergeant retorted testily. "Pa, from now on you do exactly what I say or I'll have your ass shipped back to Kansas if the krauts don't kill you first."

The barrage was half hearted compared to others we had experienced, so soon we were able to resume our patrol, circling back toward Niedermendig on a parallel road about half a mile north of the Moselle. We stopped in one pretty little village of tidy houses surrounded by orchards and vineyards where a party seemed to be in progress in one house. We stopped where the music and laughter wafted from the open door and before we could get out of our vehicles several celebrants emerged smiling and gesturing for us to join them.

When we entered the place we were greeted by the host, a young man about 25 or so who told us he was Dutch. His English was quite good and we soon learned that he had worked in the area and lived in the house with a German woman, who hung on his arm and smiled warmly at us. There were more Netherlanders and a few other foreign workers in the house, most with German women, and all were celebrating liberation, or the end of the war, or whatever the arrival of the Americans meant to them. They had a large supply of schnapps and were guzzling it like lemonade. The revelers urged us to join the party and seemed distraught because we did not drop everything and devote full attention to merriment. A couple of men sampled the schnapps and reported that it was powerful stuff, but Pa Conger swigged it down with zest and asked for more.

"God damn, that stuff has a little kick to it, not like that damned 3.2 beer in the PX," he declared.

"Be careful that kick doesn't knock you out," Robarge warned.

To the dismay of the hospitable Dutchmen we departed just when they had rounded up more women to help entertain us. As we drove away Hunk grumbled about our early exit from the party.

"Jeez, I don't know why we had to leave so soon, hell, that looked like fun. Is Robarge always like that?"

"How do you mean, 'like that'?" I asked. "We haven't been to any parties until now. I guess he thinks we should complete the mission."

"Well, I just hope he's not some bluenose who doesn't want us to have any fun. It looks like there's goin' to be a lot of humpin' and hollerin' ahead unless Sarge is a turd about it."

"Yeah, you're right, Hunk," Spada chimed in. "I think a man'll be able to fuck himself to death over here soon, and I want my share."

I laughed at my comrades' concern that the sergeant would cramp their social lives. "He won't interfere with anyone's fun, but he might tell you you're a damned fool if he thinks so. He always puts duty first, he won't allow anyone to goof off, but after the work is done you'll be on your own."

Hunk's mood changed abruptly when he pointed to the other jeep. "Look at Pa weaving all over the road. The old fart must be drunk from all that schnapps he drank."

Sure enough, the other jeep moved erratically, and we chuckled about it all the way to Niedermendig and relished what fun it would be to bait the bombastic little rooster about his drunk driving.

We were hardly back to the billet when two jeep loads of military government men drove into the yard and four cops strode into the house. The officers soon emerged carrying the radio and boots taken from the house where Rutt had tried his power play on the SS officer's wife. A little later I met Moore, one of the drivers in Samuels' section, and he was almost bursting to tell me what had happened.

"You should have seen old Rutt and Sam when those guys walked in. They were shitting in their pants, Rutt was even sweating. I guess he thought they'd go after him for attempted rape or something, but they were pretty easy on him, just a little lecture about controlling the men and that kind of crap. They said they'd take the stuff back and not to let it happen again."

"They didn't say anything about the woman and her kids?" I asked.

"Naw, I mean, what could they say? He just made her leave the house; oh, he was worried all right, but, hell, they weren't going to bother him for trying to get a little German pussy so long as he didn't use a gun."

Another day we set up a checkpoint in a village half way to the Rhine and were to patrol from that location to the river by jeep. The checkpoint was a welcome relief from life at headquarters, but the two women who lived in the house we requisitioned posed problems. Both were young, attractive and friendly. One was a widow and the other had not heard from her husband in over a year. They saw no reason to leave the house and insisted that they should stay and "take care of us", which seemed to mean whatever we wanted it to mean.

I explained their offer to the sergeant, who pursed his lips and gave me his most cynical and knowing smile.

"Holme, you tell those tarts that the rules say we can't have anything to do with them except to kick 'em out of the house. I'll be damned if I'll be the pimp in a German whorehouse for the pleasure of the guys in this section."

I conveyed his message to the women in somewhat softer terms. They looked at each other, shrugged, smiled quizzically, and said they would stay with a friend across the street in case we needed them.

"Jeez, Sarge, we coulda had a nice little deal, why'd you make 'em leave?" Hunk complained.

"Like I said, the rules say no fraternization. I'm responsible for you, so that means I don't let you hang around any Germans, you understand?"

"Well, yeah, but I wasn't going to talk politics with 'em. I mean, the army can't be against a little fucking can they?"

"Look, Hunk, if you're that hard up you can step out back and pound off or just sit down and cool off. I don't care what you do when you're off duty, but when you're on a mission we'll do things right, you got that?"

Hunk nodded, but I knew he would sulk the rest of the day. When Robarge asked if anyone wanted to run the jeep patrol, Caulkins and I quickly volunteered, glad to be away from the wrangling and tedium of the house. We had not gone far when a jeep approached from the other direction, and the driver signaled for us to stop. When we got out we recognized the passenger as Captain Smithson, our new troop commander. He had arrived two days earlier, but we knew nothing about him except that he was from Alabama and his uncle was the general in charge of division artillery. We saluted and Caulkins explained our mission.

The captain's face became grave as he spoke in a solemn voice, "I just came from up near the Rhine, men. I warn you, we must keep your eyes open, there's a lot going on around here. See that wagon load of straw over there?" as he pointed to a German farmer with a load of manure in a nearby field. "I hope you men realize that all these people are our enemies, why that man may have a couple of SS troopers hidden in that straw, you understand what I mean?"

I was glad at that moment that Caulkins was the corporal and obliged to answer the CO, because I would have had a hard time keeping a straight face while discussing such absurd nonsense.

DJ looked at the officer with a cherubic smile and replied, "Oh yes, sir, we'll watch everything, that's exactly what Sgt. Robarge told us to do."

"Where is Robarge and the rest of your section?" the captain asked.

"They've established a checkpoint in the next village, sir."

"Well, you men look like good troopers, carry on with your mission and remember what I told you. I'll drop in on the rest of your section," the captain said approvingly as he climbed back into the jeep.

"Oh cob, what a CO!" DJ exclaimed. "I declare, he must be as dumb as Onderdonk."

We could not stop laughing because every time we saw a farmer with a load of manure one of us would chirp, "Better check that straw for SS troopers."

On the way back to the checkpoint Caulkins suddenly slammed on the brakes and pointed to a railroad track running beside the highway. There next to the rail sat the largest hare I had ever seen. The creature looked the size of a cocker spaniel as it crouched immobile, apparently oblivious to our attention.

"Sarge said he would cook any game we shot," DJ said hopefully.

"OK, let's get that rabbit," I replied.

We slipped out of the jeep, lifted our carbines, and fired almost simultaneously. The hare seemed to explode in a cloud of fur and blood, and when we reached the rail embankment to retrieve our prize the carcass was such a macerated mess of gore neither of us would touch it. We must have stood blinking at the carnage for half a minute.

"We only fired two bullets, didn't we?" I asked.

"I thought so," DJ replied, "But it looks as though we hit it with a .50 caliber."

"I don't think we can do much with that, maybe we'll see a deer, something better than that chewed up rabbit," I added soberly.

DJ nodded and we returned to the jeep with new respect for the carbine.

When we reached the checkpoint the babble was still going on, but nobody mentioned the women. The captain's surprise visit seemed to have chilled all enthusiasm for open fraternization. Pa was holding forth in a windy diatribe about politics and his reasons for being a New Dealer, which I finally interrupted because I could not wait any longer to get my comrades' reactions to the new captain.

"What'd you think of Capt. Smithson?" I asked.

Painful grimaces crossed each face and Henry blurted out what could have passed as the consensus opinion.

"He came in here acting like Jesus Christ on a glass bicycle, but when he got through yapping I knew he didn't have enough sense to pour piss out of a boot."

The others hooted their agreement with this early assessment and they nearly convulsed with laughter when Caulkins told of our conversation with Smithson.

"You guys just don't appreciate Southern gentlemen like Parker and Smithson," Robarge said sarcastically.

"Nothing but crackers," Henry snorted.

"Well, they sure as hell think they're something special," Reardon chimed in. "You've all seen that picture of his wife that Rutt digs out every chance he gets? Well, I told him once that she looked like a girl I knew once and asked if she was from Ohio. You know what happened?"

We all shook our heads, so Jack continued.

"He got all red in the face. I could tell he was sore as hell for some reason, and he looked down that big old nose of his at me and said, 'You couldn't have known her, Reardon, she's a society girl.' It was like I was dirt and couldn't possibly know anyone connected with him."

Pa then settled all questions of status when he exclaimed, "Hell, them Southern trash are all lower than whale shit. I don't give a damn what Parker or Smithson or any of them sharecroppers think."

When we returned to Niedermendig we found the motor pool crew playing with the motorcycle and halftrack, but they were stymied by the little car. The entire place exuded a relaxed, almost festive air, and even the "old boys" were cordial for a change. The only excitement that night resulted from Hunk Wilson playing with a flair gun while on guard. After he fired a few into the air the division was alerted for possible night attack by paratroopers until someone discovered it was just a Washington lumberjack getting ready for Independence Day. As usual, the big guy was all apologies and assurances that it wouldn't happen again when he was reprimanded, but we all knew that it was only a matter of time before he would be in some other scrape. It was after this that Rutt Parker began to call him "Big Stoop" after a comic-strip character.

The next day some of the men shot a deer in the nearby woods, but they didn't know how to clean and dress the carcass. Robarge and Hunk agreed to butcher it for a share of the meat, so a deal was struck and the pair disappeared into a little room upstairs to perform their grisly task. They had hardly started when the general paid us a surprise visit. Cota was in a jovial mood, in contrast to his threatening attitude when he visited us in the forest. Still, I hated to think what would happen if the old martinet went inside and found my friends butchering a deer in quarters. Cota waved off any formation or formal inspection and said he just wanted to walk around and talk to "his boys". I thought he might stay out of doors, but he seemed to have an obsession with disease infested old houses, so he finally turned toward our billet. Even Capt. White was more affable and joked with the men caught tinkering with the German halftrack. I waited for something to happen after the entourage moved into the house, but all was quiet and the general emerged in a few minutes still smiling and chuckling to his aides. As Cota drove away I hurried into the house, half expecting to find that Robarge had lost his stripes.

"What happened when old Cota came in here?" I asked.

"Hell, I didn't bother looking up," Robarge said, "but I yelled something about giving me a hand 'cause I thought it was you. Then someone yelled 'attention', and I thought I'd get it for sure when I saw the old bugger standing there. But he just laughed and said it looked good, so I offered him some. I think he would have liked to take it but didn't think he should, so he just laughed again and said to carry on as he walked out. I think the captain was ready to kill me until he saw that it was OK with Cota, then he loosened up too."

Hunk nodded in dazed wonder, affirming everything the sergeant had said. The war must be nearly over, I thought, if Cota has mellowed this much.

As if to confirm my anticipation of peace, a dozen Red Cross girls arrived the next afternoon to share dinner with us and raise our morale. I had a chance to visit with one girl from Michigan, but it didn't go very well. She wanted to hear about nothing except blood and thunder adventures, while I wanted to talk about home, and a dozen other men just wanted to talk to her regardless of the topic. I don't know what effect the girls had on morale, but for that one meal the food and language were dramatically better.

The women had hardly left when Lt. Parker summoned me to his room and announced that I should be ready to leave early in the morning as part of the advance party to someplace east of the Rhine.

10

BEYOND THE RHINE

Cold, cloudy weather seemed an inevitable part of an advance party, but I was delighted to be part of that crew once again, if only as the lowly interpreter for Lt. Baker and Sgt. Carey. The sergeant was uncharacteristically quiet as we chugged away from Niedermendig in the blustery dawn, his new taciturnity a consequence of a too convivial night before, a fact evidenced by his bloodshot eyes, hoarse voice, and lingering odor of alcohol. Baker, a self assured little dandy, exuded a sense of superiority and spoke in a pretentious manner as though each utterance was a precious bit of wisdom that his less worthy companions should commit to memory and file for future reference. In spite of my companions' deficiencies as comrades, I was elated to once again be on the way to new sights and to have a break from the monotony of the troop.

Only a few units of the 28th Division crossed the Rhine, and our convoy consisted of but three other jeep loads of special troops in contrast to the vast caravan that marked our move from Alsace to Belgium. We lined up behind a large truck convoy to cross the pontoon bridge at Andernach but soon left them after gaining the east shore of the river, where we verged off the main highway onto a secondary road. The narrow two lane route wound among wooded hills and passed through occasional tiny villages, whose inhabitants glanced at us warily from the corners of their eyes. The jeeps stopped at a succession of intersections so that the officers could climb out and ponder over their maps spread on one of the hoods. When our leaders were satisfied that we were on the right route, the little procession moved on to the next decision point. Finally one of the jeeps turned off on a side road, and then another, and soon the last vehicle departed down one of the mysterious byways and left the recon contingent alone on the quiet road. It was nearly noon, and we had traveled a good distance since early morning in spite of our many stops. We were now in heavily wooded territory and had not seen a village for several miles. Concerned by the possibility that we had missed a turn Baker ordered a stop.

With an air of casual boredom the lieutenant spread his map across his lap, studied it briefly, and then announced confidently, "We are right here, perhaps 2 or 3 kilometers from Wilsonroth. Just drive on, Carey."

I did not know or much care where we were, but I wished someone would get as hungry as I so we could stop and eat a ration. I was tempted to open my C ration and eat regardless of the others, but somehow I didn't think Baker would approve of my early lunch. I then decided that the lieutenant was less sure of his position than he let on, as I noticed him fidgeting in his seat and scowling as though the dark woods conspired to bar him from his destination. He ordered Carey to stop at the next crossroads, where he got out and spread his map on the hood to give it his full attention. The sergeant seemed to be recovering from his hangover, but he still experienced a diuretic effect from his bacchanal and headed for the ditch to urinate.

"Hey, lieutenant," Carey shouted. "There's a road sign lying here, says Wilsonroth 5 kilometers, but I'll be damned if I can figure out which road it's on. Damned krauts must've knocked it down to confuse us."

"Does it give distances to other places?" Baker asked.

"Yeah, here, I'll pull it up 'n' we can take a look at it. Yeah, it's got them other names." Then as though a light suddenly flashed, Carey exclaimed, "Yeah, I getcha, if we know our directions 'n' how far it is to them other places we should be able to figure out the way to the place we're goin'."

Baker gave him a supercilious look as he pulled a compass out of his belongings and laid it on the ground. I watched in amusement from the jeep as the lieutenant scanned his map, compared it to the road sign, and then triumphantly announced, "It's 5 km that way," pointing east on the cross road.

I knew that Carey was just as able to determine the direction to our destination as the lieutenant, but his mind was still slowed by his binge. In any case, my companions now seemed satisfied that we were close to our target when they climbed back into the jeep and Carey accelerated away from the intersection. Instinctively I disliked the pompous little pretty boy officer, and yet I hoped he was right so that we could soon eat. Sure enough, after covering what seemed about 5 km the road curved and suddenly we were out of the forest and in a quaint little town of half timbered houses populated by people who on the surface seemed untouched by war. I spotted what I thought was the rathaus and suggested that we stop there to discuss our needs with the burgomaster. Baker approved of my suggestion with a windy statement about the desirability of exerting our influence through the local authorities.

Almost before we were out of the jeep the door opened and a paunchy middle aged man in lederhosen emerged, smiling and jabbering excitedly as though we were his long lost relatives.

"What's he saying, Ostrander?" Baker asked.

"I don't know, lieutenant. I'll try to slow him down so I can catch it."

A cloud of irritation crossed Baker's face at my admission of linguistic weakness, but at least he did not launch into a tirade as Rutt Parker might have. The burgomaster quickly grasped my limitations in German and slowed his speech to a ludicrous one word at a time pace. He said he was indeed the burgomaster, he was not a Nazi, and he would consider it a privilege to help us in any way that he could. I translated this unlikely statement for the lieutenant, who nodded with a smile of satisfaction.

"Tell him we need quarters for 150 men in the best houses in town," Baker said.

I conveyed the lieutenant's order to the German, expecting excuses and evasions for housing the Americans in crowded and uncomfortable billets, but instead the burgomaster's face lit up and he vowed that the Amerikaner would have the finest that his humble dorf could offer. Still looking for some sort of deception to protect his constituents, we followed the officious little popinjay as he ordered the inhabitants out of the largest and most elegant houses and proudly presented them to us. His brusque treatment of his countrymen was no better than Rutt's behavior, and I would not have been surprised if he had procured women for the victors if we had asked. The obsequious rascal was obviously trying to curry favor in order to protect his petty position as burgomaster of the insignificant town.

Baker and Carey were visibly pleased with the results of my "negotiating", and I probably edged up a notch in the lieutenant's estimation. We staked out space for the three platoons and headquarters, an easy task since the lieutenant and sergeant represented second platoon and I was from third. Not surprisingly, our units would occupy the best of the billets, but in truth all the quarters were far superior to our usual housing.

After concluding this business and finally eating our lunch ration, we were free to patrol the town while the lieutenant busied himself with some reports. He cautioned us to be alert for German treachery and to stay together in our reconnaissance of the village. Carey nodded amiably, but I knew he would agree to anything and then go his own way in his quest for interesting diversions in the town.

As we set off on our patrol his face lit up like a small boy on the first day of summer vacation, and he turned to me with a broad smile on his amiable Irish mug. "Well, Ostrander, let's see what we can find in this burg besides talkin' to that fuckin' burgomaster."

The words were hardly out of his mouth when we rounded a corner and were abruptly confronted by an M4 tank parked in front of a house. At first we thought it was abandoned, because one track was off the sprockets, but when we reached the vehicle a disheveled American emerged from the adjacent dwelling.

"Hey, Mercans," he called unenthusiastically. "You fellows just passing through or what?"

"No, we'll be here a while. We're the advance party for the 28th Recon," Carey replied.

"Oh, shit, that spoils everything," the tanker exclaimed. "Our outfit went through here like a bat outa hell three days ago, but "C'est le Guerre" there," pointing to the tank with the French name stenciled on the side, "decided she'd had enough of the damned war and threw her track right here." Now a slyly gleeful look crossed his face. "Would you believe it, we were stranded in front of this house where four young widows were livin', well I can tell you it's been the biggest fuckfest and drinkin' party you could ever dream of."

Looking at the man I was sure he was telling the truth. He was unshaven, red eyed, and reeked of alcohol. His untidy clothes had been hastily thrown on, were only half buttoned, and even his shoelaces were untied.

"Jesus," Carey almost whispered, "Is there any more of that around here? I mean, the troop won't be here until tomorrow. I could stand some of that pussy 'n' drinkin'. How many of you are in that house? How long do you figure to be here?"

The tanker laughed, "Hell, there's only four of us, there's lots of women in this town just dyin' to get what you boys can give 'em. I hope we stay here until the damned war is over, but we'll have to leave when they get time to fetch the tank. We just check in by radio a couple of times a day, the rest of the time we just eat, drink and fuck."

Carey's eyes sparkled in anticipation as he let out a low whistle. "Damn if that don't sound like heaven itself. How about introducin' us to some of them frauleins or whatever the hell they are?"

I interrupted, "Mike, I think the lieutenant will expect us back soon. Let's finish the patrol, we'll have to tell him about the tank." Turning to the tanker I added, "Our lieutenant is fussy about discipline, shaving and all that, so be careful how you look and act around him."

"Ostrander, why don't you report to Baker, 'n' I'll see if I can do any good right here," Carey suggested hopefully.

"Well, suit yourself, but I think the lieutenant will be mad if you don't show up," I countered. "Let's report, and then you can do what you want."

"Dammit all, I guess you're right. Hell, maybe we can get Baker all fixed up, and then we'll all have a party until the troop comes tomorrow."

I said nothing, but I could hardly imagine the lieutenant entering into any such arrangement, not because he was any paragon of virtue, but I thought he would consider it unmilitary and of course it would be a violation of the antifraternization law. Apparently Carey came to the same conclusion, for he carefully omitted any reference to the tankers' ongoing orgy in his report to Baker.

"You men keep your eyes open, but we seem to be fairly secure here," the lieutenant said. "If that tank crew has been here for three days it's unlikely that there are guerrilla forces in the vicinity. Just check back in a couple of hours."

With this Baker returned to whatever he had been doing, and Carey and I left the house. The sergeant was nearly pawing the ground and snorting in his eagerness to return to the tankers' pleasure palace. I begged off from that excursion and started to walk in the other direction. I had only gone about 100 feet when a middle aged man softly called and motioned for me to come over to where he stood in a doorway. I cautiously approached the German, a thin fellow of medium height wearing work clothes that bore the stains of farm labor. He was very nervous, apparently fearful that our meeting would be observed, and begged me to come into his cottage. I refused mainly because of the fraternization rule, but partly because of uneasiness about possible treachery. Although the man appeared to be just an ordinary peasant, the incessant warnings about the actions of the German irregular forces made me reluctant to enter a house in an area where only a handful of Americans were surrounded by many potential enemies.

The farmer seemed dismayed by my refusal to enter his home,

but, then, looking first right and then left along the deserted street as though he envisioned a hundred pairs of eyes following his every action, he whispered that he wanted to tell me some things. He started by confiding that he was not a Nazi, by now standard practice for every German, and went on to say that he was a social democrat whose life had been in constant danger because he opposed the Hitler regime. He then lowered his voice to a barely audible whisper, as though the very walls had ears, and informed me that the burgomaster and half a dozen other men of the town were Nazis. It was all I could do to keep from laughing at the poor, cowering rustic, who seemed so proud of himself for screwing up enough courage to expose his neighbors for their political affiliations. I thanked the man and tried to convince him that he had nothing to fear for fingering Nazis, but I also advised him to save his information for military government, which would appear later and know how to deal with political questions. He again asked me wistfully if I wouldn't come into his house to meet his family and have a glass of beer, and he seemed truly disconsolate and uncomprehending when I tried to explain that it was verboten for Americans to fraternize with Germans.

    The rest of my walk in and around Wilsonroth was uneventful. People on the streets looked at me with curiosity mixed with shy smiles for the most part, and I detected no hostility from the timid inhabitants.

    I purposely avoided the locale where the tankers and Carey were cavorting and returned to the third platoon house where I picked out a comfortable bed and settled down for a nap.

    Except for the C ration meals the interlude before the troop arrived was like a vacation. The region was heavily wooded and consisted of low hills sprinkled with villages even smaller than Wilsonroth.

Baker thought that a reconnaissance of the area by jeep was necessary, and the job fell to me. Carey spun some truly virtuoso blarney, so that the lieutenant gave him permission to help the tank crew who were "working like dogs to repair their tank so they could catch up with their battalion."

As I drove along the deserted roads it was hard to realize that the war was still going on not too far away. Occasional farmers were preparing their fields for planting or tending their livestock, and between hamlets I caught glimpses of deer feeding in the clearings. The fir trees were arranged in rows in which all the plantings seemed about the same size, clearly the result of planned forestry, so that the entire area resembled a park. The only hostility I encountered came from the huge white geese that paraded about the hamlets and even stood in the road scolding the approaching jeep. Sometimes they refused to move, and I detoured around the hissing creatures. In this bucolic setting I had to force myself to pay close attention to the pavement and avoid suspicious areas that might conceal a mine. I realized I would be just as dead if I struck a booby trap here as if a crack Wehrmacht mortar squad caught me in one of their murderous barrages in an active combat zone, but I saw nothing to suggest a military presence in the 4 or 5 mile radius around Wilsonroth. Somehow this area was different from any of my preconceived ideas about Germany, a peaceful, rural countryside of quiet beauty and charm.

Shortly after I returned from patrol Mike Carey appeared, a red eyed, whiskery, disheveled apparition with a hoarse voice and emitting the pungent odor of beer. I grinned at him and could not resist a little gibe out of earshot of the lieutenant.

"It looks like you worked all night on that broken down tank,

Mike."

With a lascivious smirk he replied, "Yeah, an' she ain't done yet, not by a damned sight she ain't. We can use some more help too, got a job just right for you, buddy, if you can see your way clear to pitch in."

I laughed and replied softly, "You better get cleaned up and take a nap before you go back to work or you may not last the day."

Mike nodded wearily and flashed his big smile as he disappeared into the third platoon house, apparently hoping to avoid Baker's scrutiny. He was still snoring loudly when the troop arrived and the town was suddenly transformed from a tranquil, otherworldly oasis to a noisy collection of vehicles and troops, racing engines, shouts, and a din that sounded like far more than 150 soldiers.

"You did a good job," Robarge said approvingly as he inspected our quarters. "I couldn't have done better myself. What kind of burg is this?"

"It's nice, but I think we'll get tired of it in a hurry," I replied. "There's nothing around here except woods and little villages. It's pretty and there are deer in the woods, so with a little luck we'll get some venison instead of Spam for a change. Carey is in there sleeping because he tried to screw himself to death in a whorehouse on the other side of town where some tankers have been shacked up for three or four days. Nothing else to tell you except that the krauts are all squealing on one another. Everyone is a Nazi except the guy you're talking to."

"Where'd you say those tankers are?" Hunk asked. Everyone laughed as I started to give the impatient driver directions.

"Hold on, Hunk," Robarge cautioned. "Better wait and see what the lieutenant wants us to do before you head off to get your asses hauled. And when you do go, remember be careful, we don't need to have you out of action with the clap."

"Oh Sarge, nothing will happen to me, you're not going to keep us from having any fun, are you?"

Just then Gorlitz entered the parlor from a bedroom holding aloft a ball.

"Hey you guys, look what I found. I was just looking around when I found a box of toys in a corner and this ball was right on top. It feels like hard rubber, but it'll do until we can get something better. Now all we need is a bat."

He passed his trophy around among the other members of the section, but before anyone could be further distracted by sex or softball, Rutt's screech for Robarge told us that we must have an assignment of some sort. As expected, we were soon on the road to reconnoiter an area southeast of town, where we were to be on the lookout for arms, Nazis, and large numbers of displaced persons, The countryside consisted of densely wooded hills with occasional lush green meadows in the shallow valleys. Only a few abandoned German military vehicles reminded us that this was still a war zone. The inhabitants seemed curious but timid. We saw a few men of military age and guessed they had mustered themselves out of service by donning civilian clothes, but there was no sign of uniformed troops. We did not venture off the paved road and could have missed arms caches or other military equipment, but Robarge wisely limited our patrol to those tasks specifically mentioned in our orders. We all shared a healthy fear of blundering into a mine field if we extended our reconnaissance to unimproved roads where the devices could be easily concealed.

The weather had become damp and chilly with a solid canopy of gray clouds adding to the somber atmosphere of the seemingly endless blanket of fir trees. The place now depressed me and I yearned for the sunny days and open fields we had enjoyed before we crossed the Rhine.

"I hope we get out of these lousy forests and see the sun soon," I griped.

"Yeah, these are toothpick farms," Hunk replied in an airy tone, "But man, this reminds me of home. If they just had some real trees it'd be more like Washington. It rains there all the time too, but it's good for the trees. Damn, I'd just like to get out and do some cutting."

"Hunk, you must be kidding," Spada interjected. "This place is like a wet sock and yet it reminds you of home. I'm sure as hell glad I'm not from your neck of the woods."

I laughed at John's comment while Hunk launched into a long recital of the glories of the Pacific Northwest. He was still going on when we suddenly entered a clearing where a village had nestled below a railroad bridge that spanned the little valley. Proximity to the trestle had been the village's undoing when aircraft had rained bombs on the area in attempts to disrupt the railroad. Miraculously, the bridge was undamaged, but the village was destroyed. Only piles of rubble interspersed among gaping bomb craters marked the site of the hamlet. We stopped and stared at this terrible scar of war in the otherwise peaceful countryside. Not a living soul remained in the village, and we could only conclude that any survivors must have been removed to other towns. Nobody spoke for several minutes as we gazed at the stark destruction, but then Hilton asked the question that must have been on everyone's mind.

"Jesus, all this, but they missed the damned bridge. How could they do it?"

"Well, we've seen it before," Caulkins replied. "It must be easier to blow up houses than to knock out a bridge."

"Hey, look," Indy interjected in more excitement than awe. "See those round pieces of wood over there? In the pile of stuff just past the first crater. Looks like part of a railing or something, but it looks like one of those pieces would do as a bat."

I saw what he meant, and soon we had found a piece of wood that would never have been mistaken for a Louisville slugger but that would do for our projected games. We passed it around and took practice swipes with the new toy with the enthusiasm of small boys on Christmas morning.

"Hey, look, you guys," Reardon called out, "There's a dog over there behind that piece of roof. He looks like he needs something to eat. See him?"

"Cob, he's the mangiest cur I've ever seen," DJ replied. "He's got his tail between his legs just looking at us, and we're not even near him."

"Well, let's see if he'll come out if we give him something to eat," Jack countered.

Gorlitz found a can of meat from a K ration and tried to coax the animal from its lair in the rubble. When he tossed a small portion of the greasy concoction toward the mutt, the pathetic creature crept forward and retrieved the morsel while keeping its tail tucked between its legs and trembling like a leaf. It was so thin that every rib could be counted. In the open I could see that it was a male of mixed breed, but probably more fox terrier than anything else. I pitied the dog and wanted to help him survive, and this same sentiment must have moved the others as well. Almost before he had bolted the piece of ration half a dozen hands were trying to coax him closer, and several men were talking of taking him with us.

"Well I'll be damned," Pa Conger exclaimed. "You boys mean you wanta take that godawful cur with us? Why the best thing you can do is put the mutt out of his misery."

Nine men turned and looked at Pa in horror, as though he had suggested killing a member of the section.

"Look, Pa," Jack replied testily, "You just mind your own business. If you don't like the dog, leave him be, but the rest of us want to take him along."

As I looked up I saw Robarge grinning and could only guess at his thoughts. Before I had time to ponder that enigma he put himself squarely on the side of the dog.

"Pa's right about one thing, he's not much of a dog, but if you guys want him, bring him along, but make it quick. We can't waste any more time nursing a mangy mongrel."

By this time the dog had summoned enough courage to accept more pieces of ration, and the next move was to the M8, where the mutt was hoisted to the rear deck.

"He can't come inside this car until we know if he's house broken," Robarge announced. "It's bad enough walking in your buddy's shit, I'm not going to walk in dog shit in my own armored car."

We continued the patrol in high spirits and eagerly anticipated some ballgames and training the dog. The reconnaissance was uneventful, and the dog clung to the deck of the M8 without difficulty.

As we parked in the town, Robarge cautioned us not to mention the dog to Lt. Parker and to house the animal in a corner of the kitchen where the lieutenant was not likely to see him. Inside of an hour the dog's tail came up, and he even wagged it as the troopers continued to feed him. I was confident he would not leave us under any circumstances, particularly in light of the food we were cramming into him.

"Better not overfeed that cur," Pa warned. "He'll throw up all over and maybe even die if you feed him too much right away."

That sage advice halted the feeding for the moment and all our attention turned to naming our pet. I don't recall who actually suggested it, but from a welter of more mundane names we chose to call him Himler. Somehow that appellation tickled a macabre sense of humor in most of us.

"Can't you just see the krauts, scared to death of that son of a bitch for years, and here's a little cur dog with the same name," Robarge chuckled. "You can bet your life he's the only dog in Germany with that name."

The dog gave every indication of being very smart and quickly answered to his name and demonstrated that he was house broken as well.

The next day was April 1 and Easter Sunday. We had been told that a chaplain would visit the troop and hold a service at 1 PM in the village church. All members of the section except Pa and Robarge set out for the church with the mutt trotting along behind us. Robarge saw him and yelled for the dog to come back without result except to attract Lt. Parker's attention. He popped out of his quarters and grasped the situation instantly.

"Don't tell me you men are trying to make a pet of that mangy cur. Who the hell said you could have a goddamned dog? Where the hell do you think you are, back home in your mama's yard?"

We stopped and shifted uneasily until Robarge interjected, "Oh come on, lieutenant, he doesn't bother anything and the men want to keep him. If he causes any trouble I'll get rid of him myself."

"But damn it all, Robarge, we're still in a war and that dog doesn't belong here. Besides, he's the worst looking mutt I've ever seen." Then after a pause that seemed to last an hour Rutt continued, "Tell you what, I won't say anything more, but the first time that dog gives us any trouble, I'll shoot it myself, you all understand?"

I recognized this as vintage Rutt Parker, more bark than bite, and reassured by Himler's status I went on to Easter worship. The church was small but had a rather ornate sanctuary for such a tiny community. The chaplain was already there arranging an altar cloth and various items for use in the service. Dave Morton had joined us on our way, but his joy at the prospect of a church service evaporated at the sight of the chaplain and his paraphernalia.

"What kind of service is this?" he asked me.

"I don't know, maybe he's Episcopalian," I replied.

"I don't like the looks of it, those people aren't real Christians," Dave muttered.

"Well, we don't have any choice, do we?"

He mumbled something and settled back into a sulk while the chaplain completed his preparations and the church filled with men of the troop. My surmise was correct, and the service was read from the Episcopal book of worship, a brief, impersonal ritual that left many of the men as unhappy as Dave. It wasn't the preacher's denomination that irked me but his cold indifferent attitude toward his congregation. The man exhibited no warmth and made no apparent effort to reach the men on a personal level. At the conclusion of the 20 minute service he packed his equipment, folded the altar cloth, and told his driver, a sad looking corporal, to put it into his jeep. I thought he would shake hands with the men and inquire about any needs of the congregation, but he departed without a word leaving us puzzled and more than a little indignant.

"See, I told you, he's no Christian at all," Dave reminded me. "I bet he's in a hurry to get somewhere he can get some booze, see, look," Morton exclaimed triumphantly. "He could hardly wait to get out so he could light up a cigarette."

Sure enough the preacher was enjoying a smoke as his driver maneuvered the jeep out of the church yard and onto the road.

"Look, Dave," I remonstrated, "in some churches the ministers smoke and drink alcohol; you can't judge him on that."

"You don't really feel like he brought Christ into that church to you and to me, do you?" he persisted.

"Well, I have to admit he isn't my idea of a good minister," I replied sheepishly. "I just don't feel that he was interested in us or whether we got anything out of the service. But I think we should be fair, maybe he had to do that in 10 or 12 places today, we don't know."

We continued the discussion on the way back to our billets, and the grumbling of other troopers matched Morton's. It seemed that everyone who attended the service came away empty, surely an indictment of the preacher. Unfortunately, this experience was not unique for me during my time in the army. Most of the chaplains I encountered were very poor ministers of the Christian faith. Some seemed to be more interested in their status as commissioned officers than their duties as spiritual advisers to soldiers. Others were so intent on being "one of the boys" that they were indistinguishable in their behavior from the least pious of their flock, an attitude that surely undercut any chance they might have had to exert moral leadership.

When we reached our quarters I was surprised to see Pa Conger scratching Himler's ears and talking to the dog as though he were his master.

"Hey, I thought you wanted to shoot that dog, Pa," I said. "You're pretty friendly with him now."

"Oh, he's a good enough little dog, hell of a lot better than listening to some damned preacher. I thought you was a smart college boy, I didn't think you believed in that religion shit."

Surprised by what sounded like the words of the village atheist I stammered, "What've you got against religion, Pa?"

"Hell, I don't care if people want to waste their time on it, but I'm surprised when a smart man goes for it. I just think it's a fairy tale, not one damned thing to it."

Caulkins overheard this last and looked as shocked as though he were face to face with the Antichrist. "Do I understand that you deny Jesus Christ and God himself?" he asked incredulously.

Pa looked uneasy at this verbal onslaught but nonetheless replied, "Well, when you say it like that it makes me sound pretty bad, but I gotta tell you, I just don't believe any of it."

"But that makes you an atheist!" DJ gasped.

"Well, I guess it does, but it don't make any difference what you call me, I just gotta be honest with you."

"But Pa, it's your immortal soul, don't you want to save your soul? Don't you want Christ to save you?"

"Dammit, DJ, I don't mean to upset you, and if I thought Christ or God or anyone could save my soul, I guess I'd want him to, but I don't believe there is a God, so He sure as hell can't save me from anything."

Caulkins seemed thunderstruck. I don't think he had ever met an avowed nonbeliever before, and it was almost as though he was conversing with the devil, but I could tell that what really bothered him was that Pa didn't look or act like the devil was supposed to. He was still the same lovable old coot we had all grown fond of in spite of his eccentricities.

Robarge had listened to his conversation in silence, and DJ turned to him almost in desperation in the hope that someone would say or do something to dispel the awful fact of Pa's unbelief. "Sarge, Pa says he's an atheist. He can't be serious, can he?"

"He's telling you what he believes. You don't want him to lie, do you, DJ?" the sergeant replied quietly.

"No, I guess not, but I just didn't dream there was anyone in the section who didn't believe in God. Is that why you didn't go to church?"

"I wouldn't go unless I believed in it," Pa replied.

"But you didn't go either, Sarge, you're not an atheist too, are you?" Caulkins continued with a note of desperation in his voice.

"Take it easy, DJ," Robarge answered with a more serious expression than usual. "No, I'm not an atheist, but I have a hard time with church. I was raised a Catholic, and I used to go regularly, but when I used to see all the priests going to the races at Narragansett I decided I didn't want any more of that church. I believe in God, but I just don't like most of the ministers and priests I've known."

Caulkins relaxed a little after this lukewarm endorsement of religion by the sergeant, and he may in fact have derived some comfort from the knowledge that Robarge was no longer a follower of the Pope and was not affiliated with the devil either. I don't think the two were far apart in the thinking of Protestants of DJ's persuasion.

"Chaplains like that guy today could almost turn us all into atheists," I said in an effort to lighten the atmosphere. "My grandfather often excused himself from going to church because he claimed that 90% of the ministers were in the wrong line of work."

This elicited some smiles and easing of tension until Pa felt impelled to add another stick of dynamite.

"Sounds like a damned smart man. What's he do for a living?"

"He's retired, he was a railroad conductor."

"A railroad man! Now I just bet he's a dirty old devil. I never knew a railroad man who wasn't just like a sailor, had a woman at every stop and spent most of his time fighting the clap."

I should have taken umbrage at Pa's assertion and rushed to defend the family honor, but instead I could not control my laughter as the feisty old rooster rattled on almost as though he enjoyed shaking up his younger comrades.

"I'm afraid you missed a few railroad men in your time, Pa. He's as much of a popoff as you are, but he's no lady's man," I answered when I stopped laughing.

"Oh hell, you're not going to know about your grandpa's fuckin', but you ask your pa some day, I'll bet he'll tell you a lot you didn't know," Pa persisted.

I just grinned and let that one pass. It seemed the only way to shut off the old blatherskate was to ignore some of his bombast. By this time everyone, including Caulkins, was chuckling at the little gamecock and his loose tongue.

Before we could continue the verbal jousting we heard the sound of what seemed to be distant rifle shots and then shouts from outside. We dashed from the house to join the rest of the second and third platoon troopers in the street, where the officers seemed to be in a frenzy, shouting orders and gesticulating wildly. Finally the captain ordered two jeeps from each platoon to follow Lt. Baker in a rapid reconnaissance to find the source of the rifle fire. Robarge, Caulkins and I represented our section in the third jeep of the procession as it left Wilsonroth and drove up the low hill leading southeast from the town.

"Those shots sounded like M1's," DJ observed.

"Yeah, it's probably some GI hunting deer," Robarge added. "The captain seems pretty nervous, he probably still thinks there are SS troopers in every haystack. He strikes me as a real horse's ass."

I darted a look at him, hardly able to believe my ears. Although our sergeant would grumble and even question an officer about an order, I had never heard him utter a disrespectful or disparaging remark about one of our commissioned ranks. He caught my surprise and looked uncomfortable as he continued.

"Well, I shouldn't say that, just forget what I said, but somehow I just don't trust him."

"That's OK, Sarge," Caulkins interrupted. "We all feel the same way. Leon and I knew he was a dumb old boy from the first time we met him. I know I could hardly keep from laughing in his face."

"Yeah, don't apologize. Everyone thinks he's a half wit," I added. "You've always been overly loyal to assholes like Rutt and the captain. Don't be embarrassed to call a fool a fool."

Robarge mumbled something, but I didn't catch it because the line of jeeps stopped at a small clearing. Lt. Baker and the occupants of the first jeep were already out of the vehicle and walking across the glade with weapons at the ready by the time we stopped. The lieutenant motioned for everyone to follow so we climbed out and started out on the boggy meadow. We had only gone a few yards when several dark figures appeared out of the trees, and we quickly recognized them as GI's. They waved and we returned the greeting, but the lieutenant suddenly became animated as the men turned to reenter the forest.

"You men, halt, come over here and identify yourselves," he shouted.

The men seemed surprised by this imperious challenge but obeyed and slowly made their way across the soggy glade. As they neared the officer one gave an awkward salute and the other seemed undecided. Both had M1 rifles slung on their shoulders, and they looked like typical infantrymen.

"What can we do for you, lieutenant?" the leader, a sergeant, asked as he stopped about three yards from Baker.

"Identify yourselves and explain what you are doing here, sergeant," the lieutenant replied irritably.

"I'm Sgt. Whittaker, and this is Pvt. Sloan, B Company, 214th Infantry, sir. We just moved into a little town about a mile from here and went out to hunt deer," the puzzled noncom answered.

"Were you firing your rifles about 20 minutes ago?"

"Yes sir, but we missed the buck," Whittaker replied.

"You're sure you've had no encounters with German troops in this area?"

"Oh no, sir," Whittaker continued with apparent relief as a smile crossed his face. "We haven't seen anything of the krauts except a few uniforms they ditched. They're long gone from around here."

"I must warn you, sergeant," Baker continued in a condescending tone, "you are close to the 28th Recon Troop, and you are fortunate that your careless use of firearms for your so-called hunting did not bring down heavy fire on you. I suggest that you return to your unit and confine the use of your weapons to encounters with the enemy."

The two infantrymen looked dumbfounded by this insulting assertion by the pretentious little officer, but they held their tongues as Whittaker saluted and said "Yes sir" in a tone that did not completely hide his contempt. I was embarrassed to be part of this silly little encounter, even though I was only an unwilling member of the cast.

As we turned back toward the jeeps Baker mused aloud, "I wonder if that pair were telling the truth. I think we better continue the patrol until we are completely satisfied that there is no other explanation for the firing."

We then chugged through the deepening shadows of late afternoon in the somber, dripping forest, and my feet began to tingle and pain as they had not for several weeks. The immersion in the boggy meadow was enough to rekindle the problem that had plagued me most of the winter, and to make matters worse we were driving around in the damp twilight looking for who knew what.

My irritation boiled over, "What's that silly little shit think he's doing? Did you ever hear anything like that? He's as dumb as the captain."

"Cob yes, those two make old Rutt seem like a genius," Caulkins added.

"He'd like to know you called him a genius, DJ," Robarge interjected with one of his most cynical smiles. "He really likes you, thinks you're the best young noncom in the troop. If he thought you called him a genius he'd find a way to make you a sergeant."

"Well, I didn't mean he is a genius, you know what I meant, he's just better than Baker or the captain."

Leon D. Ostrander, Jr.

Poor DJ wished he had never mentioned the word genius in any way related to Parker because Robarge and I would not let him forget it as we finally returned to Wilsonroth after Baker decided that we could not find any dangerous Nazis in the cold spring night. It had been a disappointing day, and the final blow fell when I learned that I was on guard duty from 2 to 4 AM. I hated that shift more than any other. It seemed to disrupt sleep more and was colder, quieter, and more boring than any other two hour segment of the night. When we were not in combat nothing stirred at that hour, there wasn't even the distraction of watching fraternizers and other night owls going about their mischief.

My post was at the edge of the town where the road snaked along a little stream and passed close to a barn where the sentry could spend some of his time sheltered from the weather in the doorway and still control the road and the troop area. I was still grumpy from the disappointing Easter when I took my place in the doorway. I paced about, gazed in every direction, patrolled the street, and then tried to kill time by thinking of all the things I would do when I got home. After what seemed at least an hour of such efforts to pass time I could not resist a glance at my watch, a temptation I should have resisted. 2:20! I had been on guard exactly 20 minutes. Then I realized that I was hungry, but I had not thought to bring a ration. I could not leave my post to ransack the kitchen for something to eat, but neither could I stop thinking of the new frankfurter and bean C rations that had just begun to appear. If only I had one of those I could build a little fire inside the barn to warm it and pass some of the time enjoying a tasty snack. But just as my imagination soared to the point that I could almost savor the delicious franks and beans, I realized there was no way for me to procure such a ration. I must wait until breakfast to satisfy my mounting hunger. Still, the idea of a little fire appealed to me. It would not only give me something to do, but it would provide a little warmth as well. I used my flashlight to round up some discarded pieces of wood and an old seed catalogue in the barn. In short order my blaze was crackling merrily while I enjoyed toasting myself in between trips outside to look for whomever one might expect in the dead of night in this remote corner of Germany. When most of the wood had been consumed I thought it must surely be time for me to awaken my successor, so I looked at my watch again. 3:05! I thought the time piece must have stopped, and yet I could see the second hand creeping around the dial. Could it really be that I had only been at my post for an hour? I looked at the watch again: 3:08. It seemed to be functioning perfectly, so I did indeed have another 50 minutes to kill. I threw the last of the wood on the embers and looked almost desperately for something to do.

Earlier I had noticed that someone had left a grenade on the ground just inside the door, and I had wondered idly who would do such a stupid thing. I concluded that some of my buddies had no sense at all. Of course the grenade was harmless unless someone pulled the pin, but why would anyone leave it here? The device seemed to cast a spell over me; I could not take my eyes off it once I became conscious of its presence. Before I realized what I was doing I had picked up the grenade and carefully inspected it, noting every detail of the wicked little "pineapple". It had a nice feel, a solid sensation conveyed by the cast iron body with its serrations. The lever fit well into my hand, and the other hand played with the ring on the pin that held the lever down and kept the device inactive. I remembered how Sgt. Renker had us pull the pin and replace it on live grenades at Ft. Riley, so we would understand that nothing would happen even after the pin was pulled unless one's grip on the body and lever was released so that the detonating device could literally spring into action. Well, why not pull this pin and then replace it? It was tight but came out with a good pull, and then I casually slipped it back into place rendering the grenade harmless again. Then I thought I might as well unscrew the body of the grenade from the activating mechanism and see if it was full of powder. I had done this in training too, and, like all the others, this grenade was filled with explosive granules. Then another whim seized me. Why not empty the powder, replace the detonator, pull the pin, and toss the device around the side of the barn? I wondered just how strong the detonator charge was, and this little experiment would give me the answer. Like the rest of this foolish little game, thought was soon deed, and I flipped the grenade around the corner of the building and waited for what I expected to be a loud pop. The report was more like a shotgun blast at close range, and the grenade fragments bit deeply into the wall of the barn, an explosion that rocked me back to reality and a shaky awareness of how my idle play with the grenade had been a case of flirting with death. I trembled as the bizarre episode sank into my consciousness, but then as now I have no explanation of why I played such a foolish game with so lethal a toy. I can only conclude that boredom is a powerful stimulus to mischief. Hunk Wilson's silliness with the signal flares under similar circumstances seemed far more rational than my tinkering with a hand grenade, and I now regretted laughing at his discomfort when he was reprimanded for the impromptu fireworks. I was thankful that the explosion had not awakened any of my comrades, so that I was spared the embarrassment of trying to explain my childish behavior.

When I looked at my watch it was 3:58, so the time had finally passed, and I could turn the post over to my relief. I fell to sleep as soon as I hit the sleeping bag, but I never forgot my folly with the grenade.

The next several days were spent in a series of patrols of the area around Wilsonroth either at platoon or section strength. We played a few innings of softball when we could find a meadow that was dry enough, and some of the men tried deer hunting with only modest success. The few deer that were bagged were quite small and did not dress out into very appetizing cuts of meat. I went on one such expedition and came face to face with a young deer in a glade. The creature looked at me with its trusting and curious gaze, so that I could no more have shot it than a member of the section. I suspect others may have had similar experiences to explain in part the small number of deer that were taken.

One day the entire platoon was dispatched to a tiny hamlet at the junction of two secondary roads in the dripping, fog enshrouded forest, where we were to establish a check point. Parker and Samuels promptly grabbed the best looking house for their section, so the other two sections were obliged to crowd into a shabby place across the road. The elderly residents quickly relinquished their home and left us in charge of the chilly, musty smelling old place. In spite of our best efforts to coax more heat out of the stove the house remained dank and cheerless. We occupied the few chairs and much of the floor, a sullen group of men whose moods matched their surroundings.

It seemed as though we had been there for hours, but it was probably more like 20 minutes, when the door opened and a fat, untidy looking young woman entered. She looked around the room and then smiled in what could only be interpreted as a seductive way. She spoke no English, but by gesture and repetition of the phrase "gehe oben mit mir" made it clear that she was soliciting sex from the men in the room.

"What in hell is she trying to say?" Robarge asked irritably.

"She wants someone to go upstairs with her," I replied, "And I don't think she wants to show off her knitting."

"Tell her to get the hell out of here," the sergeant exploded. "I don't know how many times I have to say it, I'm not running a cat house for this section."

"Hey, you speak for your section, but we have something to say about it too, Robarge," Mel Reicher, a radio operator in Nelson's section interjected. "I think I might like a little of that German pussy right about now, so you boys just look the other way."

Several other men murmured their agreement, and I could see that Robarge was disgusted but resigned to the fact that he could not impose his rules on the other section. Their sergeant was in the other house with Samuels and Parker, but he might not have objected anyway.

"Ostrander, who the hell is this pig?" the sergeant asked. "Where did she come from way out here in this God forsaken forest?"

I asked the woman, and to my surprise she said it was her husband's house, but she had no idea whether he was alive or dead, and she was tired of being harassed by her husband's parents, the old couple whom we had evicted from the house. She added that she had not had a man in a long time and would take care of as many of the men in her house as wanted to go upstairs with her.

As I recounted what she said a silence fell over the room. The whole episode seemed so bizarre that nobody knew what to make of it.

Reicher leered at the woman and grabbed some cigarettes and

candy from his musette bag before he followed her up the ladder like stair to the upper story.

"Jesus, I'm as hard up as anyone, but I wouldn't touch her with a ten foot pole," Hunk whispered to me. "She's the dirtiest looking pig I've seen in a long time. I'll just wait for something better to come along."

Apparently the same feeling gripped the rest of the men in the room, because there was no rush to be the next in line to "gehe oben" after Reicher concluded his business.

After about a half hour I heard footsteps and then Reicher appeared at the head of the stairs. As he slowly descended he was greeted by catcalls, leers, and inquiries about "how was it". His face wore a perplexed expression as though he had just come from a difficult examination rather than a sexual tryst.

"Well, aren't you going to tell us about it?" one man asked.

Reicher turned to the questioner, shook his head slowly, and a sheepish grin replaced the quizzical expression on his round face. "Well, I'll tell you, it wasn't like anything I can recall. I guess I made a mistake when I gave her the candy and cigarettes before I fucked her. I mean, as I was mounting up that fat cow was stuffing a candy bar into her mouth, and after that she started another. She was a lot more interested in the candy than in my peter, and about the time I was ready for another go she lit a cigarette. I mean it was about as exciting as fucking the pillow."

It took a moment for his report to sink in, but then the room rocked with laughter and ribald comments about Reicher's encounter. Not surprisingly, there were no takers when the fat slut came down and offered herself for whomever else wanted to "gehe oben".

Another example of the growing behavior problems among the troops at that time came to my attention a couple of nights later. The platoon had established a check point in another small cross roads community, and I had drawn sentry duty from midnight until 2 AM. When my stint was nearly over I went to our billet to find my relief, but to my surprise his bedroll was empty, and the other three occupants of the room were also missing. Perplexed and irritated by the absence of my relief I thought of waking Samuels but then decided to find the man myself. I walked down the main street of the town, but all was still and dark. As I was about to return and awaken the sergeant, I heard the sound of voices from a partially bombed out store. I approached the place cautiously and then caught a glimmer of light from the rear of the building and recognized a few words in English. As I entered I saw four figures bent over something only faintly illuminated by flashlights, and I called my relief's name.

There was no reply, so I advanced farther and again called, "Is that you, Michaels?"

The activity stopped abruptly and Michaels replied guardedly, "Yeah, who is it?"

"Ostrander," I replied. "It's time for you to relieve me on guard duty. What're you doing?"

"Oh hell, I forgot all about that, you mean it's two already?"

"Yeah, it is, and I'm going to hit the sack. What're you guys doing in here in the middle of the night?"

"Hey, maybe you'd like to help us," one of the men interjected. "This is a jewelry store, 'n' we're finding all kinds of good loot, watches, rings, bracelets, just look."

When he turned the flashlight on several drawers the looters had pried open I saw a collection of cheap looking trinkets more like what I would expect in a five and ten cent store than a jewelry. And yet, these four Americans were feverishly stealing such junk. I thought it was bad enough to be a thief, but stealing trash was not only contemptible but pathetic. I could understand, if not condone, young men succumbing to temptation when an opportunity appeared to filch something of real value, but some men seemed to revel in stealing for the sake of stealing. It was not as though there was no opportunity to acquire legitimate souvenirs, because we were under orders to confiscate all kinds of arms, cameras, and binoculars from civilians as well as military personnel. Such "loot" exceeded anyone's ability to carry it off, but still the theft of everything else imaginable burgeoned.

The most surprising and amusing occurrence during our stay in the area of Wilsonroth was the metamorphosis of our dog, Himler. I had laughed at stories of dogs adopting the behavior and attitudes of their masters, but Himler seemed to be living proof of a linkage between dog and master psychology. The little mutt ate voraciously and quickly filled out his bony frame. Even more remarkable was his transformation from a cringing, fearful, whipped cur type of dog into a cocky and indeed bellicose member of the section. He apparently considered himself one of us and gave the men all of his affection. He was friendly to other Americans, but Germans were another matter. He growled, snapped and snarled at any civilians who approached our billets or vehicles, and he put to flight any local dog that dared to come near his territory. After each act of bravado he would turn to see if his multiple masters were watching his tough dog behavior. In short, he had become a true chowhound and brash cavalry dog, and the men loved it. The more belligerent and arrogant the little terrier became, the more the GI's egged him on until he was the feistiest mutt any of us had ever seen.

Himler had great balance and loved to ride in or on any vehicle. He stood on the deck of the armored car and surveyed the world as though he were a general. Already we were trying to figure out how we would get him back to the states, and, perhaps more important, who would get the dog when we were discharged from the army. Even Rutt had taken a shine to Himler after we cleaned him up and put some meat on his bones and spirit in his heart. The lieutenant never missed a chance to pet him or talk to him when he was near the dog.

While at Wilsonroth we had our second visit to a shower point since our arrival in Europe three months earlier. The baths were welcome and much needed, but we did not evoke the same comments from the quartermaster troops manning that facility as on our first visit, so I think we had managed to keep a little cleaner with the onset of warmer weather and the opportunity to sleep in houses and take sponge baths with heated water on a fairly regular basis.

11

ODD JOBS

We thought our adventures beyond the Rhine were over when we were ordered to move west to Limburg for a special assignment. We were to meet important but unnamed American generals at an airport and escort them to Fort Ehrenbreitstein for a ceremony commemorating withdrawal of the last American forces from that same installation after World War I. The old fortress overlooked the Rhine opposite Coblenz, so we would be almost back where we had crossed the river a few days earlier. The entire troop was involved in the ceremony in one way or another, for picked crews were to provide the actual escort while the rest of the troop occupied positions along the road from the airport to the fort. I was the jeep commander of one escorting vehicle which was driven by a recently arrived first platoon man named Juan Gonzalez. He was an eager, wide-eyed young man from rural Texas who was painfully anxious to do the right thing while being very deferential to "old-timers" like me.

Juan and I spent several hours cleaning mud off his jeep and touching up a few bumps with olive drab paint, and we would have spent as much time on ourselves except we had so little to work with. I suspected that our recent trip to the shower point may have been because of our assignment to escort the generals.

The day of the ceremony was dark, cold and blustery, with intermittent rain showers. Much of our painstaking effort to tidy up the jeeps and ourselves was undone by splashes of muddy water that Juan could not avoid on our way to the airport. There were five escort jeeps and one command vehicle in our detachment, but I have long ago forgotten which men crewed the other jeeps. At the airport we pulled up behind a row of large American sedans of a sort I had not seen since I left the states. We huddled with the officer in charge and learned that Bradley, Patch and each of the American army commanders were to participate in the flag raising ceremony at the fort, but the generals would arrive separately and then be transported in one of the waiting sedans. Juan and I were to escort General Patton, whose driver was taking shelter inside the Buick that had been provided for his use.

The airport was not much of a facility, consisting only of a couple of runways large enough to accommodate transport planes, but there was no shelter or anything that remotely resembled a terminal building. Juan and I waited in the cold drizzle and watched the arrivals and departures for the fort of all the illustrious commanders except Patton.

Just when I thought that our general might be a no-show, a tiny Piper Cub approached the field and swept in for a landing. The plane came to rest a few feet from the waiting Buick, the door of the craft swung open, and Patton alighted with his polished helmet and its gold stars gleaming even in the murk of the rainy day. I could not miss the pair of ivory handled revolvers that protruded from holsters at his sides, and I could not help but think that he looked out of place, a caricature of a general right out of Hollywood.

Patch did not give a flicker of a smile to the greeting officer but strode briskly to the waiting car, which he approached from the left side. The driver had been standing on the right holding the rear door open for the great man, but "Old Blood and Guts" curtly motioned the startled driver to get into the front passenger's seat while he took the wheel himself.

Patton gunned the big Buick sedan and raced out of the parking area and onto the road, while Juan and I jumped into the jeep and set off in hot pursuit. The highway was full of pot holes and rough spots which made it very hazardous for anyone driving a short wheel base, top heavy vehicle such as a jeep at a high rate of speed. Still, Gonzales had the little buggy at 60 miles per hour, about its top speed, and yet the general kept pulling away. I knew we could never keep up with the Buick, and I did not want to be a casualty to some foolish attempt to catch up to the grandstanding commander, so I yelled and motioned for Juan to slow down. He glanced at me in wide eyed fear, as though we both might be court martialed if we did not make every possible effort to guard our reckless client, but I insisted, and he slowed to a more reasonable speed.

When we reached the fort the generals were already in the courtyard where security was provided by MP's and we were not even allowed to watch the ceremony. On the other hand, it had started to rain in earnest, and we were able to take shelter in a tunnel while the guards and brass were soaked by the shower.

Patton repeated his road race act on the return trip to the airport, so that his escort arrived after his plane was out of sight. When we were in our billets that night the Third Army commander's showboating was the main topic of conversation.

"The old bugger must be crazy," Pa Conger declared. "And he's the meanest looking cuss I've ever seen, looks like someone's squeezing his nuts all the time."

"I'd hate to be under him," Robarge added. "He looks as cold as ice. I don't think he'd give a damn about anyone as long as he got what he wanted."

"The son of a bitch should be in the movies with his shiny helmet and pearl handled revolvers," Juan exclaimed. "I wonder if the old bastard thinks he's going to have a gun fight with Hitler?"

The conversation continued in this vein until Spada changed the subject. "I hear we don't have to worry about old Georgie boy because we're going back across the Rhine. He'll be up trying to kill the last kraut or start on the Russians or some other hare brained scheme."

"Where'd you hear that?" Gorlitz asked.

"I heard a couple of officers talking in the latrine after the big shindig at the old fort."

"Did they say where we were going?" Henry asked.

"No, they just said all the 28th would be west of the Rhine."

"Yeah, but did they say when?" I asked. "Do they mean right now or when the war is over?"

The answer came in the morning when we headed northeast, away from the Rhine and toward the rapidly moving front. No effort was made to disguise our move, so we drove rapidly over a series of main highways and entered the city of Marburg before noon. Most of the city was intact, a charming old university community set in a region of gently rolling hills, neat villages, and large tracts of forest.

Our destination was a large building, apparently an apartment, on a pleasant boulevard, where we evicted the residents and moved into quite sumptuous quarters. I dropped my belongings in the corner of the room assigned to our section and then started to explore the place. I was pleasantly surprised to find a very attractive yard in the rear of the building, where the residents maintained a garden in which they had already started spring cultivation. As I wandered about this peaceful retreat I was surprised to hear a male voice speak to me in English.

"Sir, may I speak to you?"

Turning, I saw a rotund, gray haired man standing at the gate separating the yard I was in from that next door. He benignly beamed such a friendly smile at me that I completely forgot the ban on fraternization as I smiled back and walked over to the gate.

"You speak English very well," I said. "Have you lived in America or England?"

"No, but I have traveled to England many times in my work before this dreadful war," he replied. "I am a professor of history at the university, and I had many colleagues and friends among scholars in England. I wanted to visit your country but never had the opportunity. From what I have seen of the American soldiers it must be the most wonderful country in the world."

I laughed and asked, "Why do you say that? We aren't very good soldiers, our officers say we are sloppy and unmilitary, and they are probably right."

"Oh, but many of you are very young. May I ask how old you are young man?"

"I'm nineteen, but there are many men my age or younger in the German army too," I replied.

"Yes, yes, you are right, and it is such a pity, yes, it is a crime that so many fine young men are wasting their youth at war. Were you a student before you were a soldier?"

I laughed again and nodded at the old fellow's astuteness. "Yes, I was a student at the University of Michigan. Are you familiar with it?"

"Oh, but of course, it is one of America's great universities. Tell me, is your unit a special company of the better educated men?"

"No, it's not special, there are all kinds of men in our troop. Why do you ask?"

"I see so many young men like you, but they all seem so proficient in operating mechanical things. They all drive autos and are so comfortable with such equipment. I watched the first troops enter Marburg, and I was struck by the same thing. I have never seen so many large machines, and yet you young Americans are obviously used to operating such things. Young Germans must be taught to drive an auto before they can hope to operate more complex equipment. That is why I say America is so marvelous. It is almost as though you were born with the ability to handle all kinds of mechanical devices. And you have so much, you must be able to operate it. It is something we Europeans can hardly comprehend. If only our ignorant and evil leaders had appreciated America's amazing power, perhaps they would have been less eager to go to war."

The old professor's genuine admiration for Americans and his enthusiasm for conversation captivated me, but our discourse was abruptly terminated by a familiar voice hailing me from the rear door of the apartment.

"Ostrander, what in hell are you doing bull shitting with that old kraut son of a bitch? Don't you realize that's fraternizing?" Rutt Parker screeched.

"Ah yes, the officers, always the same in all armies," the professor muttered sadly as I turned to answer the lieutenant.

"It's all right, lieutenant," I replied. "I was just asking him if we could park some of our vehicles over by his place if we don't have enough room here."

"Jesus Christ, Ostrander, since when do we ask these goddamn people where we can park. We do it, and if they don't like it, fuck 'em."

"I'm sorry, lieutenant, I didn't mean to break any rules," I lied.

"Well, I know you didn't," Rutt answered in a conciliatory tone, "But I just don't want any of my men getting into trouble on account of the damned krauts. You're too kind hearted toward these people, don't trust any of 'em. Why that old bugger may be the biggest Nazi in this whole damned town."

I knew that in some ways the lieutenant was right, and the professor could indeed have been anything. And yet, even if he were not quite clean I failed to see the harm in talking to him. Our conversation had been far more interesting than any I had ever had with the lieutenant. Still, I told myself that I must avoid any future contacts with Germans that would get me in trouble with the authorities.

We only spent one night in Marburg and then split into sections for the next several days to search villages to the north and east for German troops trying to escape from the Ruhr pocket. I learned more than I ever wanted to know about the life of the German farmer as we searched scores of modest houses and barns for fugitives. We found a few uniforms hidden in hay mows or attics, and the householders always expressed amazement that such articles could have turned up in their homes. We failed to apprehend a single soldier in or out of uniform, although there were a scattering of men of military age who may have discharged themselves from the Wehrmacht. We were in no position to investigate such cases, and I even felt sympathy for those who had enough sense to return home by the most direct means. We encountered many displaced persons, most of whom were Polish,

Ukranian, or Russian. At least in these rural areas the DP's seemed fairly happy and were well fed and clothed.

We stopped in one hamlet where the houses were built on a slope between the road and a small river. Our orders were indefinite as to the length of stay, so we requisitioned a house after our usual search of the community. For some reason Hunk was sure that the river teemed with fish, a belief fed in part by a small boy with a fishing pole trying his luck on the bank. I asked the youngster if he had caught anything, and he nodded vigorously, a response that fired Hunk's urge to catch some fish. I asked Wilson what he intended to use for tackle and bait, but he only smiled enigmatically and told me to wait and see. He went to the M8, rummaged through some little used compartments on the side of the vehicle, and returned carrying a concussion grenade. I wanted no part of any more grenade play, but before I could say or do anything he had tossed the bomb into the stream and rushed for shelter behind the house. At least he had enough sense to do his fishing a safe distance from other people, but the thunderous explosion and geyser of water frightened everyone in the hamlet, both German and American.

"Jesus Christ, what's that?" Robarge shouted as he ran out of the house.

"Don't worry, Sarge, I just got us a mess of fish," Hunk replied proudly.

Everyone was thunderstruck by this boast, not knowing whether to praise or scold the wild woodsman.

"Well, I hope you didn't get something besides fish," the sergeant said as he walked down to the river.

"Aw Sarge, I wouldn't take any chances on hurting anyone, you know that," Hunk replied defensively.

By the time we reached the spot on the bank where the grenade had exploded the little German boy had recovered enough from his surprise to join us, and most of the adults of the town were talking excitedly in the street.

"Where are all your goddamn fish, Hunk," Robarge asked irritably.

"Well, I don't see any," Hunk stammered. "Hey, wait, here's one."

He picked up a small fish that looked like a blue gill from the shallows on the river bank and sheepishly waved the four inch specimen in the air. Everyone laughed derisively at his tiny catch, and to add to his humiliation the small boy who had started the fishing fervor looked at the fish and declared that it had been floating in the stream since morning. When I translated this the hoots and jeers reached a crescendo, and poor Hunk looked completely crest fallen. Fortunately we were ordered to another village and the episode of the grenade fishing was forgotten.

During these forays through German villages we were under orders to confiscate all firearms, cameras and binoculars, and these search missions provided most of the "loot" that men were accumulating as souvenirs. Many items were of little value, some were plain junk, but occasionally we would seize something of real worth. The day after the fishing episode we collected some treasures, including a fine hunting rifle, a Leica 35 mm camera, and another better than average camera. We drew lots for the pieces we considered valuable and then searched for a place to dispose of the rest, not an easy task. Some of it we were able to destroy, and some we threw in rivers or down unused wells. I wanted the Leica, but Weiner won it, and I felt fortunate to get the other camera, while Pa was as happy as a boy on Christmas morning when he won the rifle.

We had so many arms that could not be easily disposed of that we were almost desperately casting around for a place to get rid of them. We were several miles outside of our designated patrol area when we saw a crude sign in English that read "Collecting Station." Robarge assumed we had found the elusive place to dump our unwanted hardware and led us up a dirt road to a point on a hill side where we could see some Negro troops working.

As we rounded a curve and drove into a clear area in the woods I was stunned to discover what the crew was collecting. The graves registration troops were stacking corpses in neat piles, Germans in one row, Americans in the other. The bodies were stacked like wood, as grim a sight as I have ever seen. Even on the front where men were being shot and killed constantly, one does not get the same shock as when the dead are collected, identified, sorted and prepared for transfer to a burial place. The bodies had been collected from a wide area and numbered no more than 45 or 50, but they made a powerful impression on me. I could not help but reflect on how many times in innumerable places this same grim task had been and continued to be performed, and how fortunate I was to survive this nightmare. We spoke briefly to the sergeant in charge of the detail, who was amused at our error about his collection, and then we departed.

On the morning of April 13, while on our way to the town of Frankenberg, we learned of the death of President Roosevelt. I was surprised and saddened by the news, but it affected me far less than the grisly collecting station. There was little discussion of this event, other than speculation about the ability of the new president to conclude the war successfully and negotiate a lasting peace. The Germans showed no sign of either elation or despair on hearing the news. A few asked us for verification, but none exhibited any particular emotion that I could detect.

We requisitioned a nice house on the edge of Frankenberg for our billet. The place had enough beds and couches so that nobody slept on the floor, and thus promised to be a pleasant stop, except for the woman of the house. She appeared to be in her late 30's, a hatchet faced vixen with flaming red hair and a temper to match. At first she flatly refused to leave her house and told me imperiously that we could sleep in her barn if we promised not to smoke. My laughter at this offer only enraged her, and I was glad Rutt was not there to witness my discomfiture, which he would have attributed to taking too soft an approach to the Germans. At last the spitfire's parents and neighbors convinced her to leave, but she kept a watchful eye on the house from her refuge next door. I could understand her concern, because the house was well furnished and modern by German standards, and she had no assurance that we would not leave it in shambles.

Robarge had stood aloof from my negotiations with the redhead, smiling in his enigmatic way and enjoying my difficulties. When she finally left he led the raucous ribbing of my lame efforts to be boss of Frankenberg.

"Well, Holme, she's one who wasn't charmed by your German or your innocent face. She had your number; you've been around the lieutenant long enough that she decided she better go after you before you ordered her into bed."

The others hooted at this, and Caulkins had to top the sergeant.

"Cob, she was all right until you said something to her, and then she got mad. I won't tell Dave Morton, but I was shocked that you'd say anything so indecent that it would make a woman take on like that."

"Jesus, Leon, you didn't need to bargain for all of us, I mean, she's just one woman," Hunk added with a wicked leer.

The comments continued but the house was comfortable enough to make it all bearable. Among the well polished pieces of furniture was a desk with the key to a drawer still in the lock. I had run out of writing paper, so I rummaged through the drawer until I found about 25 sheets of stationery with envelopes. I started to fold these supplies so they would fit into my musette bag when I noticed an imitation leather object in the bottom of the still open drawer. I pulled it out and was delighted to find a portfolio that would hold the stationery and also serve as a lap top desk. I laid it by my belongings and closed the drawer.

As we loaded our gear in preparation for departure the following morning the redhead stood like a bank guard watching our every move. I could see my companions smirking in anticipation of another encounter with the fire eater.

"Better hide that thing under your coat, Leon, or that bitch will raise hell," Gorlitz cautioned.

"I'm not a thief and I won't act like one," I replied. "I just take what I need, I didn't ask to be here and I don't care what she says."

I walked out carrying the portfolio and my musette bag in one hand and my bedroll in the other. I laid the smaller objects on the seat while I adjusted the bedroll, and then I heard Hunk and Juan yell. I turned to see the woman reaching for the portfolio, but I grabbed it and tore it away from her. This prompted an explosion more violent than I could have imagined. I did not understand what she said, but she kicked me and tried to bite my hand, while I shoved her away with one hand and clutched the portfolio with the other. We drove away with the woman still shrieking after us, her face contorted by rage and hate.

"Man, she's some cunt," Hunk exclaimed. "How'd you like to be married to her?"

"Her husband was probably glad to go to the Russian front after living with her," Spada added.

"You know, if she had asked me nicely I would have given her back that cheap portfolio, but she was such a nasty bitch that I wouldn't do anything for her," I admitted with more than a little shame. I didn't like to think of myself as a thief, but I also had to admit that I had taken the portfolio without really needing it.

We had been ordered to a nearby town where we rendezvoused with the rest of the third platoon and were reinforced by two infantry squads. Parker and Samuels huddled with Robarge and Nelson, and then the lieutenant had a few words for the rest of us.

"We're going into that woods over yonder," Rutt said, pointing toward a fir forest just beyond the village, "And I want a picked force for this reconnaissance. Sam will lead, and I will put the men I want in each quarter ton. There may be krauts holed up in that woods, so everyone better be awake."

I was to drive a machine gun jeep with Caulkins in command, and we carried a machine gunner from another section and an infantryman armed with a Browning automatic rifle in the back seat. There were two other machine gun jeeps with similar arms and a mortar jeep in which Samuels rode and led the little convoy into the forest on a rough wagon track. We bounced along through the woods for about 30 minutes before Samuels signaled a halt. We got out and walked forward to where the lead jeep had stopped at the edge of a small clearing. To my amazement the entire area was a clutter of German arms and ammunition. It looked as though a convoy had just dropped its load there and fled, for it was not arranged in the order we had come to expect of German supply dumps. Samuels was pawing through the stuff, apparently looking for souvenirs, when he found a pair of metal snips, which the Germans had used to cut links of their machine gun belts. The sergeant, who had child like fascination with all weapons, picked up some armor piercing bullets and tried to cut them with the snips without success. Grinning, he turned to several of the strongest men in the group and insisted that each try to cut or even scratch one of the bullets. Of course, all such efforts were futile, and he smirked triumphantly as he gave us a lecture on the hardness of armor piercing bullets.

This impromptu discourse on ballistics was interrupted by a sudden hissing sound, and we turned to find that one of the infantrymen had inadvertently fired a signal flare into a pile of large mortar shells, where the projectile scooted around erratically spewing forth its incandescent particles over enough explosives to kill us all. We stood transfixed in horror watching the flare dart and sputter among the projectiles before it finally died. This frightening episode seemed to sober Samuels enough so that he turned away from the weapons, cursed the guilty infantryman thoroughly, and then resumed our reconnaissance of the forest.

As we crossed a little meadow between two stands of trees I was suddenly assaulted by a sound as though someone was bouncing .50 caliber bullets off my helmet. Indeed, it was almost that, for the machine gun and BAR were both firing with their muzzles directly over my head. I had no way of knowing the cause of the firing, I had been so intent on following the narrow track that passed for a road, but I assumed enemy had been sighted. I immediately stopped the jeep and slipped down and out the right side after Caulkins. The firing ended after a single short burst, but I was aware of severe pain in my ears, and I could not hear.

Finally, I gasped, "Who was it, who were you shooting at?"

I could not hear what the excited men said, and it was a minute or two before I realized that the fools had fired at a deer and missed at that. My hearing was noticeably impaired for several days and the ringing lasted for at least two weeks afterward.

I was relieved when Samuels announced a short time later that we would end our patrol and return to the rest of the platoon. It seemed the expedition was destined for trouble of one kind or another, and the next foolishness might have more serious consequences. I kept thinking that we were very near the end of the war, and I wanted to take no unnecessary risks. Death or injury because of someone's error or thoughtlessness would in some ways be more bitter than falling victim to enemy fire.

When the platoon reassembled we learned that a first platoon jeep had hit a mine while on a mission similar to ours, and the three man crew had been killed. This news further reinforced my determination to be extremely careful about where I drove, but it was not easy to spot trouble on dirt roads in the forest.

I felt better when Lt. Parker announced that the platoon was to separate into sections, and each unit was to proceed to a different village where we were to "maintain order". "Order" seemed to be one thing the Germans had in abundance, and I wondered what we would contribute. I was even more pleased when we reached our destination, a community of perhaps 500 people situated on a grassy slope bounded by a sparkling little stream at one end and a fir forest at the other. The bright green meadows around the village were made even more picturesque by the cattle contentedly munching grass and a couple of farm wagons drawn by oxen. Chickens and geese moved about among the houses, and a few farm people tended to their chores or talked in doorways. The bright spring sun cast the idyllic scene into sharp contrasts of light and shadow giving it an artistic quality that was almost like an impressionist painting. As we drove closer I felt a sense of detachment from the world as though we had left the war behind and were entering a peaceable land where nothing ever changed.

We stopped in a little square at the center of the village, and Robarge asked me to go with him to find a suitable house for the section. As we walked along the crooked lanes twisting among the houses, women and children smiled shyly, but our presence did not seem to disturb the atmosphere of the place.

"That looks like the best place in town," Robarge said while pointing to a whitewashed house on the edge of the village. "There's plenty of room for the M8 and jeeps and it's in as good condition as any."

I nodded agreement and replied, "Yeah, it looks good to me too. I just hope the owner is friendlier than that redhead in Frankenberg."

Robarge was about to knock when the door opened, and a woman who appeared about 60 years of age smiled at us and signaled for us to enter. My German had improved enough so that our use of the house was arranged quickly, and the woman actually seemed pleased that we had selected her home for our headquarters. She asked if she might stay in a small room on the lower level which adjoined the stable where she kept her cow, an arrangement that we agreed to because the apartment was separate from the rest of the house, and we could not be considered guilty of fraternization because of living in the same dwelling with a German. This lower level was part of the cellar, but because of the slope of the land it opened on ground level at the rear of the residence. The interior of the house was spotlessly clean, well furnished, and equipped with as many utensils as one could find in German homes of that time. The woman assured us that she would be available if we needed anything, so we felt very fortunate as we unloaded our belongings and moved into a place that seemed as hospitable as the home of an old aunt. We had a generous supply of "Ten in One" rations, and our hostess offered us all the milk and eggs we could use, so our stay in the village promised to be a lark.

We had hardly settled into our quarters when Henry brought a middle aged German man into the house. The farmer was obviously distraught about something, for he waved his arms and jabbered so rapidly that I could understand nothing. When I succeeded in slowing the torrent of words I learned that a mob of Russians was threatening his neighbor, who needed our help immediately. The man's anxiety suggested that there was indeed an emergency, so Robarge, Hunk, and I drove the German to his house, where the neighbor did in fact seem to be under duress. The farmer was surrounded by at least a dozen displaced persons, who gave every indication of wanting the German's hide. The angry shouting stopped abruptly as we approached, and then the German and the DP's vied for attention as each party sought the Americans' support in their dispute.

After a tedious ascertainment of the facts, it seemed that a young Russian man had approached the German demanding food, wine and a radio. When the German refused his demands, the DP threatened to take what he wanted, whereupon the German seized an ax and swung it at the youth, striking a glancing blow to the young man's head and precipitating the ruckus that we had interrupted. The German claimed that the Russian was drunk and very hostile, while the DP's denied this and said the youth was asking for handouts in a courteous fashion.

Robarge said we must go to the Russian camp and talk to the injured man. When I translated this to the DP's and the German, all parties nodded and smiled, so at least we had managed to separate the hostile groups without more trouble. Other Germans looked on from a distance, apparently ready to go to the aid of their beleaguered neighbor if we had not intervened. At this moment Lt. Parker's comment about maintaining order seemed more appropriate than I had anticipated.

We drove slowly up the valley for about half a mile accompanied by the smiling, talkative Russians until the road took a sharp turn behind a grove of trees where a series of rude barracks housed a large number of displaced persons. There were men and women of all ages, but most were quite young. At first glance it seemed that a huge party was in progress, complete with dancing, drinking, shouting and singing. A distinguished looking gray haired man appeared from one of the buildings and addressed us in perfect English, a shock to me because in my ignorance I could not conceive of any Russian being more than a peasant. He said he was a professor from the Kiev area and explained that most of the people in the camp were Ukrainians, not Russians. The Germans referred to all Soviet displaced persons as Russians. He took us into one of the barracks and to a cot where a young man lay with a blood stained rag wrapped around his head. Robarge asked the old man to have the youth remove the rag, and to our relief it appeared that he had a small laceration which did not look serious. The young man admitted that he had been drinking and added that the German had struck him with an ax handle, not the blade. The old man told us that he was leader of the camp but had trouble maintaining discipline after German troops left the area. The young people were very unruly, in part due to widespread drunkenness, but they seemed more intent on partying and petty pilfering rather than taking revenge on the Germans. In fact, according to the old man, the people in the camp had been treated fairly well by the villagers and had no reason to seek retribution for their forced labor in the area.

Robarge and the camp leader inspected the installation while the young Ukrainians crowded around Hunk and me. They were very friendly and urged us to drink and dance with them, and the women giggled when we sheepishly begged off from trying their fast and intricate dance step.

"Jeez, it looks like we came to the right place," Hunk said with a wide grin. "These girls are built more for comfort than speed, but they're sure as hell not Germans and they couldn't be friendlier."

I laughed and said, "I guess we can take our pick."

Hunk was right about the Ukrainian girls. They were stocky and buxom but so friendly that I could not hold their lack of beauty against them. By the time the sergeant returned we each had a girl by the arm and were trying to talk to them.

"Jesus Christ, I turn my back for one minute and you guys go crazy over those big boobies and asses," he exclaimed in mock disgust.

"Hey, Sarge, you're not putting them off limits too, are you?" Hunk asked plaintively.

"No, they're not German, so you can do what you like, but don't get any of the men down on us. They've got some guns, and there are a hell of a lot of them. We don't need any jealous husbands or boyfriends giving us trouble."

When we returned to our quarters and told the others about the camp, Caulkins and Gorlitz said they would like to see the place for themselves and meet some of the Ukrainians. We returned to the stalag in two jeeps and delighted the young people by passing out candy and cigarettes and giving them rides in the vehicles. So far as I could tell none of them had ever ridden in a motor vehicle other than perhaps the rear of a truck. It was both humorous and pathetic to watch their excitement when riding in the jeeps, a reaction similar to that of small children going to an amusement park for the first time.

The others were limited by the language barrier in trying to communicate socially with the young Ukrainians, but I could make myself understood in German and catch at least the drift of what they said to me in their heavily accented German. The girl who had gravitated to me while we were waiting for Robarge seemed to have gotten all the wrong ideas about my intentions and clung to me affectionately at every opportunity. Whatever I said only seemed to fuel her ardor, in spite of my efforts to disengage myself from her grasp. As we were about to leave she embraced me and said she wanted to live with me. She insisted that she would cook and clean for all the men but she would only sleep with me.

I must have blushed and looked uncomfortable because my companions burst into laughter and started to give me advice even though they could not catch her exact meaning. I finally convinced her that I must return to the sergeant, but I would come back to see her as soon as I could. Smiling broadly she promised that she would be waiting for me, and then we would make love and be very happy.

The others could hardly wait to tell of my encounter with the buxom Ukrainian when we reached our billet, and from then on the kidding was relentless.

"Seems none of you boys except Ostrander made much of a hit with those girls," Pa declared. "Course I don't know why in hell you wanted to go up there anyway. They sure as hell ain't nothin' to look at."

"Now Pa," Robarge replied with his most sardonic smile, "Ostrander seems to be a big ass, big tits man and that Ukrainian babe sure has those. Why I bet he marries the first girl who wiggles a big ass and boobies at him once he gets home."

I knew that whatever I said would only make it worse, so I tried to ignore it, but they were having too much fun to stop.

I finally interjected, "I just don't want to go near that camp again; I don't want to have anything to do with that girl. The old man speaks English, so you don't need me to translate. I'll do anything else, I just don't want to go there.

"Oh you heartbreaker," Robarge chided. "You're just going to leave that love sick little flower to pine away and not even say good-bye? I should make you face your responsibilities, but if you're not up to it, I guess we'll have to protect you from the Amazon."

More hoots and laughter, and so it went as long as we were in the village. Just when I thought they had forgotten, someone would make a pointed remark that sent the others into gales of laughter. In all other respects it was an ideal place. The old woman of the house treated us like sons, so we had every possible comfort.

I was outside the house cleaning weapons the next morning when I heard a woman address me in perfect English.

"Young man, I wish to speak to your officer."

Turning, I was amazed to see a very attractive and well dressed woman about 40 years of age looking down at me with a haughty and indeed arrogant demeanor. I was too surprised to do more than gape, obviously not the response she wanted.

"I said I wish to speak to your officer. It is quite urgent."

"Oh, ah, yes ma'am," I stammered. "I'll get Sgt. Robarge, just a minute."

I called for Robarge as I entered the house, and hoped he was there to deal with our overbearing visitor.

"Yeah, what's the matter?" the sergeant answered from the direction of the kitchen.

"There's an English speaking woman outside, says she has to talk to you, says it's urgent."

"Is she German or what?"

"I don't know, but she speaks English as well as any of us."

We walked out the door, and Robarge introduced himself to the woman, who seemed disappointed that he was only a noncom.

"You must help me, a woman of the village is having a baby, but the delivery is not proceeding properly and we must have the doctor. He is in Siegen, but we have no way to summon him, so you must dispatch one of your men to fetch him immediately."

Robarge seemed surprised by the woman's dictatorial manner, but he recovered quickly and replied with a courteous inquiry.

"And who are you, ma'am?"

"I am Frau Werner. My husband and I are temporary residents of this village, but our home is in Dusseldorf where he is a well known chemist."

She said this as though even we barbarians from far off America should have heard of the great Herr Dr. Werner, the renowned chemist.

"I can have Pvt. Ostrander drive to Siegen to get the doctor, but you better go with him so he can find the doctor's office," the sergeant replied in a friendly but not obsequious way.

"Very well, let us go," Frau Werner replied.

We set off immediately for the larger town which was about 10 miles away. The woman sat in the front passenger's seat with her nose in the air as though I was the most menial chauffeur to whom she would not condescend to speak. I was stubborn enough to refuse to initiate conversation, so we drove in silence until we entered Siegen, where she issued curt directions to the doctor's office. It was a comfortable looking home with the physician's clinic attached to one side. I could see a few people in the waiting room, so I thought the doctor must be in. My passenger alighted and sailed into the clinic as though she owned it and soon returned with the stocky, middle aged physician puffing after her. To my surprise he climbed into a small Opel sedan and drove away as fast as the little car would go. Unlike the case with Patton's Buick, I had no trouble keeping up with the doctor as he drove his flivver for all it was worth along the winding road to the village. I deposited my passenger where the doctor parked and returned to the section's quarters. It was a relief to be rid of the overbearing German woman and her superior airs.

"How'd you like that dame, Sarge?" I asked.

"I suppose she warmed up to you with all your education and way with women," Robarge replied sarcastically.

"Yeah, just like she'd warm up to a colored cab driver. As Pa would say, she acted as though I was lower than whale shit."

"You gotta admit, she gets what she wants, we did exactly what she told us to do," Robarge added.

"Well, now that she has gotten what she wanted we probably won't see any more of her," I said.

"Don't be so sure, she may have some other plans for us," the sergeant replied.

How right he was. Late that afternoon Frau Werner again came to our door, but her demeanor had changed dramatically. She was friendly without being patronizing and accorded Robarge appropriate deference as the man in charge of our unit.

"Sergeant, I am most appreciative of what you and your young soldier did for me and my friend this morning. My husband and I would be honored if you would visit us this evening. We live in the house next to that of Frau Sattelmeier, the woman who had the baby. Thanks to you, she and the baby are doing well, but the doctor will return to see her in the morning. Would you be so kind as to accept our hospitality?"

I was half hoping that Robarge would tell her that the law prohibited us from fraternizing with Nazi trash, for I was convinced that the Werners must be party members, and yet I was curious enough to wonder what her husband was like and how they would behave in a social setting. The sergeant did not hesitate.

"Thank you, Frau Werner, we will be pleased to visit you. What time would be convenient?"

"Could you come at 2000, or as you say, 8 o'clock?"

"We will be there," Robarge replied graciously.

This development lent interest to our humdrum lives and diverted attention from my encounter with the Ukrainian girl. In spite of my prejudice against Frau Werner, I was excited by the prospect of visiting an influential German couple whose views might be quite different from those of the common people to whom we had talked previously. I was sure they would say something besides "nicht Nazi".

We gorged on one of chef Robarge's fabulous dinners before setting out for the Werners. The sergeant took pride in stuffing everyone so that even Hunk could not eat another mouthful. In addition to incredible quantities, the food was tasty and far from monotonous, considering that he had limited resources. I belched in satisfaction as we approached the Werners' house, and Robarge warned me to watch my manners since we were visiting the upper crust. I chuckled at that as we reached the door, where one knock brought Frau Werner. She exuded charm and hospitality as she ushered us down a hall and into a sitting room, where a gray haired man who looked to be between 45 and 50 rose from his chair and greeted us warmly.

"I am so glad you could come," he said in a heavily accented English. "My wife has told me about you. Come, sit down, can I get you something to drink, some wine or perhaps some beer? I apologize, we have no whiskey, gin or vermouth, the war has compelled us to drink the local beverages."

"Thank you, but we thought you might enjoy some coffee," the sergeant replied. "I brought some with me, if Frau Werner would like to brew it."

The Werners were as delighted by the coffee as the humbler folk with whom we had shared our precious beverage. We always had more than we could use because Robarge was the only avid coffee drinker in the section, and the younger men hardly drank any. Frau Werner took the coffee to the kitchen, and her husband looked at us quizzically.

The Werners pried into our backgrounds as though we were two interesting specimens of some rare genus never before seen in these parts. At first they professed not to believe that Robarge was a truck driver with an eighth grade education. Of course he was far more articulate and polished than one could expect of a man with so little formal education, but he seemed to fascinate the German couple. They also claimed to be baffled by my status as a lowly private in the army when I had been a student in good standing at a prestigious university. They claimed that such young men were not drafted in Germany, but I doubted that assertion. I appreciated Werner's obvious respect for my school, a fact that was not lost on Robarge. Finally the conversation turned to our hosts, a far more interesting topic.

Werner had been an academician but entered industry and became an important man in the Ruhr. To my surprise he admitted membership in the Nazi Party but equated it to becoming a Republican or a Rotarian in the United States. The Werners then told at great length of the hardships and privations they had endured due to the war and particularly the bombings of the Ruhr area. Hitler came in for scornful denunciation, but more because he blundered and lost the war than because he was evil. It was a virtuoso performance of self justification and one that could easily sway the gullible. We did not agree with our hosts, but neither did we take issue with most of their assertions. Frau Werner served some little cakes with the coffee and excused their poor quality on the grounds that she was not used to baking and the ingredients for first class pastries were not available. Whatever the reason, the things were barely edible.

As we were about to leave the woman revealed what was surely the main reason for inviting us to visit. She eloquently begged us to keep the barbaric Russians away from the village where they could terrify and probably harm innocent women and children. Her husband nodded emphatically throughout this appeal and underscored her assertions with a few comments that revealed his utter contempt for the displaced persons as human beings. Robarge patiently explained that our task was to maintain order, and that meant to protect all the people of the area from abuse of any kind. He made it clear that we would not allow Russians or Germans to threaten anyone, so the Werners had nothing to fear. Werner then interjected that there would be no trouble from the Germans, who were an orderly and peaceable people, but the Slavs were so primitive that they might do anything unless strictly supervised.

When we got outside Robarge said, "That son of a bitch and the rest of these krauts should have thought of what those DP's might do before they brought them here. Those two are real corkers."

I agreed, and we tried to think of some way to humble the arrogant couple without getting in trouble ourselves.

"You know, they'll find a way to land on top of the heap no matter what anyone does," the sergeant said. "They'll cozy up to all the right people, and old Werner will get his job back or maybe a better one."

"You're probably right," I said. "I bet they'll be thick as thieves with military government as soon as they get here, unless she tries to feed them some of her cakes. That was the only part of their act that wasn't slick."

"Hell, by then she'll have a maid again who can bake the damned cakes or anything else," Robarge grumped.

We stayed in the village another day, and Frau Werner continued her efforts to ingratiate herself by bringing more of the awful cakes to our billet. With this offering she cautioned us that several of the Russians had been walking about the town. While they had not threatened anyone, their presence was enough to frighten the villagers. Somehow she could not comprehend Robarge's statement that the DP's had as much right to circulate as the Germans so long as they did not cause trouble.

A squad of infantry relieved us, and we were ordered to join the rest of the troop in Eibelshausen, a larger, nearby community. It was the usual scene of crowding and confusion in the town, where not only the 28th Recon but several other units were quartered. However, the third platoon was assigned to a large house at one end of the main street where we had more space for the vehicles and were away from the congested part of the town.

I hoisted my bedroll and other gear and climbed the stairs in hope of finding a bed or couch that was not already claimed by one of the early arrivals. I flung open a door and walked into a scene that stopped me in my tracks. Samuels had his pistol drawn and was closing in on a little blond girl in the corner of the room. She looked to be no more than 14 or 15, a pale, trembling youngster facing the brutal sergeant and his ominous .45. Samuels wheeled when he heard me, and I was afraid he would shoot, particularly since his quarry seized this diversion to make her escape.

"God damn you, Ostrander," he snarled. "What's the idea of busting in like that?"

I gulped in fear, an emotion that must have shown on my face, as I stammered, "I didn't know there was anyone in here."

To my relief Samuels holstered his Colt, spit out a few more oaths, and growled, "You better not cross me again, dammit. When I catch that little blond again, I don't want any interruptions, you hear?"

I retreated in haste, glad that I had inadvertently foiled a rape but eager to get away from the angry sergeant. The intended victim had fled across the street to a neighbor's house where she and her family took refuge while the Americans occupied their home. Her father glanced out the window fearfully from time to time as though he half expected the fierce American sergeant to continue his pursuit of the girl in broad daylight.

The town was a noisy, unpleasant place, and I was glad to learn that we would not be there long. Before dinner that night we were told that the next day, April 23, we would leave Eibelshausen and move to Kaiserslautern in the Saar region, where we would serve as occupation troops for an indefinite period. This was the first and only time that we had been told exactly where we were going and what we would do there. At least we had official notification that the war was over for us, a little over four months after we arrived in France, a period that seemed much longer because of all that had occurred.

12

OCCUPATION DUTY

At Kaiserslautern we were billeted in an apartment building near the outskirts of the city. The place was large enough to house the entire troop without crowding, and the bathrooms featured coal fired hot water heaters so that we could take regular showers. A large vacant area behind the building was quickly converted to softball diamonds, where many of us were soon playing games with real balls, bats and gloves. The billet was back far enough from the street so that long tables were set up near the kitchen for use as an outdoor dining area. The vehicles were parked in a lot across the street and in spaces at either end of the apartment. Troop formations were held in front of the building, but our military activities were very limited.

It was soon obvious that no American would perform any task that could remotely qualify as work, because Russian displaced persons were willing, indeed eager, to take over all the onerous chores in the kitchen, motor pool, and housekeeping areas in exchange for food, shelter, old clothes and cigarettes. There was so little to do that even the DP's had plenty of spare time, which they spent pursuing women, drinking, and performing personal tasks for some of the Americans.

Many men had acquired huge quantities of "souvenirs", items as varied as Nazi flags, weapons, clothing and household articles pilfered from homes and best described as "loot". Incredibly, the army allowed any officer or enlisted man to ship home without charge as much plunder as he wished so long as it was properly packaged. The Russian workers spent much time building boxes and crates to ship the swag to the states. Pa Conger was the champion souvenir collector in our section, and his boodle filled two boxes the size of small coffins. Even after that he had so much junk that it was doubtful whether he would be able to carry it all home.

With menial work in the willing and capable hands of the Russians the soldiers had nothing to do except run a few road patrols, take turns on guard, and loaf. The officers departed each evening for a hospital in a nearby town where the nurses seemed to be staging a marathon party, so everyone rose late and did little until noon when the military day ended and recreation began.

In spite of this pacific atmosphere the apprehension and incarceration of dangerous Nazis remained a military priority. I had two experiences with such villainous types, each more humorous than dangerous.

The first occurred soon after our arrival in Kaiserslautern when the men began to complain of a foul odor emanating from a mound of debris next to the kitchen area of the building. The putrid stench became stronger by the day until it could not be ignored. It was obvious that some creature was decomposing in the warm spring weather, a problem that could only be corrected by excavation of the remains and proper burial. No American was even considered for this revolting chore, and nobody would have thought of foisting such a task onto our friends the Russian DP's, so a decision was made to requisition a squad of Nazis from the division stockade for the burial detail. Because of my linguistic ability I was put in charge of three other men to fetch and supervise the unfortunate supermen. The division M.P.'s released half a dozen very ordinary looking men to us with the warning that they were SS troopers suspected of war crimes and thought to be very dangerous. The six were docile enough in the truck and smiled shyly at us; one even tried to ingratiate himself by muttering something about Hitler being "ein schwein".

Their affability turned to sulky resentment as I explained the job and they got their first whiff of the smell. A couple of the supermen began to sweat, and before they could turn a shovel of dirt their leader informed me proudly that he was an officer and could not be forced to perform manual labor under the Geneva Convention. He was, of course, prepared to help supervise the enlisted men. I guess I became a war criminal at that moment because I laughed in the cocky little rooster's face and told him to get to work with the others. For once my modest ability to speak German was a liability because I had to stand close enough to the excavation to get frequent drafts of the putrid stench even though I stationed myself upwind. I must admit that it was a rotten job for the POW's; they sweated and each retched at least once before they finished uncovering and burying the rotting carcass of a horse. In spite of their reputed crimes I sympathized with them as I struggled with my own queasiness. I think my companions on the detail shared my compassion for the unfortunate Nazis, because none of us gloated at their discomfort and one man gave them cigarettes on the way back to the stockade.

My only other experience with "dangerous Nazis" came several weeks later. We were just finishing dinner when Robarge asked Juan Gonzalez and me to accompany him to an apartment a few blocks away where a war criminal was said to be hiding. As we pulled up in front of the place the sergeant told Juan to stay by the jeep and cover the front of the building while we entered from the rear. Whoever had fingered the fugitive had said he was in the second floor apartment at the top of the stairs. We did not pause for any formalities but burst into the place with our carbines at the ready, catching the family by complete surprise as they were eating dinner. If our quarry had any thoughts of fight or flight they must have been fleeting, for the occupants of the room, two men, a woman and a boy about 6 or 7 sat impassively while I asked their names. The SS fugitive readily admitted his identity and asked us to leave the others alone. He said they were his sister and her family and insisted that they had no party connections but had sheltered him because he was a relative. The man was small yet lean and wiry, and on casual inspection he failed to impress one as a dangerous war criminal. He had dark hair, almost a swarthy complexion, and nondescript, ill-fitting clothes giving him the appearance of a simple workman caught by mistake in a raid for bigger fish. It was only when he rose from his chair and turned to face us that I was struck by his pale blue eyes, an incongruity in his dark face. They stared at me coldly with just a hint of arrogant disdain, so that I had the feeling that the man would snuff out my life with no more thought than swatting a fly if given the chance. Perhaps it was my youthful imagination, but I was immediately convinced that the German was indeed a cold, menacing fanatic capable of whatever atrocities were attributed to him. He remained quiet and cool on the way to the stockade and seemed completely unfazed by his predicament.

From comments of the M.P.'s I guessed that he was a more important catch than the hapless crew who had buried the dead horse. They were SS troopers, but part of the combat forces, while our prisoner was in the political arm of that evil organization, a post which conferred an additional aura of mystery and menace.

As we drove back to our quarters I was relieved to hear Robarge say, "I'd sure as hell hate to be at the mercy of that son of a bitch, did you guys notice those eyes? If the shoe was on the other foot he'd probably have shot us by now. At first I thought he was just another small fry kraut, but I bet he's more than that."

"I'm glad you thought so too," I replied. "I thought maybe I'd seen too many movies, but that guy was scary."

These incidents with Nazis stand out in my memory because they were about the only military duties I performed at Kaiserslautern. My main preoccupation was the platoon softball team and frequent trips to a huge outdoor swimming pool where we swam around in our undershorts. Of course we had no swimsuits and nude bathing was prohibited because the pool was in the middle of a residential neighborhood whose inhabitants had an unobstructed view of the entire complex. Consequently the men had to gauge accurately the time necessary for the drawers to dry and stay out of the water for that interval before our departure by truck for the recon billet on the other side of town if they did not want to endure the discomfort of wet underwear beneath their uniform pants. Orders were explicit that men were not to appear on the streets in anything but the regulation uniform, so we could not ride home in our shorts and carry the outer clothes.

After an afternoon of softball or swimming, troopers could find entertainment in the center of the city where the division had requisitioned a theater and a large house. Nightly shows, mostly movies, were presented at the theater, and the Red Cross opened a service club in the mansion.

The biggest event at the theater was the appearance of Freeman

Gosden and Charles Correll, better known as "Amos 'n Andy" of radio fame. Their show was an outstanding success for men who had grown up listening to the antics of their Harlem characters each evening on the radio. By modern standards "Amos 'n Andy" was an incredibly racist caricature of Negroes, but in 1945 I found the gentle clowning of the warm and generous Gosden and Correll innocent and amusing. The theater rocked with laughter and applause, and the performers responded with encore after encore.

The Red Cross Club was a great place to play ping pong, shoot pool, read books, write letters and eat doughnuts. The few hostesses were haughty and distant, at least with enlisted men, but rumor had it that they were much friendlier to officers. Still, it was a good place to go once in a while for some tame entertainment.

These places were in easy walking distance from our quarters, and most of our section visited one or the other establishment almost every night. It was on the way back to our billet one evening that tragedy struck. Himler, our dog, often accompanied us on our trips to the center of town and provided as much entertainment as the movie or the games. He had become an incredibly arrogant, cocky, and spoiled terrier who seized every opportunity to assert his dominance over the local animals and even some of the civilian pedestrians. On this particular evening he had just chased a local mutt into an alley on the opposite side of the street when one of the men called to him. The little bully dashed into the street just as a six-by truck rounded the corner, and suddenly our mascot and pet lay dead on the pavement. The truck didn't stop, which was probably fortunate because several men were angry enough to punish the driver, although I did not see how he could have avoided the dog.

I mourned the loss of our pet, but fate may have been kind to remove him before he got us into trouble. As his bellicosity had increased the little tough had started to nip at passing civilians, apparently just for the joy of inciting fear in his victims. Perhaps more ominous for his future he started to run barking through and around our occasional military formations, a gambit that irritated the captain as much as it amused the men. It was clear that Himler was not a garrison type of military dog; he belonged in the field, riding on the M8, standing guard with his multiple masters, and lifting our morale with his macho antics.

My greatest thrill during this brief stint in the occupation army was a three day pass to Paris. I could not believe my luck in drawing a high enough card to win one of the first two passes to the French capital. The only drawback was that Samuels was the other winner; I could think of no travel companion I would enjoy less than my platoon sergeant. The problem was solved when Samuels got into some sort of trouble that resulted in his demotion to private, loss of pay and removal of all privileges including leave. To my amazement Dave Morton was the next in line. I had not thought that he would touch a playing card let alone participate in a drawing for the trip, particularly to Paris with all its reputation for sin. Still, I was glad that his religious scruples did not prevent him from competing for the trip and looked forward to his company. However, at the moment of departure I was afraid that Morton too would miss the trip. Just as we climbed into the truck bound for Luxembourg City, where the rail line ended, the troop clerk dashed out of headquarters waving prophylactic kits for us. An order from division stipulated that no man could leave his unit on pass or furlough unless he was properly protected against venereal diseases. Since nobody had gone on pass in the clerks memory, he had forgotten this requirement until almost too late. Of course the soaring VD rate had little to do with infections incurred on leave, but rather to contacts with women in the occupation area, mostly Germans, but the military bureaucracy decided to apply prevention where it was least needed. My friend was insulted and angry at this requirement, indeed his mixture of shock and disgust suggested that he felt as though General Eisenhower himself had said, "Morton, you will sin in Paris, so take this and at least protect your body!" He refused the kit with a sullen anger that I would have never expected of him, and the dumbfounded clerk didn't know what to do.

"Oh, come on, Davey, take the damned thing," the corporal cajoled. "You can give it to one of your buddies or throw it away when you're outta sight, but I gotta report that I supplied you guys with pro kits."

Still Dave refused and I could tell by his expression and tone of voice that this was not only an issue of honor but of his very soul.

Just when I thought he would have to get off the truck one of the impatient riders exclaimed, "Gimme the damned thing, I'll carry it for him. Anything to get this show on the road."

The clerk handed the infantryman the kit, and with that we were off to Paris. It was a marvelous three days. Dave was a good companion, and we must have walked 50 miles in our ceaseless sightseeing. Of course Morton was the butt of a lot of banter for his scene about the pro kits until we dispersed in the city. One man in particular took it upon himself to conduct a constant patter about what kind of woman a young and inexperienced fellow like Dave should contact. Like all similar harassment in the troop, the soldier's remarks seemed to have no noticeable effect on Morton, and he even managed a few faint smiles in response to the fellow's outrageous comments.

The trip produced one other humorous incident. Our friends had given us a generous supply of cigarettes, candy and soap to assure a well funded trip, although almost everything necessary for our enjoyment was available without charge. As a result we planned to sell our goods on the black market and send the money home along with a few months back pay. I had wondered how my righteous friend would view such an illegal transaction, but I need not have worried. He was as avaricious as I, an attitude we rationalized as a way to build educational funds. My plan was simple: we would stroll along a side street off Boulevard Houseman with our musette bags bulging from trade goods and a carton of cigarettes sticking out of one corner like a flag until a dealer accosted us to do business. This scheme appealed to me as safe, quick, and remunerative enough if we haggled a little, but Dave shocked me by wanting to retail the stuff to make a bigger profit. When I thought of how long it would take to peddle the merchandise I feared that we would spend our three days selling and would run a much greater risk of arrest. This latter point finally convinced my friend to do it my way, and once we made the decision our entry to the black market took all of 15 minutes. A wonderfully furtive, almost sinister looking, Frenchman on a bicycle approached us just off the Boulevard Houseman and led us to the vestibule of an old apartment building that seemed to exude intrigue. We quickly came to terms and stepped out into the sunshine, each with $200 more than we had a few minutes before. Dave's beaming face must have reflected mine as we headed to the army post office where we could send money orders home.

I sent nearly $400 and by return mail received a letter from my mother in which she begged me not to let temptation lead me astray.

Soon after a letter came from my minister with a not very subtle exhortation to pray when tempted by sin. I found out later that just before my money order arrived with the unlikely story of how I had made so much money on my $60 a month salary, the local papers had run some lurid tales of black market rings in Europe and how they corrupted innocent service men. Of course, all American servicemen were portrayed as innocent by the papers, and the foreigners were ever ready to lead these lambs to perdition.

The major pastime in Kaiserslautern was fraternization. In one way or another it was almost universal and surely inevitable. It is hard to imagine what kind of bureaucratic mind ever thought that healthy young men could be cloistered from the community around them. Whoever conceived the fraternization ban needed introductory courses in biology and psychology. Transgressions of the law ran the gamut from flagrant, foolish pursuit of women to the most subtle intrigues. A few men actually cruised the streets in jeeps, picked up girls, and drove them to their apartments where they parked and retired inside until the patrolling M.P.'s spotted the jeeps and arrested them. Some just slipped away after dark to a collection of hovels on the far side of our ball diamonds where half a dozen frumpy bawds displayed their unattractive bodies each afternoon. That area became known as the "left field foul line" when so many of the floozies' customers developed gonorrhea. Indeed, at one time it was claimed that the 28th Recon had the highest incidence of venereal disease of any unit in the ETO. Besides the risks of infection, those caught fraternizing were usually punished by reduction in rank, a fine, and loss of privileges.

There were some who yearned for a better class of female companionship, a small, naive group who thought there must be some "nice girls" even in the ruins of the Third Reich. Caulkins and I fell into that group and decided to conduct our quest for decent girls in a large city park near a good residential area not far from our billet. It was a pleasant place to meander even if the girl crop was nonexistent. On our second visit we discovered the principal reason for the paucity of Germans in the park. As we rounded a clump of bushes we found ourselves on a grassy slope stretching down to a large pond where a score of Russians were bathing in the buff. We must have stood blushing and dumbfounded by the sight, but the jovial folk surrounded us and in unmistakable sign language urged us to join the fun. Any inhibitions they might have felt had been dissolved by a copious supply of some sort of moonshine, which they also urged on us. The friendly Russians were genuinely disappointed when we declined their invitation to a drunken nude frolic on the grounds of our important duties elsewhere. After we told others of our experience a steadily increasing group of voyeurs loitered near the pond, and soon the Russians realized what the Americans were doing there and discontinued their frolics. With nothing to watch, the leering peepers sought thrills elsewhere, so DJ and I resumed our pleasant but lonely walks among the pretty ponds, trees and meadows of the park.

Gradually Germans reappeared, mostly old people and mothers with children at first, but then we saw an occasional young woman or girl. One day we came upon two young women sitting on a bench in a little glade well hidden from the gravel drive where M.P.'s occasionally patrolled in jeeps. DJ must have flashed one of his most captivating smiles at the attractive member of the duo because she blushed slightly and tittered in an inviting way. I knew my role as the interpreter, so we were soon engaged in some cumbersome small talk. The girls were close friends who lived in the good neighborhood near the park, neither was married or engaged, and both expressed great fondness for Americans. They were very well dressed, so they or their families were probably Nazi Party members, but we didn't think of that at the moment. Caulkins' target was very pretty, bright and witty, while her friend was a fat, phlegmatic lump without one attractive feature. I told DJ that I would do my best to put him in right with the pretty girl, but under no circumstances would I have anything to do with her dumpy friend.

My uncooperative attitude complicated an already awkward situation, but at last we got to the point where Caulkins was to meet the attractive fraulein about dusk, and she would take him to her home to meet her parents and for whatever entertainment the place afforded. The fat one was not included in any of this and I had made it clear that the date would have to be kept without the benefit of an interpreter. Just as we were about to leave a voice behind us brought us up short.

"What the hell do you guys think you're doing?" an M.P. demanded with a smirk on his face. "You think you're back home pickin' up babes in the park? Nobody'll bother you if you just go out quietly at night and get laid, but this socializin' shit is just what'll get you in the stockade."

I was petrified, not because I had much to lose in a tangible sense, I was only a PFC, one tiny step above a private, and my pay was a pittance, but my family were bound to learn of my disgrace and were sure to be terribly upset, particularly in light of lurid stories in the press about fraternization. This term was used to cover all sorts of sin, but mostly sexual misconduct on a grand scale. How would I ever explain that I was only arranging a date for a friend, seemingly with a decent girl? Who would ever believe that when the *Detroit News* reported that the troops were debauching themselves among the amoral dregs of Nazi society in spite of the efforts of their superiors to protect their morals?

The speaker and his partner started grinning at our consternation, and then the partner spoke in a more conciliatory tone. "Look, we don't want to get anyone into trouble, but the old man is a bear on fraternization. We won't turn you in this time, but get out of this park and don't make any more dates with krauts."

It was only then that I realized that the M.P.'s had approached in a jeep which we had not heard as we concentrated on getting DJ a date with the pretty fraulein. The police departed and we turned to go, but Caulkins stopped, looked at the little German girl and then at me, and I realized that he still intended to keep the date.

"Leon, you tell her I'll still be there this evening. Would you do that?" he entreated.

Reluctantly I agreed and began to explain the situation to the girl when the irate voice of the first M.P. struck me dumb.

"I'll be goddamned, I thought I told you two wise guys to leave those two kraut bitches alone and shag your asses outa here. We gave you a break, but now we'll have to take you down to headquarters, and you can tell your story to the lieutenant."

I could not have uttered a word if my life depended on it. I was frozen by a combination of fear, remorse, and anger at myself for letting DJ talk me into this folly.

Suddenly Caulkins found his tongue and exclaimed in an almost tearful, pleading tone, "Please, don't do that, it was my fault, I asked him to tell her that I'd be back, but I was wrong, and he was just being a friend. I won't do it again, I promise. Why my daddy's a preacher back in Texas, and it'd just kill him if I got into trouble over here.

Please, won't you give us another chance?"

In spite of my other emotions I could hardly keep a straight face at DJ's virtuoso performance. I knew that Texans were a lot like the Irish in their ability to talk their way out of almost any predicament, but I had no idea how talented my friend really was.

The M.P. looked at us quizzically as though he didn't know whether to get angry or laugh, but then after a moment that seemed like an hour he replied gruffly, "OK, I don't know why, but I'll give you guys one more chance, but don't let me catch either of you in this park again or I'll run you in for sure. Now on your way and don't even look back at the dames."

"I thought your father was a deacon, not a preacher," I said when we were safely out of earshot.

"Well, it's almost the same, and I wasn't sure that old boy would know what a deacon is," DJ replied, his jaunty effervescence fully restored.

We only stayed in Kaiserslautern until early July, when the division returned to the United States for amphibious training in preparation for redeployment to the Orient. While we were on our thirty day furloughs the Japanese surrendered, so the training and trip to Asia were canceled, but I still faced months of dull duty in the United States before I was eligible for discharge. After my adventures in Europe any duty would have seemed dull, but being in the States reminded me constantly of my lack of interest in military life.

• ──────── •

The events and people that crowded into my brief seven months in the European Theater of Operations almost six decades ago, are still sharply etched in my memory, as they always will be.

This experience hastened my maturation from a naive and bookish young student to an adult who recognized and appreciated the amazing variety and uniqueness of people, an understanding which surely contributed to my empathy for patients and students during my career as an academic physician.

I have always treasured my lifelong friendship with Arthur Robarge and appreciated my good fortune to serve with a man of such extraordinary character.

Finally, I hope this collection of anecdotes provides later generations of Americans with a better understanding of those eventful but increasingly remote times.